The **CSS**
DETECTIVE GUIDE

*TRICKS FOR
SOLVING TOUGH
CSS MYSTERIES!*

DENISE R. JACOBS

The CSS Detective Guide: Tricks for solving tough CSS mysteries
Denise R. Jacobs

New Riders
1249 Eighth Street
Berkeley, CA 94710
510/524-2178
510/524-2221 (fax)
Find us on the Web at www.newriders.com
To report errors, please send a note to errata@peachpit.com
New Riders is an imprint of Peachpit, a division of Pearson Education

Editor: Wendy Sharp
Production Coordinator: Myrna Vladic
Copyeditor: Jacqueline Aaron
Compositor: Rick Gordon, Emerald Valley Graphics
Indexer: Emily Glossbrenner, FireCrystal Communications
Cover and interior design: Charlene Will

ISBN-13   978-0-321-68394-6
ISBN-10   0-321-68394-3

9 8 7 6 5 4 3 2 1
Printed and bound in the United States of America

This book is dedicated to those who touched my life with love and guidance and have moved on to another place: Dennis R. Jacobs, Daniel Lev, Kay Corbin, Charles Jacob, Michael Fajans, Ferne Carpousis, and Leah Moussaioff.

It is further dedicated to all of my former web students at Seattle Central Community College from 2000–2005. You all were an absolute delight to teach. For those of you who suggested that I should write a web book, well, you got your wish.

Acknowledgments

They say that it takes an entire village to raise a child, and this is true for a book as well.

It started with a seemingly innocuous conversation with Robert Hoekman Jr. at a SXSWi 2009 party where I met his editor, Wendy Sharp. That brief meeting and business card exchange set in motion a series of events that have produced this book.

I can't thank Wendy enough for taking the overly ambitious writing schedules that I created for myself with a huge grain of salt, for maintaining my voice while magically cutting away half the words, and for appreciating my oddball sense of humor. I am indebted to my technical editor Estelle Weyl for invaluable feedback that kept my code clean and for being even more of a web standardista than I am. I thank our copy editor, Jacqueline Aaron, for her hard work and for going beyond the call of duty by editing the content of the website examples. Myrna Vladic was the book production manager extraordinaire, generous with her time and energy in answering my questions and responding to my needs. Thanks go to our designer, Charlene Will, for running with the book concept and giving the book a fun and snappy look-and-feel. And Rick Gordon provided great page layout, and I really appreciated his praise for the concept of the book when he said that it's "the CSS book I've needed, and so far, hadn't found."

When plagued by doubts at the beginning of the project, I received amazing support from peers, mentors, and former colleagues (my own personal version of Webgrrls): Tiffany B. Brown, Cecily Walker, Elaine Nelson, Leslie Jensen-Inman, Jen Hanen, Yvette Ferry, Cindy Li, Glenda Sims, Lynne D. Johnson, Gillian Reynolds, Kathy E. Gill, Anna B. Scott, Molly Holzschlag, Erica Mauter, Eris Stassi, Shawn Lawton-Henry, Alison Cramer, Sara Newman, Kimberlee Jensen-Stedl, Andrea Pruneda, Melissa Acedera, Stephanie Sullivan, and Christine Van Valey.

Speaking of Webgrrls, thanks by association goes to Aliza Sherman for creating Webgrrls, and to Betsy Aoki, Anne Baker, and Honora Wade and for starting, growing and expanding Seattle Webgrrls and DigitalEve Seattle. Being a part of that community gave me one of the best starts in the industry that anyone, female or male, could ever want. I am pleased to still be connected with DigitalEve Seattle and NWR lists, whose members were extraordinarily supportive when I needed it the most.

Deep thanks goes to the Web Standards Project Educational Task Force members for cheering me on through the process and being understanding about my schedule constraints: Aarron Walter, Chris Mills, Nick Fogler, Christopher Schmitt, Virginia DeBolt, Terry Morris, Jinny Potter, Jeffrey Brown, Zac Gordon, Lars Gunther, Jessi Taylor, Rob Dickerson.

Similarly, I want to thank the members of Social Media Club South Florida for their interest in and excitement about this project, and cutting me slack on event planning: Agustina Prigoshin, Ulises Orozco, Alex de Carvalho, Murray Izenwasser, Angie Moncada, Toby Srebnik, Jay Berkowitz, Neil Bardach, John Prieur, Matthew Chamberlin, Michelle Catin.

I am excited to be a part of the growing tech community in South Florida, fast becoming known as Silicon Beach. Compatriots include Maria de los Angeles, Robert Murray, Brian Breslin, Davide de Cecillo, Willie Morris, Stefani Whylie, Chris Fullman, Ines Hegedus-Garcia, Tami Stillwell, Steve Roitstein, Alisha Vera, David Bisset, Ben Bewick, Josue Rodriguez, Amanda Stewart, Patrick Barbanes, Enzo Balc, Miguel Lopez, Lisa Sparks, and Michelle Villalobos.

My BXSW peeps and SXSW and TODCon buddies supported me indirectly, largely without them knowing it. Just being associated with these folks is reward enough: J. Smith, E.J. Flavors, Baratunde Thurston, Rhazes Spell, Jason Toney, George Kelly, Twanna Hines, Michael Moss, Jeffrey Bowman, Dave Shea, Hugh Forest, Jim Turner, David Stiller, Kris Krug, Tara Hunt, and Dori Smith.

Mentors, former teachers, and people who have always believed in me also get due thanks: Julia A. Davis, Mary MacDonald, Cynthia Mapes, Pam Conine, Rebecca Llyod, Wadiyah Nelson, Carlene Brown, Merri-jo Hillaker, and Beth Wilson.

My long-term Lovefest and YS chosen family have stuck with me for at least seventeen years and hopefully they will stick around for a few more: Andrew Lambert, Jessica Meistrich-Gidal, Lisa von Trotha, Stephen Moses, Stephanie Graham-Lvovich, Carole Vacher, Jeremy Dragt, Lenny Rede, Emilie Zuffrey, Corinna MacDonald, and Michael Harris.

Local-yocals checked on me to make sure everything was on track and often provided occasional necessary diversions away from writing: Brent Knoll, Natalie Morales, Melissa DeCastillo, Marlon Norris, Tricia Bannister, Terry Toney, David Fernan, Martin Eschvarria, Mike Reynolds, and Caroline Gaudy.

I would be remiss not to acknowledge the 24/7 kitty companionship provided by Gheri and Malcolm (who are both on loan), Aashika, and Zealand (who are with me for the long haul).

Invaluable emotional support, preliminary readings, feedback, happy dances, and quite a few good dinners came from chosen sisters and close friends: Amber Zimmerman, Elizabeth Williams, Stephanie Troeth, and Julia Wakefield.

This book would not have been possible on so many levels without the support of my family: my sister, Diane Jacobs, my grandparents, Robbie Mae and William James Lowe. Most important, however, was the unwavering support on multiple levels from my mother, Deloria L. Jacobs. I only hope I can return the gesture one thousand-fold, Mom.

I want to give thanks in advance to all of the wonderful people who are coming into my life on all levels—professional, social, and personal. I am looking forward to meeting you.

An ultimate thank you goes to all of the people who read this book. I hope you can get something out it and that it helps you in way.

Contents

Chapter 3   GIVING THE THIRD DEGREE 51

Chapter 4   THE USUAL SUSPECTS. 75

PART 2   The Game's Afoot

Chapter 5   THE CASE OF THE DEVILISH DETAILS 123

Chapter 10   THE CASE OF THE LOL LAYOUT 229

PART 1

The Detective's Apprentice

YOU SIT LOOKING AT THE SCREEN, trying to understand why your code is giving you the visual equivalent of gibberish instead of the clear visual diction of your original design. Criminal CSS and browser rendering have gotten the best of you again, but for the last time. You are ready to start your training with the CSS Detective.

IN CHAPTER 1, "Investigating the Scene of the Crime," you'll learn how to go over the evidence in the code, discovering what you're looking at and what you're looking for.

IN CHAPTER 2, "The Tools of the Trade," you'll learn techniques and tips that will go a long way toward preventing coding crimes before they happen.

IN CHAPTER 3, "Giving the Third Degree," we will cover methods of isolating suspicious rules and lines of questioning techniques to get your CSS to 'fess up as to where the rendering problems are coming from.

BY CHAPTER 4, you'll be ready to see the lineup of "The Usual Suspects": common bugs and problems that almost everybody who wrangles CSS has had the misfortune of encountering face-to-face.

Investigating the Scene of the Crime

1

RUSHING INTO A CRIME SCENE TOO HASTILY CAN cause us to miss picking up important pieces of evidence, so we'll start your apprenticeship by going over HTML best practices: document structure, good semantics, and tag structure. From there, we'll move on to CSS, including rule structure, getting the styles into your documents, and commenting.

WE'LL ALSO TAKE A GOOD LOOK AT THE CLUES POSED by inheritance, the cascade, and the vast array of selectors you can employ to target the desired elements in your HTML document.

HTML Document Structure

As you know, HTML (Hypertext Markup Language) is the basis for all things web. And you also probably know that HTML has different version numbers, and that there is a character on the block known as XHTML. Without going into lengthy detail about the version histories and differences, I'll cut to the chase: HTML 4.01 is the latest version of HTML. The W3C (World Wide Web Consortium) is working on a draft of HTML 5.0, which is slated to be released "soon." XHTML was created to be an "extensible" version of HTML, which means that it conforms to the XML syntax and can be made modular (divided into usable components).

To learn more about HTML, see http://www.w3.org/TR/html4/.

The main difference between the two forms of markup is that XHTML by definition needs to be well formed; therefore, all elements need to be in lowercase, all elements need to be closed, and attributes are case-sensitive. By contrast, HTML, technically, does not *need* to be all in lowercase, empty elements do not have to be closed, nor are the attributes case-sensitive. However, just because the specification says you can be loosey-goosey about those items doesn't mean you should be. To conform to best practices and industry standards, you should create consistent, well-formed, semantically correct documents.

Here are the underpinnings of a "well-formed" HTML document in a nutshell:

1. All elements are closed.

2. All tags are in lowercase.

3. All attributes values are enclosed by quotes.

4. All elements are properly nested.

note

See Chapter 3 for an in-depth discussion of doctypes and their importance in an HTML document.

A basic HTML 4.01 document using the strict doctype definition looks like this:

```
<!DOCTYPE HTML PUBLIC "-//W3C//DTD HTML 4.01//EN"
➥ "http://www.w3.org/TR/html4/strict.dtd">
<html>
<head>
<title>HTML 4.01 Strict Document</title>
</head>
<body>

</body>
</html>
```

A basic XHTML 1.0 document using the transitional doctype definition looks like this:

```
<!DOCTYPE html PUBLIC "-//W3C//DTD XHTML 1.0 Transitional//EN"
➥ "http://www.w3.org/TR/xhtml1/DTD/xhtml1-transitional.dtd">
<html xmlns="http://www.w3.org/1999/xhtml">
<head>
<title> XHTML 1.0 Transitional Document</title>
<meta http-equiv="Content-Type" content="text/html; charset=utf-8">
</head>
<body>

</body>
</html>
```

 note

Please refer to the Resources section for a detailed explanation of the differences between HTML and XHTML.

HTML TAG STRUCTURE

HTML tags can be distilled into this syntax:

```
<tagname attribute="value"></tagname>
```

The tag always has a tag name, may have an attribute, and when there is an attribute, the best practice is to always give the attribute a value.

Keep this syntax in mind for later; being able to recognize patterns like this one makes it easy to detect when tags fall outside the pattern.

Here's a little quiz for you. What's wrong with the HTML tag below?

```
<p class, highlight>Hunting for clues</p>
```

I know you caught it: the attribute and value were in the wrong format. Rather, it should be like this:

```
<p class="highlight">Clues found!</p>
```

The CSS pattern is analogous, which you will soon see. With both HTML and CSS, once you have the patterns down, you'll be able to recognize them and know when a tag or a style declaration has gone wrong.

Tags vs. Elements

You may think that the terms *tags* and *elements* are interchangeable, but in fact, they are not. Tags refer to the HTML tag itself, including all of its properties and values. Elements refer not only to the tag, but also to the text and other elements that are enclosed by the tag. An element is a complete entity that starts with the opening tag and ends with the closing tag.

POSH, OR PLAIN OLD SEMANTIC HTML

Standards advocates have coined the phrase "Plain Old Semantic HTML," or POSH, as a mnemonic term to encapsulate the idea of using HTML as it was originally intended: to present information so that it conveys meaning and significance to the reader as well as the reader agent.

So what does that mean for you? It means that you must remember and practice the key concept: semantics over presentation. You've heard the term "separating presentation from content" before, right? It simply means making sure the markup that creates visual effects, but lends no meaning to the structure of the document, is stripped out and put into a style sheet.

To support separating content from presentation, you need to use your tags for their meaning, not for how you would like them rendered by the browser. Think of using the correct tags to convey meaning as adding the right intonation and facial expressions when you talk. Proper semantics are the key to getting the point across with HTML documents.

For example, while the following code snippet is syntactically correct (there are no actual errors), from a semantics standpoint it needs major help:

```
<p>Greatest Detectives of All Times</p>
<p>These have proven to be some of the best detectives to read and
learn from in literature.</p>
<p>Sherlock Holmes<br>
Encyclopedia Brown<br>
Hercule Poirot<br>
The CSS Detective</p>
```

What's wrong with it? There is no indication of what the elements are in relationship to each other, and what they truly are themselves. With the corrected snippet, you can clearly see their identities and the code hierarchy.

```
<h1>Greatest Detectives of All Times</h1>
<p>These have proven to be some of the best detectives to read and
learn from in literature.</p>
<ol>
<li>Sherlock Holmes</li>
<li>Encyclopedia Brown</li>
<li>Hercule Poirot</li>
<li>The CSS Detective</li>
</ol>
```

And trust me, it is truly a boon for both you and your markup. Your HTML will be easier to read, you will be able to better control the visual display, and you will be that much farther on the road to becoming not only a CSS detective, but a CSS pro.

Practices for Achieving POSH:

- Avoid using tags for display instead of meaning.
- Avoid use of <b> for making things bold; use <strong> or <em> instead.
- Avoid use of <br> to create space between elements or paragraphs; use
 only for forced line breaks with paragraphs, for example, with lines of poetry.
- Use semantic id and class values that speak to their function, not their display.
- Stop using tables for layout; use them only for tabular data.
- Use as little HTML as possible to get the job done.
- Avoid using more <div>s on the page than necessary.
- Validate your HTML with an approved validator (see the Resources section).

 **note**

Did you know that semantics helps with accessibility? Having accessible pages means that more than one audience can extract meaning from the page. For example, a screen reader would actually read a word enclosed by <em></em> with vocal emphasis to convey the meaning to a blind user. Not only is using semantic instead of presentational markup the right thing to do, Stevie Wonder would appreciate your efforts.

What's in it for me?

POSH isn't just a nice idea, nor is it solely promoted by a small contingent of well-intentioned groupies. Semantic HTML has become the standard, not the exception, for serious web professionals who care about their craft. What's more, standards-based markup has many immediate and far-reaching benefits such as these:

- Your pages will be easier to maintain.
- Authors, users, and browser agents will find it easier to determine document and content hierarchies and relationships.
- Your pages will get a better search-engine ranking, as document content hierarchy is distinguishable.
- Your pages will load faster thanks to less code.
- Your pages will be more accessible to people seeing the document in an environment where CSS cannot be applied (text-only readers, other media).
- Your pages will be understandable to users who have it read to them through a screen reader.

But finally, writing HTML any other way makes it harder to see where the problems are in your code. Make life easy on yourself and write semantic code!

General HTML troubleshooting tips

When I troubleshoot, I start with the area that I think the problem is in and then work my way out of it in a spiral or concentric circles. I also tell myself "it's something simple," which helps me relax and find problems more easily.

Here are my guidelines for troubleshooting HTML code.

1. Check the <tag> name—is it spelled correctly? You'll know it isn't if you have one or both of these problems:
   - Tag contents (ie, the tagname itself) show up as text.
   - The text or section of the document is not affected by the tag the way you intended.

2. Check that the tag has its ending bracket (>). You'll know it's missing if:

- The tag name shows up as text with a < in front of it.

3. Make sure the start tag has a closing tag—for example, `<tag>word</tag>`. You'll know this is the problem if:

- text—text from the start tag on has that formatting.

- lists—any new lists indent after the initial one.

- tables—the new table is nested within the first table.

4. Check the `<tag attribute="value">` syntax. Check the spelling of the tag name, attributes, and values, and make sure the attribute value has an ending quotation mark. You'll know this is the problem if:

- Contents of the tag don't show up at all.

- Contents of the tag don't have any of the formatting.

- Contents of the tag have some of the formatting, but not all of it.

5. Check that you have placed the attribute you want in the proper tag. You'll know this is the problem if:

- Contents of the tag don't have any of the formatting you wanted.

- Contents of the tag have some of the formatting, but not all of it.

6. Check the order of nested tags. Make sure that tags are nested properly, like parentheses: ([{ *word* }]). For example, `<a href=http://www.something.com><em>this is a link</em></a>`. You'll know this is the problem if:

- This may not show up as a problem—the browser may render it anyway.

- The text may not show up.

7. Check that you have placed the tags in the proper place. You'll know this is the problem if:

- Content is affected in a different area than you intended.

If you are really stumped and can't find the errors in your markup, then validate your page using an HTML validator (see the Resources section for a complete list). Validation for both markup and CSS code is covered in further detail in Chapter 3.

CSS Document Structure

In the most basic form, a CSS style rule or "rule set" has the following syntax:

```
selector {property: value;}
```

Doesn't that look suspiciously like the structure of an HTML tag? Earlier I mentioned that the tag syntax and rule syntax were roughly analogous. The image below (**Figure 1.1**) illustrates what I mean:

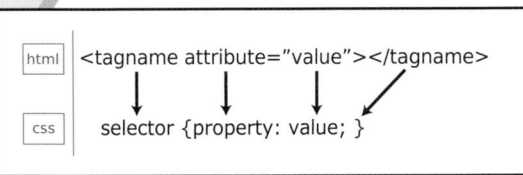

Figure 1.1 *Analogous tag and style-rule structure*

The tag name of the HTML tag and the selector of the CSS style rule are similar, and sometimes even the same if you are using the tag name as the selector. The CSS property is similar to the HTML attribute, and like the tag/selector, may share the same name.

In a style rule, the selector targets the HTML element that will be affected by the rule set. The selector is everything that comes before the curly brackets.

The declaration block is everything that is between the two curly braces, and the style declaration itself is the `property: value` pair. The semicolon at the end is not required for a single declaration, but is used to separate declarations from each other and to end a list of multiple declarations. Therefore, it is a good habit to end all declarations with a semicolon.

Just as HTML tags can have multiple attribute-value pairs in one tag, you can have multiple property-value pairs per style rule:

```
selector {property: value; property: value; property: value;}
```

For some properties, you can also have multiple values for one property:

```
selector {property: value, value, value;}
```

And you can have multiple selectors for a set of properties and values:

```
selector1, selector2, selector3 {property: value; property: value;}
```

In contrast to HTML, the CSS style rule always has a selector, the selector always has a property, and the property always has a value. This is important to keep in mind as it leads to some of the very first clues to hunt for when troubleshooting CSS. Forgot a selector? Then the declaration has nothing to be applied to. Don't have a property? Then the browser can't determine where to assign the value. Missing a value? Then the selector and property are all dressed up with nowhere to go and won't render in the browser. Leave off the opening or closing curly bracket? Then the style won't render, and the style declarations following it may be affected as well. Remember also that misspellings, use of improper terms, and unaccepted values will all have the same effect: your CSS won't work as expected. These sorts of errors are among the most common problems when your pages don't render as expected.

EMPLOYING STYLES IN YOUR DOCUMENTS

Now that you know the syntax, let's look at where to place the style rules. There are several techniques for getting style rules into your HTML pages.

External styles

External style sheets are the modern-day workhorse of standards-based websites. Most websites have at least one style sheet for rendering the page on various media including standard monitors, cell phones, audio browsers, and printers.

Linking to an external style document with `<link>`

Connecting your style sheet to your HTML document is as easy as using the `<link>` tag, which establishes a relationship between documents. Here is the code:

```
<head>
<title>Black and White Page Example</title>
<link rel="stylesheet" href="stylesheet.css" type="text/css">
</head>
```

When the browser renders your page, it reaches the link tag, then retrieves the style sheet document and renders the styles. After the style sheet is downloaded, it is cached and reused without a new call to the server.

The external CSS document should not contain any HTML markup in it at all. The only content it has is style rules and comments. So if you got all riled up and put some `<style></style>` tags in the .css file, remove them! With HTML markup in the style sheet, the browser cannot properly render the page styles.

Obviously, using external style sheets is the best method for a website of any number of pages greater than one. Every page will call the style sheet and apply the styles, making the styles consistent throughout the website. If you ever want to change any piece of presentation, you just change the style sheet and the whole site changes. How in the world did we ever survive without this? Those were dark days pre-CSS!

Linking to an external style document with @import

Like using the `<link>` tag to link to an external CSS document, you can use the `@import` directive through the `<style>` tag to link to external CSS documents.

```
<head>
<title>Black and White Page Example</title>
<style type="text/css">
    @import url("stylesheet.css");
</style>
</head>
```

tip

When linking to a style sheet document from an HTML page, the URL is relative to the location of the HTML page. However, when linking to another file from a style sheet, the URL is relative to the location of the style sheet or the style sheet document.

The Importance of type and rel

One of the most common errors for beginners is to omit the `type` or `rel` attributes. So keep these points in mind:

1. Always indicate `type="text/css"` in the `<link>` or `<style>` tags. Never use `type="text/plain"`.

2. In the `<link>` tag, always indicate `rel="stylesheet"`.

Forgetting either could end up causing your browser to render your pages incorrectly.

The `@import` directive can also be used in an external style sheet. In this case, again, no HTML tags are needed. Simply use the directive as the first declaration in the document:

```
@import url("stylesheet.css");
```

If you use the `@import` directive in any of your style sheets, it needs to be the first declaration. If it is after any other style rules, the browser will ignore it.

A useful advanced technique is to import multiple style sheets from one CSS document using the @import rule in that style sheet.

Document-level or embedded styles

Document-level styles are a great way to create and test all the styles you create for your pages before you export them to an external style sheet.

You place document-level styles in the head of the HTML document using the <style> tag.

```
<head>
<title>Black and White Page Example</title>
<style type="text/css">
body {background-color: #000000; color: #ffffff;}
</style>
</head>
```

The <style> tag always needs the type="text/css" attribute and value, and always needs to be closed.

As mentioned above, document-level styles are great for when you create your initial page or template document, and you want to work in one place to access both your styles and your markup. All of the styles can be reused within the document (as opposed to inline styles, which are only applied to the tag it is in). However, document-level styles add to the size of the page, and the styles are not applicable to any other pages in the website.

Inline styles

Inline styles are valid in HTML 4.01, but are so strongly recommended against that they are practically verboten, while in early proposed drafts of XHTML 2.0 the style attribute is fully deprecated and dropped from the specification altogether. In HTML 4.01 and XHTML 1.0, with the style attribute, you can insert style declarations directly into any HTML tag.

Before you use an inline style, however, think about it: what is the difference between that and, say, using the deprecated <font> tag? The answer is, not a whole lot. Don't use inline styles: the styles themselves are not reusable by other elements on the page, they can't be overwritten by embedded or external styles without the use of !important, they increase page-rendering time, and they quickly become a maintenance nightmare. Implementing your styles in other places will be a lot more powerful and portable for you in the long run.

Comments in Styles

You'll probably use comments in your styles, whether to help you organize and notate what you have created (and why) or to make logical sections of the styles. Commenting your code is a really good practice and well worth a little extra time. When you come back to the code three months (or even three days) later, you'll be happy that you did. After all, you want to be solving CSS mysteries, not creating them!

The comment syntax in styles is as follows:

```
/* comment */
```

Comments can be single words up to multiple lines. You can break lines and have carriage returns inside of the comment tag, and it won't affect the styles one whit.

```
/* A comment with
multiple lines of text. */
```

The one thing you shouldn't do is nest style comments inside each other.

The comment element is also incredibly useful for creating titles for groups of styles, and for temporarily removing a style for testing or troubleshooting.

CSS Foundations

To really troubleshoot CSS, we need to understand a few foundational concepts—specifically, document hierarchy and element relationships, inheritance, the cascade, and specificity.

DOCUMENT TREE, HIERARCHY, AND ELEMENT ANCESTRY

The best way to understand the document tree, document hierarchy, and the relationships between elements is to see them. So let's start with the code:

```
<html>
<head>
<title>Mikey Spillane vs. Mike Hammer</title>
</head>

<body>
<h1>Mikey Spillane vs. Mike Hammer</h1>

<p>Who is the toughest, smartest, and most steely? <em>You</em> get
➡ to be the judge by taking this <a href="survey.html">survey</a>.
➡ </p>
```

```
<p>Next month's survey: Sir Arthur Conan Doyle or Sherlock Holmes?
➡<img src="doyle.jpg" alt="Doyle vs. Holmes"></p>

</body>
</html>
```

We can illustrate the document tree visually:

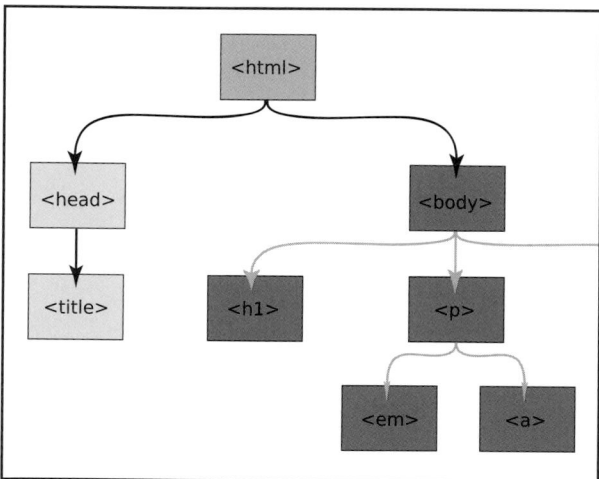

Figure 1.2 *Document tree showing hierarchy and element ancestry*

In this example, the html tag is the main ancestor of all of the tags in the document. In the <body> of the page, the <h1>, <p>, <img>, <em>, and <a> tags are all descendants of the <body> tag. The <h1> and <p> are siblings, and the <em>, <a>, and <img> are descendants of one of the <p> tags.

Did you notice the pattern? A descendant element is nested inside another element, which is its ancestor.

Let's delve deeper into element relationships to get the full picture of the "family tree."

An **ancestor** is any element that is connected to other elements but is higher up the document tree, no matter how many levels up. For example, in the document above, both the <html> and <body> tags are ancestors of the <p> tag.

A **descendant** is any element connected to an ancestor, but lower in the document tree, no matter how many levels down. In our example, the <em>, <a>, and <img> are descendants of the <body> tag.

A **parent** is an element directly above a connected element in the document tree. A parent element is also an ancestor, but an element can have ancestors that are not its parents.

A **child** element is directly below a connected element. A child is a descendant, but an element can have descendants that are not its children.

Sibling elements share the same parent, and are on the same level as each other in the hierarchy.

INHERITANCE

Just as art mimics life, so does CSS. One of the foundations of CSS, **inheritance**, is like a drama set in 18th-century England: just as in a family with descendants fighting for the fortune of a wealthy relative, in CSS, style rules often have to duke it out to be the one whose properties get expressed and displayed.

Inheritance is a process by which ancestor elements pass down selected properties to their descendants. The quality of inheritance in CSS is truly a godsend. Think about it: without inheritance, you would have to establish some of the exact same style rules for *every single element* in the page.

note

Please see the Resources section for a full list of properties that are inherited by default.

Not all the properties of the ancestor element are inherited, however, and there is a beautiful logic to the way inheritance works. Properties that are related to text display, foreground color, and list styles are inherited. These are the properties you most likely want to stay consistent throughout the document. In contrast, properties related to the box model are not inherited. These include margin, padding, borders, position (absolute, relative, and z-index), display, and overflow. You wouldn't want these styles to be inherited—pages would be practically incomprehensible if properties like margin, padding, or position were inherited automatically.

note

If you have a situation where you want a property that normally would not be inherited to be inherited, you can force inheritance by using the inherit *value.*

THE CASCADE

Understanding how the **cascade** works is one of the most important skills to have as a CSS detective. In essence, the cascade is the property of styles being applied layer upon layer to each other. Some of your issues may be fixed simply by changing the order of your styles, but knowing the rules of the cascade will help you write cleaner, more concise style declarations.

Origin and importance

What happens when two or more conflicting styles target the same element in the page?

The style that ultimately gets applied trumps all of the others based on a scale of specificity (explained below). To get a visual equivalent of the concept of the cascade, imagine styles as steps. Styles that are closer to the element are more important, and more likely to be applied.

The first part of the cascade is determined by the origin of the styles themselves. Styles can originate from three places: the user agent, the author, or the user himself.

User agent is another term for a browser. Browsers have default styles built into them that will render an HTML page a certain way whether there are styles attached to it or not.

Author styles are the style sheets attached to the HTML file either externally via a link or @import, or embedded at the document level in the <head>.

User styles are a set of styles established by the user for his particular browser. This may be the case if a user is sight impaired or has any other disability that needs accommodating for on a consistent basis.

Normal style declarations can be taken up a notch and designated as !important. Doing so causes the style to override the cascade and be implemented over any conflicting styles. Both the style author and user can designate !important styles. !important user styles will override !important author styles.

Here is the cascade for user agents, author, and user styles (**Figure 1.3**):

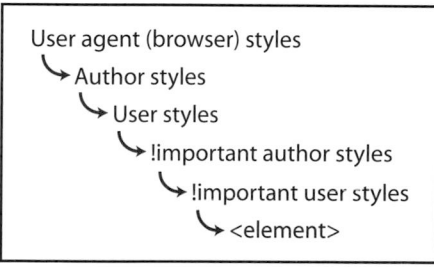

Figure 1.3 *The cascade for user agents, author, and user styles*

The second factor in the cascade is the location of the style, whether it's external, document level, or inline. This is a key factor in determining distance or closeness from the element targeted by the styles.

External style sheets are farther away from the element, document-level embedded styles are closer, and inline styles are closest.

Here is the cascade for external styles to inline styles (**Figure 1.4**):

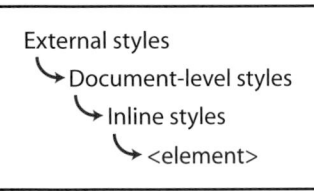

Figure 1.4 *The cascade for external styles to inline styles*

Specificity

The term **specificity** refers to how specific a style rule is to the desired element. The mechanism works like this: the more specific a rule is, the more easily it will trump other rules that may be targeting the same element. Let's use the close-versus-distant metaphor: if the selector is less specific, then it is more distant from the element, whereas if it very specific, then it is closer to the element. The closer the rule to the element, the higher the specificity weight or number, and the more precedence that rule has over others targeting the same element.

Specificity takes into consideration all of the selectors to determine the proximity of the style rule to the element. Here are the questions you would ask to calculate the specificity weight and thus see which style will ultimately get applied to the element:

1. Is it an inline style? If yes, then it has more weight. If it's not an inline style, then proceed to Question 2.

2. How many ids are in the selector? The more it has, the higher the weight. If there are no ids in the selector, then proceed to Question 3.

3. How many class names, pseudo-classes, and attributes are there in the selector? The more it has, the higher the weight. If there are none of these in the selector, then proceed to Question 4.

4. How many element names or pseudo-elements are there in the selector? This number will ultimately determine the weight of the style rule. (See the next section for a description and examples of pseudo-elements.)

5. If it has !important in the declaration, then it has more specificity weight than any other style.

Order

The order in which the styles are listed is important on all levels of styles: the order of the links to the style sheets, the style tag, and the @import directive in the HTML document; where the style is listed in the external style sheets, and where the style is listed within the style tag at the document level. The farther down the style is in the order of the documents, the closer it is to the element—and thus, the more weight and precedence it will have over any conflicting styles (**Figure 1.5** and **1.6**).

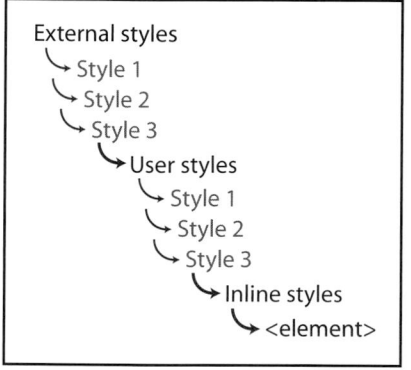

Figure 1.5 *Style order*

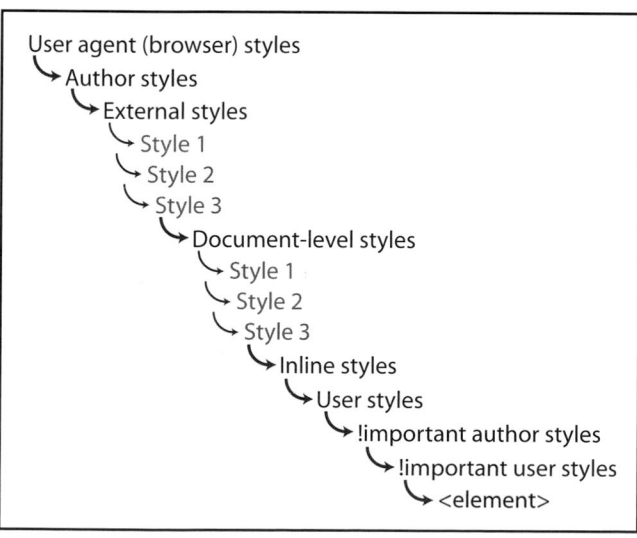

Figure 1.6 *The grand view of the cascade, taking all factors into consideration*

SELECTORS

Styles don't do us much good until they are associated with an HTML element in a web page. To enable us to target the exact elements on the page for the maximum amount of display control, the CSS 1 and CSS 2 specifications provide a vast number of selectors.

General selectors

The possibilities for applying selectors seem almost endless, but you have to know the right way to do so. Once you know the rules for creating selectors and understand the patterns, writing well-constructed CSS will be a snap. As a bonus, you'll able to troubleshoot really well and discern the root of any issues that may come up later.

Universal

The universal selector is the asterisk (*). This selector lets you select every element on the page and apply the style rules to them.

```
*{font-family: Arial, sans-serif;}
```

Element/type

The element or type selector targets an HTML element, and thus uses a tag name. This enables you to select any of this kind of element in the document.

```
p {font-size: 1em;}
```

Class

In HTML, every single tag can have the class attribute. A class selector targets the value of a class attribute of a tag. A class attribute can be used multiple times in a document and applied to different elements.

For example, both <p> and the <li> tag have the class attribute with the value of "highlight" assigned to them, so they both get the style applied to them:

```
<p class="highlight">Someone has been murdered!</p>
<p>What was the possible weapon?</p>
<ul>
<li>A candlestick </li>
<li class="highlight">A lead pipe</li>
<li>A rope</li>
</ul>

.highlight {color: #ffcc00;}
```

Because you can use a class selector many times in a document with multiple elements, it is very flexible and portable.

You can increase the specificity of a class selector by attaching it to an element selector, which would cause the style to be applied only to an element with a class attribute with that value.

So, from the example above, if you wanted only an <li> with the class="highlight" to have the color declared, you would change the selector to this:

```
li.highlight {color: #ffcc00;}
```

ID

Id selectors target an element with a particular id attribute. Ids help you zero in on a particular element, because you can only use an id once in any document. Ids have a very high specificity weight.

```
<div id="maincontent">
<p>Would Nancy Drew ever write a tell-all? <em>Yes, she would.</em>
➥In <a href="nancydrewconfessions.html">"Confessions of Nancy Drew"</a>
➥you'll find out that being a teen sleuth is not all the glitz and
➥glamour that you may think.</p>
<p>Still want to be a detective? Then keep reading. <img
src="fingerprint.jpg" alt="fingerprint"></p>
</div>

#maincontent {background-color: #eee;}
```

IDs and Element Selectors

You could use the element that the id is associated with in the selector like so:

```
div#maincontent {background-color: #eee;}
```

In this case, I added div. However, because the id that you are using is unique to the page, the addition of the element name is unnecessary. The results would be the same.

Contextual selectors (relationship-based)

There are several selectors that focus on target elements based on their relationship with other elements in the document tree. The important thing to remember about all of the relationship-based or combined selectors—also sometimes called **combinators**—is that the target element is the final element of the combinator. It is easy to get distracted by all of the selectors at the beginning, but they are only there in reference to the element at the end.

Let's take a look at the different combinations available.

Descendant

Descendant selectors select the element that is a descendant of another element in the document tree.

```
<div id="sidebar">
<h2>Missing Jewels</h2>
</div>
```

The syntax is as follows:

```
ancestor selector (space) descendant selector {property: value;}
```

So to target the <h2> that is the descendant of the <div>, we would write this:

```
div h2 {color: green;}
```

Child

A child selector targets an element that is a child of another element. Remember that a child is a direct descendant of an element in the document tree (as opposed to a more distant descendant).

```
<p>Here is text that is <strong>forcefully</strong> emphasized.
➥More text, but that is only normally <em>emphasized</em>.</p>
```

Here's the syntax:

```
parent selector > descendant selector {property: value;}
```

So to target the <strong> element that is the child of the <p> element, we would write this:

```
p > strong {font-family: Tahoma, sans-serif;}
```

Sibling/adjacent

A sibling selector (also known as adjacent) selects an element that is next to another element in the document tree.

```
<div id="sectiontwo">
<h3>Priorities</h3>
<p>Things to accomplish today</p>
<ol>
<li>Interrogate suspects for the case of the Lost Content</li>
<li>Track clues for the case of the Notorious Em</li>
<li>Clean kitchen</li>
</ol>
</div>
```

This is the syntax:

```
sibling selector + sibling selector {property: value;}
```

To target the <ol> element next to the <p> element (which are both descendants and children of the <div> element), we would write this:

```
p + ol {font-family: Georgia, serif;}
```

Pseudo-class selectors

Pseudo-class selectors let you select elements that are not part of the document tree, but rather are events or qualities of certain elements.

Link pseudo-classes

You use link pseudo-classes to target link text in its various states.

- :link targets an unvisited link
- :visited targets a visited link

Dynamic pseudo-classes

These pseudo-classes are typically used on the link element, but you can apply them to any element on the page as well.

- :focus targets any element that is in focus
- :hover targets any element that is being selected by a pointing device (such as a cursor)
- :active targets any element that is activated by the user (such as an active link)

note
We will explore more complex variations of pseudo class combinations in Chapter 2.

The order of these pseudo-classes is important as it mimics the cascade that the browser follows, and most of the states are mutually exclusive. For example, you must have a regular link state before you have a visited link state.

Many people use the mnemonic *LoVe For HAte* to remember the order `:link`, `:visited`, `:focus`, `:hover`, `:active`. Usually, all of the link styles are written together:

```
a {color: #3f0;}
a:link {text-decoration: none;}
a:visited {color: #0f3;}
a:focus {text-decoration: none;}
a:active {color: #f03;}
a:hover {text-decoration: underline; color: #636;}
```

Esoteric selectors

These selectors are part of the CSS specifications, but not as widely used because of support issues with some browsers. Over time, however, the use of esoteric selectors will probably increase. I encourage you to check recent browser-support charts to determine which browsers support these selectors. Several helpful browser-support charts are listed in the Resources section.

Other pseudo-classes

- `:first-child` targets any element that is the first child of its parent element.

  ```
  <ol>
    <li>this list item is a first-child.</li>
    <li>this list item is not.</li>
  </ol>

  li:first-child {font-variant: italic;}
  ```

- `:lang(n)` targets any element on the basis of the language that has been set for it.

  ```
  <cite lang="fr">Faites les bon temps rouler!</cite>

  :lang(fr) { font-face: Gigi, sans-serif;}
  ```

Pseudo-element

Pseudo-elements also target entities in the document that are not explicitly part of the document tree.

- `:first-letter` targets the first line of text within an element.

```
<h1>Solving your first case</h1>
<p>Make sure you act cool, calm, and collected. Remember
➥everything you have learned about deduction, and take your
➥toolkit.</p>

h1 + p:first-letter {font-size: 110%;}
```

- `:first-line` targets the first letter of a line of text within an element.

```
<p>Once you arrive at the scene of the crime, you have to start
➥gathering the evidence. Hopefully, they won't have tidied up
➥before you got there!</p>

p:first-line {font-weight: bold;}
```

- `:before` specifies content to be inserted before a given element.

```
#breadcrumbnav:before {content: "Current page:";}
```

- `:after` specifies content to be inserted after a given element.

```
<p>the crime took place at <span class="time">13:00</span>.</p>

.time:after {content: "hours";}
```

Attribute

Attribute selectors let you target an element by its attribute or attribute value.

- `selector[attribute]` targets a selector with a particular attribute.

```
<a href="http://www.mst3kinfo.com" title="Mystery Science Theater
➥3000"> Mystery Science Theater 3000</a>

a[title] {font-variant: italic;}
```

- `selector[attribute="value"]` targets a selector with a particular attribute and specific value.

```
<img src="catchathief.jpg" alt="learn how to catch a thief">

img[src="catchathief.jpg"] {border: 1px solid #999;}
```

 **note**

Weirdly, the value does not need to be quoted.

- `selector [attribute~="value"]` targets a selector with a particular attribute and value where the value is one of multiple values separated by a space.

```
<img src="csi.jpg" alt="CSI">

img[alt~="CSI"] {border: 1px #ff8000 solid;}
```

- selector [attribute|="value"] targets an element with an attribute that contains values separated by a hyphen in a list.

```
<img src="lg-rope.gif" width="500" height="300" title="large-rope">

img[title|="large"] {border: 1px solid #000;}
```

STYLES OF WRITING CSS

People have different styles for writing their CSS code. You want to aim for maximum ease of readability and scanability for yourself and anyone else who may read your code after you.

Here are some ways of writing your style rules that can make your code more readable.

Style rule all in one line

```
selector {property: value; property: value; property: value;}
```

Pro: All of the styles are on one line and thus easy to find in the document.

Con: It may be difficult to scan to find the property-value pair you are looking for.

Selector separated from style rules

```
selector {
property: value;
property: value;
property: value;}
```

Pro: The style-declaration block is on a separate line from the selector, which can make it easier to find both the selector and the declarations.

Con: Breaking the declarations onto separate lines may cause the style-sheet page to be marginally larger.

Selector separated from style rules, declarations indented

```
selector
{
   property: value;
   property: value;
   property: value;
}
```

Pros: The style-declaration block is on a separate line from the selector, and with the declarations indented, it's easy to distinguish between the selector and the styles. Style declarations are easy to scan. You can add new declarations without worrying about the end bracket.

Con: Breaking the declarations onto separate lines may cause the style-sheet page to be marginally larger.

In all the cases above, the line breaks have no effect—the page will render the same. There are many other slight variations, but ultimately, it just boils down to your personal style. The way you think and find information visually will determine what best works for you.

PRELIMINARY CSS TROUBLESHOOTING TIPS

At this point, with the core concepts of the cascade and the structure of selectors under your belt, you have a good idea of how to approach any future coding crime scenes. But you also need to be able to correctly identify the evidence. By focusing on the syntax patterns for the different kinds of selectors and style rules, we can arrive at the first set of foundational trouble-shooting tips for style declarations.

Basic style syntax troubleshooting

Selectors
- Check spelling.
- If grouped, make sure you have commas between selectors. Make sure there is no comma between the selector list and the opening curly bracket, and that you don't accidentally use double commas.
- If combinators, check that your combinator syntax is correct.

Properties
- Check spelling.
- Check that you are using the correct property name.
- Check that you are using the correct format and order (such as with shorthand properties).
- If multiple, make sure you have semicolons between the `property:value` declarations to separate them.

Values

- Check spelling.

- Check that you are using the correct unit of measure for the value.

- Check that the value is an acceptable value for the property.

- Where applicable, make sure the value is properly enclosed by quote marks.

Declaration block

- Make sure your declaration block is enclosed with curly brackets (not square or angle brackets).

- Make sure your whole style declaration ends with a semicolon (which, with the end curly bracket, essentially delimits the end of the declaration).

In the markup

- If you are linking to an external style sheet using the `<link>` tag, make sure you have `rel="stylesheet"`.

- If you are embedding styles, make sure you have a closing `</style>` tag.

Typical Tip-offs

How can you know what the culprits of your problems are? Here are some outcomes to look for:

Outcome/Problem	Possible Culprits
The style doesn't show up at all on the page	• a nonexistent or misspelled selector • a missing opening or closing curly bracket • `rel="stylesheet"` missing from the `<link>` tag • incorrect URL to the style sheet in the `<link>` tag
The styles lower in the style sheet don't show up on the page.	The previous style declaration wasn't properly closed with a semicolon or an end bracket.
The style shows up, but is applied to the wrong element.	Your combinator selector probably has improper structure and is targeting the wrong element.

These guidelines are just the beginning. As we start to review the tools of the trade, you will learn some time-honored techniques for writing better and more efficient CSS code, as well as some intermediate troubleshooting tips.

The Tools of the Trade

WHILE I WOULD HAVE PREFERRED TO ATTRIBUTE this saying to Sherlock Holmes, it was Benjamin Franklin who stated, "an ounce of prevention is worth a pound of cure." That adage is rarely as true as when it comes to troubleshooting CSS.

A STRONG REPERTOIRE OF PROPER TECHNIQUES will put you on a good footing from the start. These tools create the equivalent of a neighborhood watch, discouraging CSS felons and forestalling a significant number of potential future offenses. When the game's under way, you'll be ready!

Advanced Selectors and Style Declarations

Selectors pinpoint elements on the page, in order to apply styles to the elements. To build the components of your detective toolkit, we will take a closer look at styling elements with advanced selectors.

GROUPING SELECTORS

As you learned in Chapter 1, a selector can be a list of elements:

```
selector1, selector2, selector3 {property: value; property: value;}
```

This technique of having multiple selectors for a style declaration is referred to as **grouping** selectors. Grouping helps decrease the size of your style sheet, because instead of using the same declaration for each element, you can list them together.

For example, you could take code like this:

```
h1 {font-family: Verdana, sans-serif;}
h2 {font-family: Verdana, sans-serif;}
h3 {font-family: Verdana, sans-serif;}
h4 {font-family: Verdana, sans-serif;}
```

And condense it down to this:

```
h1, h2, h3, h4 {font-family: Verdana, sans-serif;}
```

Isn't that better? It's easier to read and find what you may be looking for, and it's only one line of code instead of four!

COMPLEX RELATIONSHIP SELECTORS

The contextual selectors—pseudo-elements, pseudo-classes, and attributes—are sometimes considered advanced selectors, which I consider complex because they combine selector types. You can create ultraspecific selectors using all of the essential selectors in combination.

For example, with any of the link pseudo-classes, you can have selectors like these:

```
a.aboutus:link {text-decoration: none;}
```

```
#unav a.aboutus:link {
```

note
The first line is a pseudo-element with a class, while the second block is a pseudo-element with a class as a descendant of an id. The third example is an element with a class as a child of an element with a class that is a descendant of an id.

```
text-decoration: none;
color: #ffcc99;}
```

```
#footer ol.firstcollinks > li.highlight {font-weight: bold;}
```

Once you identify which element to target, you can combine multiple types of selectors to create highly specific contextual selectors that will target any element on the page like a laser.

MULTIPLE CLASSES TO ONE ELEMENT

Another cool technique is to apply multiple class styles to an element. Although this is not a selector itself, it is an advanced way to use class selectors.

Say you have these two style rulesets:

```
.leftfloat {float; left;}
.thinborder {border: 1px solid #000000;}
```

And say you wanted to apply them both to a single element on the page. Easy. All you have to do is refer to both styles like so:

```
<img src="magnifyingglass.png" class="leftfloat thinborder"
alt="magnifying glass" />
```

Both styles will be applied to the image.

This technique works best with styles that are fairly straightforward and widely applicable. While you are creating your page and beginning to form your styles, see which ones can be structured as simple styles so that you can stack them up via the class attribute.

STYLE SHORTHAND

Now it's time to get tricky. I introduce to you shorthand styles.

Style shorthand was created to act as a way of condensing multiple style declarations into one. Once you understand the rules for each set of shorthand properties, you will find that they are easy to use.

Thankfully, not all properties have a shorthand equivalent—that would be a lot to remember! There are only a limited number of groups of properties that take shorthand. The main ones are border, padding, margin, background, font, and list-style.

There are three points to keep in mind when using style shorthand:

1. You do not have to state all of the values, but there are certain values that you must establish in order for the style to be applied.

2. Any value that you do not provide explicitly will be filled in by the default value for that user agent (aka browser); so if you want a particular value, you absolutely need to make the value explicit—otherwise the browser will use its own value.

3. The order of the values can be important for certain properties. Some values are dependent upon the explicit declaration of other values.

Shorthand properties

Shorthand properties are extremely consistent. Again, it's all about patterns. Once you understand the pattern for constructing shorthand styles for one set of properties, you will know what to do with the rest of them.

Margin

Have you written margin properties like this?

```
#localnavigation {
margin-top: 10px;
margin-right: 10px;
margin-bottom: 10px;
margin-left: 10px;
}
```

Shorthand can reduce the above code to this:

```
#localnavigation {margin: 10px;}
```

"But no," you say, "my code is much more complicated than that: I have four different values established, not just one." As the French would say, *pas de quoi!*—it's nothing! All you have to do is follow the logical syntax:

```
margin: margin-top margin-right margin-bottom margin-left;
```

In other words:

```
margin: 10px 5px 20px 15px;
```

Note the pattern here: it is like clockwork, literally. The positions follow the clockface starting with 12 o'clock, so if you can tell time, you can remember the order of the values. Some people use the mnemonic *TRouBLe* to remember the order, but I find the clockface image easier. Go with whatever works for you.

If you include one value, all four sides will have the same margin. With two values, the top and bottom with both have the first value, and the left and right will have the second value. If you include three values, the first value defines the top-margin, the second value defines the left- and right-margin values, and the third value defines the bottom-margin.

Padding

The `padding` shorthand property condenses the `padding-top`, `padding-right`, `padding-bottom`, and `padding-left` properties into one.

As with the `margin` shorthand property, you can establish one value for all four positions:

```
padding: 10px;
```

Or use two values, for the top/bottom and right/left positions:

```
padding: 5px 15px;
```

That's 5px of padding on top/bottom and 15px for the right/left.

Or three values—one each for the top, the right/left, and the bottom:

```
padding: 10px 5px 15px;
```

That's 10px of padding for the top, 5px for the right/left, and 15px for the bottom.

Or finally, four values, one for each position:

```
padding: 10px 5px 20px 15px;
```

You'll recognize this as 10px top padding, 5px right padding, 20px bottom padding, and 15 left padding.

These order notations work for the `margin` property as well.

Border

You may have written CSS code that looks like this:

```
#maincontent {
   border-width: 1px;
   border-style: solid;
   border-color: #eaeaea;
   }
```

You can condense all of that code into one shorthand `border` style:

```
#maincontent {border: 1px solid #eaeaea;}
```

You probably gleaned the syntax from the example:

```
border: border-width border-style border-color;
```

In this case, the order of the values is not important. You could list them in any order and the style would still show up correctly. However, if you keep to this standard order, it will be easier to detect mistakes.

What if you want to establish width, style, and color for multiple borders? It can be done! Other border shorthand properties are as follows: `border-top`, `border-right`, `border-bottom`, `border-left`.

In the case of the `border` shorthand properties, it is good to know the default values. If you don't declare them, the default values are as follows:

```
border: medium none color;
```

This means that if you want the width of the border to be `medium`, then you don't have to declare it. Similarly, if you want the border to be the same color as the text, you don't have to declare that. The only required value is `border-style`. As long as you have that one value, the style will be applied to the element.

Background

The background shorthand property can really pack a wallop, because it condenses a lot of properties into one tidy package. The `background` property encompasses `background-attachment`, `background-color`, `background-image`, `background-position`, and `background-repeat`.

Here is the syntax:

```
background: background-color background-image background-attachment
background-position background-repeat;
```

note
When declaring a background image, you will generally want to declare a background color as well.

The order is unimportant, and there are no required values.

```
background: #aaa url(maltesefalcon.jpg) fixed 50% 50% no-repeat;
```

Here are the default values:

```
background: transparent none scroll 0 0 repeat;
```

In terms of the background position, it is important to know that if you declare only one of the background position values but not the second; the declared value will be the horizontal value; and the background image will be vertically centered.

Font

Much like the background property, the font property reduces a lot of information into a little space. The font shorthand property incorporates the font-style, font-family, font-variant, font-size, font-weight, and line-height.

A word to the wise: for this property to work correctly, you do need to declare both the font-size and the font-family.

Here is the syntax:

```
font: font-style font-variant font-weight font-size/line-height
font-family;
```

And an example:

```
p.intro {font: italic normal normal .9em/1 Palatino, serif;}
```

In the font shorthand property, the one value that is dependent upon another is line-height. You cannot establish the value of line-height unless you have first established the font-size, and it must come directly after font-size, separated by a /.

The default value depends on both the element and the browser, but is generally this:

```
font: normal normal normal 1em/1.4em serif;
```

Lists

Finally, we are left with list-style. The list-style shorthand property brings together the longhand list properties of list-style-image, list-style-position, and list-style-type.

Syntax:

```
list-style: list-style-type list-style-position list–style-image;
```

Example:

```
ul {list-style: square inside url("squaretarget.gif");}
```

Default:

```
list-style: disc outside none;
```

Color shorthand

I'm sure you know that you can use either color names such as red or hexadecimal numbers such as #ff0000 for color values in styles. There are additional options.

You can use the RGB number values like so:

```
.callout {color: rgb(255,0,0);}
```

Or use RGB color percentage values:

```
.callout {color: rgb(100%, 0%, 0%)}
```

However, the true gem in color notation is the three-digit hexadecimal shorthand. With this color shorthand, a color like #ffcc00 becomes #fc0.

Do you see the pattern? You can truncate the number only if the values in each R, G, and B position are the same number. Thus, a color like #fea02c cannot be represented in color shorthand, nor can #fe3399.

SHORTHAND TROUBLESHOOTING TIPS

Shorthand is great, but like any part of CSS, it can lead to trouble. Here are some things to watch out for:

1. Know the default values.

Remember that any value you don't explicitly establish will take on the default value. You may actually want to use the default value. However, if you do not, be sure to provide the property value that you want applied instead.

2. Know your shorthand syntax.

Use references to double-check and make sure you are using the correct values for the desired result.

3. In some cases, beware of the order of property values.

The order is important when one property's value relies on the previous establishment of another property's value. If they are not in the proper order, the browser may ignore the declaration.

4. Establish all the values that are necessary for that particular shorthand property.

Some declarations will be completely ignored if any of the required values are missing.

CSS Reset

If our goal is to start off strong from the beginning, employing a CSS reset may be one of the strongest tools in our arsenal against code gone afoul.

WHEREFORE ART THOU, RESET?

Or, in modern verbiage, "Why use a CSS reset?"

Much to many a developer's chagrin, the properties for elements are not consistent across user agents. These differences between the browsers' default presentation styles wouldn't be so bad if they only affected minor, infrequently used HTML entities. But the differences are evident with the most major tags and properties, such as the padding and margins for headings and paragraphs; the indentation for headings, lists, and other tags; and line-heights. Although this may not seem like much, you will find that these differences can have a strong effect on the visual rhythm and look-and-feel of a page.

In order to avoid the rendering ills that result from the variations in browsers' style sheets, many coders explicitly reset the styles for the most common elements in their style sheets. In this way, one no longer has to fall victim to the idiosyncrasies of the various browsers, and can be more in control of how consistently the styles are rendered. In essence, a CSS reset creates a tabula rasa and paves the way for a more consistent cross-browser user experience.

TO RESET OR NOT TO RESET, THAT IS THE QUESTION

There are benefits to employing a CSS reset. Not only can you control the margin and padding of common elements, but you can also establish the font size, weight, family, and style. You can be deliberate about each element's presentation.

However, some argue that the reset is overkill, and that it makes them spend more time trying to get elements to show up the way they want. Some suggest that using a CSS reset focuses too much on trying to achieve pixel-perfect layouts, and that the errant styles don't need to be cleared completely, merely *overwritten* with your own styles.

As a CSS detective, you need to pinpoint what and where your problems are in order to solve them. To that end, starting with a clean slate will make solving your CSS mysteries easier.

AS YOU LIKE IT: APPROACHES AND RECOMMENDATIONS

You'll decide how you want to structure your CSS reset based on which properties of which elements you want to clear and reestablish.

While you could create your own CSS reset, there are many available already. I recommend finding a nice repository of them online and choosing one that fits your needs.

Here is an example of a basic, minimal CSS reset:

```
html, body {
    padding: 0;
    margin: 0;
    }
html {font-size: 1em;}
body {font-size: 100%;}
a img {border: 0;}
```

This CSS reset clears the padding and margins of the HTML and body elements, and forces a reset on the base font-size. It also removes the border from image links.

Please see the Resources section for where to find other great CSS resets.

tip

It helps to know the differences between the popular user agents' default style sheets. See the Resources section for recommendations of sites that list and compare various browsers' properties for common elements.

Beware the Universal Selector Reset

Some people use the universal selector in their **CSS** reset. You may come across this code:

```
* {margin: 0; padding: 0;}
```

This is a drastic reset: it removes the margin and padding for *every element* on the page, including inline elements that already have no padding or margin. It also removes the padding on all form elements, which you don't want to do.

Furthermore, the universal selector reset triggers some specific bugs in certain browsers. Some elements won't take the property back despite an explicit style declaration later in the style sheet.

I recommend against using this particular form of **CSS** reset. Instead, think ahead about which elements you want to control explicitly, and then use only those as the selectors for your reset styles.

Building a Solid Foundation

While it is easy to rush into trying to create and complete your website projects as quickly as possible, thorough planning will prevent many coding errors down the line and should be a key practice in your CSS detective approach.

TAILORED HTML

You want your HTML to perfectly fit the needs of the layout, reflect the proper page semantics, and create the ideal container for the content. This kind of tailored HTML is easy to achieve if you think it through.

Plan out your page from the outside in and from the top down. Sketch out the page sections and figure out ahead of time what the semantics will be. This process starts your brain thinking right from the start about how to construct the code and what styles you will need to create.

Code your HTML first

While you may think it is more efficient to create your CSS styles while you are coding the page's HTML, think again. Write the HTML markup first, before you create even one style declaration.

Why? Because by doing so, you'll thoroughly understand the semantics of the document and document tree: creating styles based on relationship and context will make much more sense.

Create semantic hooks

As you know, your styles will be applied to the ids, classes, and elements you employ as selectors. The ids and classes that tie your styles to the page elements are sometimes referred to as **hooks**.

Base your `id` and `class` names on the semantics of the page, not on the visual aspects of the design. Why? The page semantics are based on the structure and meaning of the information on the page, and thus will stay the same. The visual layout, as well as colors and other design elements, may change with a site redesign or branding effort.

For example, if you name something `redrightcolumn`, but eventually the colors are changed and the column is no longer on the right, that element will be much more difficult to identify. Instead, focus on what the content is or what the content does. A better name would refer to the content of that page section—for example, `favoriteslist`.

Generating Selector Names

The CSS specification states the following:

In CSS 2.1, identifiers (including element names, classes, and IDs in selectors) can contain only the characters [A-Za-z0-9] and ISO 10646 characters U+00A1 and higher, plus the hyphen (–) and the underscore (_); they cannot start with a digit.

This means you can't name your style by starting with a number like `101solutions {...}`, as the style would simply be ignored in some browsers. You shouldn't start a selector with a hyphen or an underscore either, although they can be used later in the selector name.

tip

When you create the markup for a page with a complex layout and many content sections, one helpful technique is to notate the end of a page section with an HTML comment. So at the end of each major page division, you can add a comment after the closing tag. This will help you see the div pairs more easily and as a unit/ single element.

```
<div id="bodycontent">
...
</div>
<!-- end bodycontent -->
```

Practice preventive medicine

Think of it this way: you are working to achieve "CSS Wellness." As you know, it is better to not catch a cold at all than to try to get over one. So let's enact some preventive measures to avoid coming down with bad cases of "divitis" and "classitis."

The `<div>` tag is intended to create logical sections in the HTML document—such as the header, main body, sidebars, and footer—for both semantic and presentation purposes. One should be able to think correctly of the `<div>` as a division in the page. However, many developers take a good thing too far, and fall ill with divitis by creating divs that lend nothing to the meaning of the page.

When creating your HTML markup, ask yourself:

- Do I really need this `<div>`? What do I really want this `<div>` to do?
- Is this `<div>` about semantics or is it just for presentation?
- Is there another element already present, one with semantic meaning, to which I can assign an `id`?

Build your immunity

- Keep in mind the semantic meaning of block-level HTML elements, and use them appropriately when creating markup.
- Leverage block-level HTML elements instead of adding an additional `<div>`.

  This code...

```
<div id="pagehead">
  <div class="strong">Heading</div>
</div>
<div id="subhead">
  <div class="strong">Sub Heading</div>
</div>
<div>This is the content</div>
```

...becomes this code:

```
<h1>Heading</h1>
<h2>Sub Heading</h2>
<p>This is the content</p>
```

- Assign multiple classes to one element, instead of targeting the element with an additional <div> with an id and a descendant element with a class.

  No-no:

```
<h2>Who has a clue?</h2>
<div id="cluelist">
<ol>
   <li class="suspects">Colonel Mustard</li>
   <li class="suspects">Miss Scarlet</li>
   <li class="suspects">Professor Plum</li>
</ol>
</div>
#cluelist {font-variant: small-caps;}
li.suspects {font-style: italic;}
```

  Yes, yes:

```
<h2>Who has a clue?</h2>
<ol class="cluelist suspects">
<li>Colonel Mustard</li>
<li>Miss Scarlet</li>
<li>Professor Plum</li>
</ol>
.cluelist li {font-variant: small-caps;}
.suspects li {font-style: italic;}
```

- Consider altering some of your design decisions if it means lightening the load of the page by removing unnecessary divs.

Classes fall prey to a similar affliction. Classitis often occurs when coders create classes for every little style instead of working with the rules of the cascade to create only styles are that are well targeted and necessary.

Build your immunity

- Understand the cascade and use it to your advantage.

  Make a rule that you will only declare a property once, then be strategic and deliberate about placing that style early enough in the style sheet so that it will be properly inherited.

- Pay attention to default values of elements.

  Unless you have done a style reset, there are many properties that you do not have to declare, such as `font-weight: bold` for any of the header tags or `margin: 0;` on inline elements.

- Keep selectors that you will use on multiple elements generic by not tying them to a particular tag.

  You can establish some basic styles for all the style sheets that you will use all the time, such as these three for applying and clearing floats:

```
.left {float: left;}
.right {float: right;}
.clear {clear: both;}
```

SLEEK CSS

At this point, your HTML should be expertly constructed to show off the assets of the content. The next step is to create CSS that completes the well-groomed and polished presentation. Challenge yourself to write the most trim and graceful CSS that you can. Some people would argue that well-written code is poetry. You may be no bard, but the tips below can guide you toward creating your own CSS masterpieces.

Know the properties and values

I'm not suggesting that you memorize *all* of the CSS properties and their corresponding values. However, you should know them well enough to know when something just does not look or feel right and you need to check a reference.

- Know your values, and remember default values (or have a great reference).
- Know the range of applicable units of measurement.

  There is a wide range of units of measurements for length, height, and font size in CSS. Be aware of what is possible for the property and value.

Zero Units of Measurement

You have probably heard this before, but it bears repeating: when you use 0 as the value, you don't need a unit of measurement. Thus, 0px, em, %, and so on are simply 0. Save yourself a little time and trouble!

- In declaration values there are no quotation marks, except when declaring a string.

  The only times you may use quote marks are with strings, and with URLs, like body {background-image: url("images/fingerprintduster.jpg");}, or multiple-word font names, like #comments {font-family: Georgia, "Times New Roman", serif;}. And even in these cases, the quote marks are optional.

Use shorthand

There was a method to my madness in presenting style shorthand rules at the beginning of this chapter: using shorthand is a great way to increase the efficiency of your CSS.

When you employ shorthand, however, keep these tips in mind:

- Remember your shorthand syntax, defaults, and order when necessary.

- Use any longhand properties to override the shorthand—for example, if you want to change only one border out of four. It is easier to write two style declarations than it is to write four.

- Employ color shorthand when possible and avoid using color names.

Go with the flow

Remember, the cascade is your friend. While CSS was designed to separate presentation from content, the cascade was expressly designed to save time and effort. Sure, you could repeat declarations, but why do so when it's unnecessary? Work with the cascade, not against it:

- Declare the styles that you want inherited at the beginning of the style sheet, and use an appropriate ancestor element.

- Create selectors using the lowest-weighted elements (see the section "Specificity," in Chapter 1) so you can easily overwrite them later if need be.

  The descendant selector, with its higher specificity, is an ideal way to target elements, and it is the most widely supported CSS selector by the popular browsers.

- Place selectors that need to override any inherited styles later in the style sheet. It is a good practice to comment them to indicate what they are overriding.

tip

Remember to place the longhand style directly after the shorthand style so you don't have to go hunting for it.

tip

Be careful with color shorthand and search-and-replace. Sometimes making a change for 333 may change a color like de3332. If you do a search and replace for shorthand colors, remember always to include the # in front of the color.

STANDARDIZED STYLE SHEETS

Now that you have written fantastic HTML and have constructed streamlined CSS styles, the last step to getting all of your CSS in top shape is organizing the style sheet itself.

Why organize?

Keeping your styles organized not only makes it easier for you to scan and hit upon the styles you're searching for, it also helps anyone else who might be looking at and even working in your code.

Tips for optimized, organized style sheets

1. Order the selectors and declarations.

- Group the selectors.

  By grouping selectors, you use your style declarations only once in the document and thus avoid code bloat.

  ```
  #header a, #unav a {text-decoration: none;}
  ```

- Indent the descendant selectors.

  By indenting descendant selectors, not only can you easily identify any given style, but also you can see the document tree hierarchy from the way the styles are listed. From this, you can leverage the cascade, as the descendant styles are listed under their ancestors.

  ```
  #unav {
     background-color: #ddd;
     border-top: 1px solid #333;
     border-bottom: 1px solid #333;
     font-weight: bold;
     text-align: right;
     }

  #unav ul {
     display: inline;
     }

  #unav ul li {
     list-style-type: none;
     display: inline;
     }
  ```

■ Alphabetize the style declarations.

This is by far one of the most useful tips that I know. Alphabetizing the declarations by property name means you don't have to hunt through a list of styles only to miss the one you are really looking for. If you know they are in alphabetical order, you can quickly zero in on the one you want.

```
body {
    background-color: #fff;
    color: #636363;
    font-family: Trebuchet MS, Arial, Helvetica, sans-serif;
    font-size: .8em;
    margin: 1px 0 0 0;
    text-align: center;
}
```

2. Organize the style sheet.

Now that you have your styles indented with the declarations in alphabetical order, organize the style sheet itself. Using the comment tags, create logical visual dividers. There are several ways you can divide your style sheet:

■ By section

Start with the reset styles, then create sections by element groups, like headers, text and link styles, navigation lists, forms, comments, and additional areas; or create sections according to the way the actual page code is laid out.

```
/*****Reset*****/
/*****Basic Elements*****/
/*****Generic Classes*****/
/*****Basic Layout*****/
```

Choose the way that makes the most sense to you, and stick with it.

■ Table of contents

Once you have grouped your styles in your style sheet, make a table of contents at the top of the style sheet so that you or any other developer working on it will know the sequence of the sections.

```
/* Table of Contents
    1. CSS Reset Styles
    2. General Styles
    3. Navigation
    4. Main Content
    5. Footer
*/
```

Mark your section title so that you can treat it like a flag, and so you can do a quick search for the term and jump right to the section.

Here are some ideas on how you can do it:

```
/* footer styles */

/* =Footer */
/* ----------> Footer <-----------*/
```

3. Provide additional information.

- Developer information

  Include the file-created date and file-last-edited date, as well as your name and email address so people can contact you with questions.

  ```
  /* stylesheet information
  File created date: 09.15.1890
  File modified date: 01.12.1976
  Developer: Agatha Christie
  Developer contact: ladymallowan(at)iampoirot(dot)com
  */
  ```

- Color-scheme information

  This is a great way to keep track of the colors that you are using in the design when you are using hexadecimal colors. I often start with the relevant section or purpose, followed by the exact hex color number, and then a color description.

  ```
  /* styles for orientation nav colors, etc.
  home {background-color:#660099;} purple
  about us {background-color:#330099;} blue
  services {background-color:#006633;} green
  fees {background-color:#660000;} burgundy
  contact us {background-color:#cc3300;} orange
  */
  ```

4. Create multiple style sheets.

   Once you have your code optimized and your style sheet organized into sections, you may consider breaking your one large style sheet into multiple style sheets, especially if your single style sheet is really long and has many styles per section. Using the @import directive, you could have the first style sheet call the rest in order for the styles to be implemented.

```
@import "styles/reset.css"
@import "styles/comments.css"
@import "styles/footer.css"
```

One advantage of doing this is it makes your style sheets modular and easier to manage. A disadvantage of this practice is that you have to hunt through multiple docs for a particular style, whereas if they are all in one style sheet, you can easily find whatever you are looking for with a text search.

It's OK to Start Off Slowly

If trying to remember all of these tips and rules is too overwhelming, then do this: first, write all of the styles for your page the easiest way for yourself, even if that means using longhand and repeating declarations. Then go back over your styles and condense them according to these guidelines.

Intermediate CSS Troubleshooting Tips

Spelling errors will still account for a huge share of CSS coding misdemeanors, but here are some additional troubleshooting tips:

PLAY BY THE RULES

1. Avoid default styles and make your selectors as specific as possible.

Instead of this:

```
a {text-decoration: overline;}
```

Target and focus like this:
```
#sponsorlinks a.topsponsor:link {text-decoration: overline;}
```

2. Watch for competing rules.

- Rules declared multiple times in the style sheet

  Nope:
  ```
  dt {padding: 0;}
  ```

  and then at the bottom of the style sheet
  ```
  dt {padding: 10px 20px;}
  ```

Yep:

```
dt {padding: 0}
```

Use the rule just once in the stylesheet, and that's it.

- Rules that compete by mistake

Nah:

```
<q id="hammett" class="hammett">I haven't any sort of plans
➥for the future, but I reckon things will work out in some
➥manner. </q>
```

```
.hammett {font-family: Century; }
```

and later in the style sheet
```
#hammett {font: italic 12px Tahoma, sans-serif;}
```

Yah-sure, you betcha:

```
<q class="hammett">Thanks for the information about what we
➥call business. </q>
```

```
.hammett {font: italic 12px Tahoma, sans-serif;}
```

Use it just once in the stylesheet, and that's it.

3. Remember to close comments.

This is straightforward. You will know this is the problem if a ton of styles are not being rendered on the page, and you *know* that you created them and they are definitely in the style sheet.

4. If using !important, make sure it always goes inside the semicolon of the declaration.

Oops:

```
h1, h2, h3,h4, h5, h6 {font-family: Garamond, Georgia,
➥"Times New Roman", serif; !important}
```

There ya go:

```
h1, h2, h3,h4, h5, h6 {font-family: Garamond, Georgia,
➥"Times New Roman", serif !important;}
```

5. Remember the naming rules for selectors.

Don't start with a number or any character other than a letter.

Not so much:

```
#23horsepower.engine {margin: 0;}
```

Better:

```
#commentblock {border: 1px solid #999;}
```

CURB YOUR CREATIVITY

1. Watch for mismatching ids and classes.

Wrong:

```
<div id="gallery">
<img src="watson.jpg" alt="Watson" class="galleryitem" />
</div>

.gallery {padding: 5px 10px;}
#galleryitem {float: left; border: 2px dotted #ddd;}
```

Right:

```
<div id="gallery">
<img src="watson.jpg" alt="Watson" class="galleryitem" />
</div>

#gallery {padding: 5px 10px;}
.galleryitem {float: left; border: 2px dotted #ddd;}
```

2. Beware of using a nonexistent property.

Take one:
```
p.copyright {horizontal-align: center;}
```

Take two:
```
p.copyright {text-align: center;}
```

3. Steer clear of nonexistent values.

Nice try, but…:
```
img.bio {float: yes;}
```

Much improved:
```
img.bio {float: right;}
```

4. Watch out for using the incorrect value for a property.

Problem:
```
li.last {font-variant: italic;}
```

Corrected:
```
li.last {font-style: italic;}
```

MORE IS NOT ALWAYS BEST

1. Check for extra commas, colons, or semicolons within the style declaration, and semicolons at the end of the style declaration, after the brace.

Not good:

```
#booklist ol.whodunit, ol.felons, {list-style-type:: upper-roman;};
```

Better:

```
#booklist ol.whodunit, ol.felons {list-style-type: upper-roman;}
```

2. Check for extra white space, especially between a period [.] and class name or between a value number and its unit of measurement; or forgetting white space between shorthand properties.

Wrong:

```
. murdermystery {color: #dec;}
#suspects {padding: 5 px 10px 15px 20px;}
#suspects.murdermystery ol li {font:
➥.9emHelvetica,"Trebuchet MS",sans-serif;}
ol .murderlist {}
```

Right:

```
.murdermystery {color: #dec;}
#suspects {padding: 5px 10px 15px 20px;}
#suspects.murdermystery ol li {font: .9em
➥Helvetica,"Trebuchet MS",sans-serif;}
ol.murderlist {}
```

3. Check for multiple units of measure for one value number.

Bad:

```
#famousdetectives {width: 90%px;}
```

Good:

```
#famousdetectives {width: 90%;}
```

3

Giving the Third Degree

NOW THAT YOU'VE LEARNED HOW TO INVESTIGATE the scene of the crime and you have the tools to crack your cases, it's time to take the next step and learn techniques to thoroughly interrogate any code and make it 'fess up as to where exactly it went wrong.

Validating Your Hunches

We'd all like to believe that our code is beyond reproach and has no issues, but most of us have also had that lingering suspicion that we've missed something. In either case, it's a good idea to validate.

Validation is a method of interrogating your code to see if it is written correctly. Validation checks the markup and style code that you write against the rules of that particular code version. A **validator** is a tool, usually online, that finds all of the instances where your code does not match the standards of the specification written for it, and then generates results to show you what needs to be changed.

The biggest advantage of validators is that they catch small errors that are often difficult to spot but that may have larger ramifications for the rest of the document and related documents. Minor problems in HTML may be negligible on their own, but when combined with a style sheet could cause major problems. In short, validation is a great error-finder and quality-assurance tool.

To validate, you need a code validator, either online or stand-alone. You can either point the validator to the location of the document that you want checked (on the web or locally on your computer), then upload the document to the validator; or cut and paste the code and submit it that way. Then, using the document type, or doctype, definition (DTD) that you've included in your document, the validator runs the page code against the DTD written by the W3C, and provides a list of results based on the comparison. The results will be a line-by-line itemized list of issues in your document (unless the page is error free).

There are many good code validators for HTML, but the one most often used is the one from the W3C, http://validator.w3.org/. In order for the validator to work properly, your HTML document must have a proper doctype declaration at the beginning of it. (I will cover doctypes in greater detail in the next section of this chapter). A list of additional HTML markup validators can be found in the Resources section.

The W3C also has a validator for CSS: http://jigsaw.w3.org/css-validator/. In contrast to the HTML validator, it doesn't require a doctype declaration in your CSS. Instead, you have to indicate which version of CSS you're using. There are also some CSS validators whose results will show which properties specific browsers support. For a list of additional CSS validators, please see the Resources section.

"HUH? WHAT ARE YOU SAYING?"

Interpreting validation results takes some practice. The output is based on the standards of the language definition, and is really geared more for standards geeks than everyday web developers. However, with a little practice, you'll get the hang of it.

For example, here is a standard output:

```
End tag for X omitted, but its declaration does not permit this
```

And here is the translation:

```
You are missing a closing tag.
```

The W3C has a great resource to help with interpreting validation results called "Explanation of the Error Messages for the W3C Markup Validator" (http://validator.w3.org/docs/errors.html), which explains many of the more esoteric results that the validator produces.

WHAT VALIDATING CAN AND CANNOT DO

Validating is perfect for finding all the little mistakes that can make for rendering problems that cause much pulling of hair and gnashing of teeth. Once you have validated your code and fixed the issues, you can rest assured that your page is free of syntax errors.

However, validating your code is no guarantee that your pages will show up the same across all browsers (would that it were so easy!). To achieve this feat, you will have to test your pages in various browsers and fix them accordingly.

Also, some of the issues that the validator points out may or may not be relevant to your particular case. You may be expressly using a style that you know will not validate, or you may choose to ignore CSS warnings if, for example, styles higher up in the document take care of the issue through the cascade.

Take a look at this warning, for example:

```
Same colors for color and background-color in two contexts #container
and h1
```

The warning resulted from this code:

```
#container {
background-color: #fff;
border-left: 2px solid #936; ➡
```

```
border-right: 2px solid #936;
margin:0 auto;
padding: 0;
width: 950px;
}

h1 {
color : #fff;
font-size : 1px;
line-height : 0;
margin : 0;
}
```

The h1 was styled with the color as part of an image-replacement technique to keep the text on the page, but invisible. In this case, then, the warning is easily ignored.

Finally, there are some mistakes that the validators just won't pick up. If you are still having problems, you will need to go over the document with a fine-tooth comb.

ERRORS VS. WARNINGS

When you first start validating, the validator may return a lot of errors in your markup and both errors and warnings in your CSS code. Errors definitely need to be addressed and fixed, for they indicate that your code is incorrect and does not conform to the standards in that instance. Warnings, however, are simply spots in your code that may cause potential problems. Many common warnings are accessibility related, such as the color warning above, and aren't related to how the page actually renders. With practice, you will learn to determine how serious a warning is and whether the problems it may cause are acceptable or not.

TROUBLESHOOTING TIPS FOR VALIDATION

- Make sure you have the correct doctype defined so that the validator knows which DTD (document type definition) to validate against.

- Start validating early. Don't wait until you've finished creating your markup and styles. You will find simple errors sooner, and avoid what might look like a lot of errors if you validate later in the process.

- Validate frequently. A good rule for HTML is to validate after you add a major section of code. For CSS, validate after you style each major section.

- Set color and background color for ancestor elements high in the document tree so that the styles cascade down to all of the descendants. Then you can rest assured that you can safely ignore any warnings.

- If you do have a lot of errors and warnings, don't freak out. Often, there is one error early in the document that causes a cascade of other errors. Start addressing the errors from the top of the document down, and then revalidate. You may find that a list of 30 errors is cleared with one or two tweaks to the code.

Bait-and-Switch Tactics: Doctype Sniffing and Switching

Not only does a doctype declaration let the validator know which rules to check your markup against, but the doctype declaration also affects how the browser renders your pages by triggering different browser modes. An unexpected browser mode could be contributing to your problem, so understanding doctypes may help you get to the bottom of your code's misdemeanors.

ANATOMY OF A DTD

Being familiar with the parts of a doctype declaration will give you a better idea of what to look for when choosing and troubleshooting your doctype declaration.

Here is the doctype declaration for HTML 4.01:

```
<!DOCTYPE HTML PUBLIC "-//W3C//DTD HTML 4.01//EN"
➡ "http://www.w3.org/TR/html4/strict.dtd">
```

- `!DOCTYPE` tells the browser that this is an element that defines the doctype definition.

- `HTML` is the root element of the document.

- `PUBLIC` specifies the availability of this DTD.

- "-//W3C//DTD HTML 4.01//EN" is the formal public identifier (FPI), which indicates the registration, owning organization, which markup language is being used, and which human language it is in.

- http://www.w3.org/TR/html4/strict.dtd is the formal system identifier (FSI)—that is, the location of the definition document.

There are many incomplete doctype declarations floating around on the web, so be sure to check the W3C's complete list of valid doctypes at http://www.w3.org/QA/2002/04/valid-dtd-list.html.

BROWSER MODES

If validating still hasn't revealed the felony in your code, there may be extenuating circumstances. Browsers can render pages differently based on the doctype declaration at the head of the HTML document. Doctypes were originally designed to enable standards-savvy developers to choose how they wanted their pages rendered intentionally, while simultaneously allowing pages that were older or created by standards-ignorant applications to render as well.

There are three rendering modes: **standards** (or **strict**), **quirks** (or **loose**), and **almost standards**. The process by which a browser reads a document to determine in which mode to render a page is called **doctype sniffing** or **doctype switching**.

- **Standards (or strict) mode**

  In compliant browsers, standards mode will render your pages according to rules of the doctype definition that you have established at the head of your document. This means that your pages will show up the way you expect them to: the markup will be rendered according to the rules of the version of (X)HTML you are using, and the CSS will be rendered according to the latest CSS specification.

- **Quirks (or loose) mode**

  Ah, quirks mode. Quirks mode is for the pages that time and developers have both forgotten: for the pages that have lost their way and are without a doctype, for the pages that have only partial doctype definitions or incorrect doctype syntax, and for the pages created by WYSIWYG editors and page generators that neglected to bestow upon their page progeny a proper doctype declaration.

In essence, quirks mode renders pages based on the browser's best guess, with some browsers rendering pages the same way they did up to circa 2001. This was an era of poorly written invalid markup and before the popular browsers released versions that conformed to the standards written for the web by the W3C for both HTML and CSS. Yes, we are talking browsers rendering like Netscape Navigator 4.0 and Microsoft Internet Explorer 5 (IE5), to name names. The exact particulars of rendering do vary slightly between different browsers.

Needless to say, having your pages rendering like those of the previous millennium would throw a huge wrench in the works of determining what the problems are in your code and making the most effective and necessary changes. Most likely, you will want to avoid having your documents trigger quirks mode.

Making Quirks Mode Work for You

Before the advent of HTML5, we used to be able to throw the browser into quirks mode by using `<!DOCTYPE HTML>` as the doctype, but that no longer works. Try it out in the w3c validator and you'll see why: your document gets validated as an HTML5 page! When HTML5 becomes better supported and therefore more widespread, writing doctypes will be a lot simpler.

But you can still activate quirks mode by deleting the doctype altogether. Why would you want to? Well, really only during testing, to be sure of what mode your pages are being rendered in.

- **Almost-standards mode**

Almost-standards mode is exactly the same as standards mode except for the rendering of images in table cells, in which case it operates like quirks mode. This mode was created to let developers have pages with sliced images in tables that can display as desired without a lot of workarounds. However, if you're not using tables to assemble sliced images and you're doing table-free CSS-based layouts, you won't really need this mode for your pages.

Choosing the right doctype

After all of the above, you may be thinking, "OK, I get that I need to have the proper doctype, but how do I choose the right one?" There are great charts on the web that list every doctype and which browser mode each triggers. However, to get you up and running quickly, here are some general guidelines:

- All doctype declarations below HTML 4.0 will trigger quirks mode.

- Documents with incomplete URLs in the FSI or FPI will trigger quirks mode.

- Documents using the HTML 4.0/4.01 strict doctype with the correct syntax will trigger standards mode.

- All XHTML strict documents (regardless of version number) with the correct syntax will trigger standards mode.

- Documents with HTML transitional or frameset doctypes and XHTML transitional doctypes will trigger almost-standards mode.

- The HTML5 doctype will trigger standards mode.

Tip-offs that an undesired browser mode may be behind your problems

Although not exhaustive, here is a list of some of the rendering you may see if your page is being rendered in quirks mode against your will:

- Text inside a table has not inherited styles as you expected it to.

- Widths and heights seem to be off.

- Default font size is small.

- List bullets do not inherit the font size of the list itself.

- Line-height does not show up as expected.

- The <hr> element renders differently than you expected.

TROUBLESHOOTING TIPS WITH DOCTYPES

While not the most dangerous character on the block in terms of wreaking havoc, doctypes are significant enough to be on the list of suspicious characters. Here is an overview of what to look for to make sure they don't make your rendered page look like it's going down the wrong path.

- Be sure to have a doctype, or your browser will render like it's 1999. Literally.

Not this:

```
<html>
<head>
<title>Hunting for Suspects</title>
</head>

<body>
...
</body>
</html>
```

But more like this:

```
<!DOCTYPE html PUBLIC "-//W3C//DTD XHTML 1.0 Transitional//EN"
  "http://www.w3.org/TR/xhtml1/DTD/xhtml1-transitional.dtd">
<html xmlns="http://www.w3.org/1999/xhtml" xml:lang="en" lang="en">
<head>
<meta http-equiv="Content-Type" content="text/html; charset=utf-8" />
<title>Hunting for Suspects</title>
</head>

<body>
...
</body>
</html>
```

- Make sure the doctype declaration syntax is correct.

  No:

  ```
  <!-- DOCTYPE html PUBLIC "-//W3C//DTD XHTML 1.0 Strict//EN" -->
  ```

  Yes:

  ```
  <!DOCTYPE html PUBLIC "-//W3C//DTD XHTML 1.0 Strict//EN"
    "http://www.w3.org/TR/xhtml1/DTD/xhtml1-strict.dtd">
  ```

- Make sure the declaration is going to a valid DTD.

  I don't think so:

  ```
  <!DOCTYPE html PUBLIC "-//W3C//DTD HTML 4.01 Transitional//EN"
    "http://www.superstandards.org/mydtd/looseygoosey.dtd">
  ```

  Definitely:

  ```
  <!DOCTYPE html PUBLIC "-//W3C//DTD HTML 4.01 Transitional//EN"
    "http://www.w3.org/TR/html4/loose.dtd">
  ```

- Make sure the declaration has the correct URL—one that is not truncated, incomplete, or relative.

Not gonna work:

```
<!DOCTYPE html PUBLIC "-//W3C//DTD XHTML 1.0 Strict//EN"
➥ "DTD/xhtml1-strict.dtd">
```

There we go:

```
<!DOCTYPE html PUBLIC "-//W3C//DTD XHTML 1.0 Strict//EN"
➥ "http://www.w3.org/TR/xhtml1/DTD/xhtml1-strict.dtd">
```

- Avoid the XML prolog if using the XHTML doctypes: it will trigger quirks mode in some browsers. Use the meta tag instead.

Instead of this:

```
<?xml version="1.0"?>
<!DOCTYPE html PUBLIC "-//W3C//DTD XHTML 1.0 Transitional//EN"
➥ "http://www.w3.org/TR/xhtml1/DTD/xhtml1-transitional.dtd">
```

Do this:

```
<!DOCTYPE html PUBLIC "-//W3C//DTD XHTML 1.0 Transitional//EN"
➥ "http://www.w3.org/TR/xhtml1/DTD/xhtml1-transitional.dtd">
<html xmlns="http://www.w3.org/1999/xhtml" xml:lang="en" lang="en">
<head>
<meta http-equiv="Content-Type" content="text/html; charset=utf-8" />
<title>Confessions of Crooked Stylesheet</title>
</head>
```

Zeroing In on the Problem

You've created your pages, chosen a doctype that triggers the browser mode that you want, and validated your code. You've even employed a CSS reset, as discussed in the previous chapter. However, your pages still don't look the way you want them to. It's time to turn up the heat on your document to expose the real culprits in your code.

DEBUGGING INTERROGATION TECHNIQUES

To help you get the information you need, here are some time-honored techniques that act like truth serum for getting your code to spill the source of its problems.

You're Going to Need Some Backup

Before you start serious troubleshooting, make sure you back up the original document. You always want to be able to start over if you ever get too far off-track during your debugging process.

Shine some light on it

To better determine where and what the problems may be, highlighting elements is often the first method for targeting areas of code.

Background

You can highlight the background of the element with a color so that you can see the element in contrast to its surroundings, and also see the element's boundaries.

Add this declaration, and the element should pop right off of the page at you.

```
background-color: pink;
```

Adding a contrasting background color does not add to the size of the element's box and does make the element easier to see. However, if there are nesting issues that you want to bring to light, then you should employ the next technique of adding a border. Also, background colors will not help you see any margin issues.

note
You can use whatever color you want, as long as it provides contrast to the element's styles.

Border

You can put a border box around an element by adding the declaration to the code of the suspicious element:

```
border: 1px dashed red;
```

As effective as this is, you do need to be aware that adding a border to an element will alter its width and height. If you use this technique on an inline element, this may not be an issue. However, if you use this on a block-level element, such as a <div> that is floated and part of a fixed-width pixel-perfect page layout, you may end up breaking the layout of the page by those few additional pixels. And again, this method does not help troubleshoot margin issues.

note
Again, use whatever color you want, as long as it provides contrast to the element's styles.

Good to Know: Universal Border

Another technique employing a border is to apply it to every element using the * selector. Adding the style declaration

```
* {border: 1px dashed red;}
```

at the beginning of the style sheet will cause every element in the page to have a dashed red border.

If this seems like overkill, then use a descendant selector to target all elements in a particular section, for example:

```
#footer * {border: 1px dashed purple;}
```

It will definitely help you see the true lay of the land in your document.

---

tip

You may have noticed that the example declarations use color names instead of hex or shorthand hex numbers. This is intentional. This way, you make a distinction between the "true" declarations versus the ones for debugging, while also visually flagging the declaration as temporary. Furthermore, it is easier to keep track of which section is which color while you are testing, and easier to do a find when you are ready to delete them.

Outline

You can also use the outline property. This method has an advantage over border because instead of adding to an element's width and height, as border does, no dimension is added since an outline is visually placed over the edges of the element's box. This method is most effective in browsers that support the W3C box model, because outline is not supported by browsers that get the box model wrong, namely IE6 and IE7.

So you can use this declaration to delineate the element:

```
outline: 1px dotted orange;
```

without affecting the layout of the page.

Get ugly

You've been playing nice guy by using border or background by itself. To take it up a notch and make an element jump out at you, make it really ugly. Change the font to one that you hate (for me, that would be Comic Sans); make the font color a crazy, brash color; and add an equally garish background color, border, or outline.

Here is an effective piece of code that you can add to a selector. It will make you want to put a paper bag over its head, but it makes it much easier to see. I like to think of it as "The Ugly Treatment":

```
/* start - the ugly treatment */
border: 1px dashed green;
background-color: yellow;
color: magenta;
font-family: MS Comic Sans;
/* end - the ugly treatment */
```

Wreak havoc with space

Another technique is to add either margin or padding values to the questionable element to see if it causes any changes in the element or surrounding elements. Ironically, the most powerful value to establish is 0. Why? Remember the earlier discussion about default browser styles? Explicitly establishing a value of 0 overrides whatever value the browser was rendering by default.

If setting margin or padding value to 0 doesn't make anything come to light, then try changing the values in very slight increments—for example, from .9em to .89em.

Because either option will cause a change in how the element renders, it may bring the problem to the surface.

Make it !important

You can also use !important to make a declaration override any conflicting styles. If the element renders differently, it can indicate that a style later on in the style sheet is causing a conflict, and that improper order of your styles may be the source of your problem.

Get specific

Another way of isolating problems in your code is to leverage specificity. By making a selector more specific, you can see if the problem is in the cascade, the selector itself, or the style rules you have established for it.

In the style sheet

For example, take this:

```
.replies {...}
```

And turn it into this:

```
#comments .replies {...}
```

This change makes the selector more specific, and will direct the styles that you think might be the problem to very particular spots in the document.

You may find that your selector is not being correctly applied to the desired element.

By limiting the target of the style, you should gain insight into the source of the issue.

Inline

Although inline styles are not good for standard page development, during troubleshooting you can leverage them and the cascade to help isolate your problems by process of elimination.

By taking a style declaration out of the head of the document (or an external style sheet) and making it inline in the markup, you can see if the problem persists or if anything changes. If something does change, it may mean that there is a declaration higher up in the document that is conflicting with the style that you changed to inline, and it's the other style that is creating the problem.

Once you have determined that the problem is elsewhere, you can remove the inline style and put it back in your external style sheet.

Incapacitate it

You might just need to eliminate parts of your markup and code to better see the root of the problem. Here are several ways to do so.

Comment out sections of the code

Commenting out certain parts of the code is another way to isolate the parts that are buggy. You can comment out either parts of the HTML markup or sections of the CSS code. In both cases it is important to remember that you cannot nest comments, so you need to keep track of where you have the comment tags, or your page will end up looking even more off the mark than when you started. Using a text editor with code coloring will help you find comments in a jiffy.

As a reminder, here are the comments:

- HTML: `<!-- comment -->`

    In action:

    ```
    <div id="container">
      <div id="header">
      <h1><a href="lineup.html">The Line-Up</a></h1>
    </div>
    ```

```
<!-- <ul id="nav">
<li class="first"><a href="shifty.html">Shifty Sam</a></li>
<li><a href="unreliable.html">Unreliable Ray</a></li>
<li><a href="doubletalk.html">Double-talking Dan</a></li>
<li><a href="alibi.html">Alibi Allen</a></li>
<li><a href="wiley.html">Wiley Warren</a></li>
</ul> -->
</div><!-- end container -->
```

- CSS: /* comment */

In action:

```
body {
background: #E2DEE5 url(bg_suspects.jpg) no-repeat 0 0;
color: #993366;
font: .85em "Trebuchet MS", sans-serif;
margin: 0;
}

#container    {
background-color: #fff;
border: 1px solid #369;
margin: 0 auto;
padding: 0;
width: 950px;
}

#header {
margin: 0;
padding: 5px 0 0 0;
}

/* temp nav removal
#nav {
background-color: #E2DEE5;
border: 2px solid #cdcecd;
margin: 0;
padding: 6px 0;
width: 100%;
} */
```

Comment out sections with the code

A less intrusive method—it's gentler on the markup and you don't have to remember whether or not your comments are nested—is to use CSS properties to "comment out" sections of the page by making them invisible while keeping the code intact.

There are two options: visibility: hidden and display: none.

The property visibility: hidden will prevent the element in question from being seen. However, the element will continue to occupy its normal space on the page.

In contrast, display: none will not only hide the element from view, but also take it out of the normal flow of the page, and other elements will take its place.

Adding either of these properties to the selector of the page section that you are trying to eliminate will help you more easily see the area that you feel is problematic. The one you use will be based on whether or not you want the element to take up its normal space on the page.

During debugging, add the style declaration to the style sheet for the section that you want to make disappear temporarily. Or, leverage the start tag of the element that starts the section (such as a <div> or a <ul>) by adding style="display: none;".

If there isn't a convenient element to comment out the part of the page you want, then it's fine to create a temporary <div> to contain it expressly for the purpose of making it disappear for a while. Give it an appropriate name like id="testdiv" to remind you that it is temporary and is to be removed once you have finished debugging.

For example, if you used the CSS property option, it would look like this:

```
#header {
margin-top: 0;
padding: 5px 0 0 0;
visibility; hidden;
}
```

If, instead, you add the style to the HTML, it would look like this:

```
<div id="header" style="display: none;>
    <h1><a href="lineup.html">The Line-Up</a></h1>
</div>
```

Quick disable

Commenting out sections both manually and by CSS works great, but if you want to dispense with the niceties and get right to the point, there is a quicker way to disable styles in both the CSS code and in the markup.

In the CSS, add an x in front of the suspicious selector to essentially switch off its rendering. (You could also add the word `disabled`, but that is more typing.) For example, if you had this:

```
.highlight {...}
```

You could turn it into this:

```
x.highlight {...}
```

Similarly, in the markup, you can disable a style from being applied to an element thus:

```
<div id="xnav">...</div>
```

or

```
<li class="xfirst">...</li>
```

 **note**
You could also write it as disabled.highight [...].

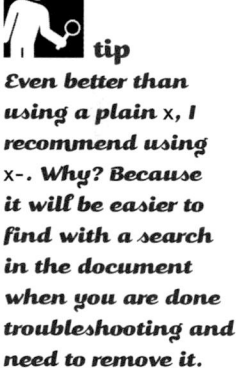 **tip**
Even better than using a plain x, I recommend using x-. Why? Because it will be easier to find with a search in the document when you are done troubleshooting and need to remove it.

Word to the Wise: Double-check

Is a problem continuing to make you crazy no matter what you do? It doesn't hurt to make sure that your style does what you think it does. Check the specification again and read up on examples of the style in action. You might not be getting the results that you expected because that property simply doesn't do what you thought!

TROUBLESHOOTING TIPS FOR DISABLING AND ZEROING IN

- Check the selector syntax and alter it to target the correct element(s).
- If the selector is not being applied, check to see if the style above it is properly closed, or that the hook you are using in the HTML document is catching the style.

- To be sure that the selector you are working with is targeting the piece of code and area of the page that you are fixing, make it stand out from the rest of the page.

- If you add styles to the selector to make it bright, obvious, or ugly and nothing happens, then the problem is that the selector is not being applied, or you have another selector overriding the one you are working with.

- If you think a selector is being overridden, check styles lower in the style sheet, as they have more cascade precedence than higher ones.

- If the problem is not in the section you thought it was, then search for the problem in the markup and styling of the section immediately before it.

Good to Know: Developer Tools

You could kick it old school and do all of your troubleshooting by hand in Notepad, but thankfully there are many, many developer tools available that make zeroing in on problem areas a whole lot easier.

Many developers swear by Firebug, the Developer Toolbar, and the DOM Inspector for Firefox, some love Dreamweaver, while others use MSIE's Developer Tools.

Play around with several to find the one that best fits your working style.

Resorting to Drastic Measures

At this point, you've spent some time trying to get the document to fess up, but it remains tight-lipped about sharing the source of the problems. When even the most reliable methods of getting the answers are only moderately effective, then you have to resort to last-ditch efforts and call in the SWAT team of techniques.

START WITH THE BASICS

If you haven't done it already, you should simplify the cascade by putting the styles back in the document. Taking the styles from external to document-level will eliminate a layer of complication and rule out problems with the link syntax, the path to the CSS document, or the @import rule.

PROCESS OF ELIMINATION

You can lull the document into a false sense of security by initially being gentle. When you are troubleshooting, often less is more. Instead of adding style declarations and potentially making the problem worse and the solution even more elusive, try taking them away. Adding styles often hides the bug under more code and compounds the problem. Instead, execute a process of elimination where you take out pieces of markup and CSS declarations until you have the bug isolated.

In a copy of the original document, remove sections of markup one by one until you have only the section where the bug is. You want to keep going until there is no code left to remove without also losing the problem as well.

Then shift your focus to the CSS and remove all the unnecessary styles. You want to reduce your declarations to the bare minimum needed to keep the bug. Many times it's the declarations you wouldn't suspect that are the ones at fault.

Create a minimal test case

When you strip out as much of your CSS code as you can to isolate the section you are dealing with, and to make sure that other elements aren't affecting it, you are creating a **minimal test case**. This process is extremely helpful in letting you see clearly all the factors that may be contributing to your bug. Sometimes margins, widths, heights, floats, and other properties can influence each other in unexpected ways. Simplifying the code can reveal any dubious interactions.

One way to pare down the code to the essentials is to follow the steps above by taking out code from the document until you isolate your area.

Another way to make a minimal test case is to put the section in question into a blank (X)HTML document, and make the styles for it inline. This converts your test case into the most compact and immediate version possible. If a section works by itself, then you know that the problem is coming from conflicting styles elsewhere in the document.

If you have multiple problems, start with the one highest in the document and work your way down, following the same minimal test case process. Just as in validating, sometimes fixing problems higher up in the document hierarchy eliminates issues in the lower elements.

DISMANTLE IT COMPLETELY

Although you are already getting tough by stripping out sections of the markup and code, you may still be holding back from really laying into the document and showing it who's boss once and for all. But you can take the process of elimination a step further and burn the document down to the ground to smoke out the true problems.

You would use this technique only in the most drastic situations, when you absolutely can't find the source of the problem through any other means. In essence, you fully disassemble the uncooperative markup and style sheet to get as close to ground zero as possible. During the process of dismantling everything you have done, you should manage to ferret out the nefarious bug.

Save your original document as a backup. In the test document, make sure all of the styles are embedded and not external. Open a new file to place all the code that you cut out of the test file.

Start cutting away sections of code from the test file and save them to the cache file. After every cutting of code, view your test file in the browser to see if the bug is still there. When you get to a point where the bug is no longer there, you know that you have found the guilty section.

If you can't isolate the bug, continue until you have stripped the document bare, and then move on to rebuilding the document.

REBUILD IT FROM THE GROUND UP

The teardown process has left you with a blank document, but still no insight as to the source of the problem. It's time to reverse the process, then, and build it back up, piece by piece, until you can reproduce your bug.

Upon adding each section back, test the file and see what changes have occurred and if the bug is triggered. By keeping track of everything you do, you will be able to pinpoint the section of the markup—and then, correspondingly, the code—where things started going afoul.

The Shakedown: A Debugging Process

Over the course of this chapter, you've hardened yourself to become a ruthless interrogator of CSS code and markup. You now have techniques to make your code waive the right to silence. But let's put them all together, for a solid debugging process.

Word to the Wise: Practical Troubleshooting Advice

A thorough interrogation takes time and patience. Remember to take breaks from the process if you need it. Some people find that a walk, a run, music, or other break can help their subconscious work on the problem and get to the *ah-ha* moment that changes the course of their problem solving.

STEPS TO FINDING THE BUG

Here is a step-by-step process for finding and isolating the code that is wreaking havoc in your document:

Start at the beginning

1. Make a backup copy of the original files in case the process goes awry.

2. If styles are external to the document, make them document-level.

Covering Your Bases

It may be overkill, but still, you might want to save a copy of every major change you make in the code so that you have revision versions. This could be very useful if you get to a point where you have the bug but then lose it and need to backtrack a few steps. However, it will generate a lot of files to keep track of. It really depends on how fastidious you want to be.

Due diligence

3. Validate both the HTML and the CSS.

Fix any errors that the validators reveal. Check your page in a compliant browser.

4. Rule out the doctype by deliberately throwing the browser into quirks mode to see if the problem is still there.

Eliminate to isolate

5. Eliminate sections of the HTML:

- Determine the exact location in the code where the problem starts. If the area is not obvious, try the various methods for highlighting elements to make it more visible.

- Remove (through commenting out or actual deletion) the markup for the sections before the problem and anything after. Remove extraneous headers, footers, navigation bars, sidebars, and so on, to create a minimal test case.

- With the target section isolated, remove the piece of code immediately before the problem to see if an element above is the trigger.

- Remove the pieces in smaller and smaller increments until something changes—if it does, you have found your errant piece of markup!

- If nothing changes, then the problem is in the styles, so it is time to move on to isolating them.

6. Eliminate sections of the CSS:

- Take out all of the styles for the areas of the page you have removed, leaving only the general styles for the page and all the styles for the section of the page you have isolated.

- If the problem is still there, then comment out the body styles. If the problem is still there, then you know the problem is probably in the styles for that section.

- Remove the styles in the test-case area one by one. When you have a change with your issue, you have found your errant style!

Rebuild to target

7. Create a copy of your original document. In this copy, remove all of the HTML in the document between the `<body></body>` tags. Yes, all of it.

8. Take out all your CSS declarations. Yes, all of them.

9. Add back the sections of the page, one by one:

- Add back the main layout `<div>`s.

- Add back the CSS declarations for the main layout `<div>`s incrementally, and view the page in the browser after every addition.

- Start with the essential CSS rules like size, positioning, `margin`, and `padding`, one at a time. Save visual styles like fonts, colors, and backgrounds for later.

- Add temporary `background-color` or `outline` to the layout `<div>`s to determine if they are where you expect.

- Add back test content in the form of headers and paragraphs. Add their spacing and `border` rules as well.

- Add back test content in the form of lists, images, and so on. Add their spacing and `border` rules as well.

- Last but not least, add back `font` and `line-height` rules where applicable.

tip
Before adding navigation menus to the rebuilt layout page, build and test the menus in a separate document to be sure they function the way you want.

THE BIG FIX

The big moment of the grand confession has come: you've finally found your bug! To fix it, you get to exercise your brain power and creativity. Here are some ideas to get you thinking:

1. The fix may be a matter of `margin` or `padding`, where either establishing an explicit value of 0 or making a very slight change in a value is all you need.

2. You may need to augment the style declaration with an additional property or several.

3. Conversely, you may need to remove properties.

4. You may need to change the property altogether to create the effect that you want.

Totally stumped and don't know what to do?

1. Double-check the property to make sure it does what you want.

2. Do a web search to see if there is a known bug for what you are experiencing and to find the solutions posted for it.

An Interrogator's Work Is Never Done

After trying the techniques in this chapter, were you able to make the shady styles squeal? Did they finally offer up the whys and wherefores of their crimes and misdemeanors? With all the ways of getting at the truth behind your coding errors, I suspect the answer is yes.

However, we've only dealt with coding errors. There is an additional group of shifty characters that you absolutely need to be familiar with before we can start solving the cases: the browser bugs.

In the next chapter, you will meet some of the usual suspects—many of the common browser bugs that trip up developers—and learn how to outwit them from the start.

The Usual Suspects

HERE THEY COME SHUFFLING IN: A MOTLEY CREW of problems and persistent bugs that every CSS developer has run up against. To become more familiar with the most pernicious of these characters, let's line 'em up so that you can study their distinguishing features and learn how to spot their modus operandi. After all, forewarned is forearmed: knowing about these bugs and their fixes should help you change them from the bad and the ugly to the quick and the dead.

Concepts to Remember

Before we begin identifying the bad guys, let's quickly review a couple of important foundational concepts. As a burgeoning CSS detective, you need to keep key concepts like document flow, element type, and positioning at the forefront of your mind. Bugs are most often found where one or more element's properties and qualities collide with a browser's rendering engine.

DOCUMENT FLOW

Every element on a standard HTML page is placed within the "flow" of the page: elements follow each other in the order in which they're placed in the markup source, wrapping to the next line when they reach the edge of the browser viewport or the edge of a parent element with a set width.

Elements are either block or inline. In the flow, each category has distinct characteristics and behavior.

A **block** element is its own entity, a contained "block" of information, which is the width of the container surrounding it, unless a specific width is given. In terms of the document flow, block elements flow after one another vertically unless otherwise specified.

You are already familiar with most of the block elements: <div>, headers, <p>, <blockquote>, <ol>, <ul>, <dl>, <table>, and several others. With a few exceptions, block level elements can contain text and other block elements as well as inline elements as long as they are properly nested.

Inline elements flow after one another on the same line as the element before them horizontally. An inline element can contain text and other inline elements, as long as it is properly nested. Inline elements cannot contain block level elements. Common inline elements are <img>, <strong>, <em>, <a>, and <span>, as well as other less frequently used elements.

Elements are in the flow unless the author of the page specifically codes them out of the flow. What does being out of the flow of the page look like? The most common instance of an element being out of the page flow is when an author attributes a position on the page to an image, usually by applying the float property with CSS, but also by using positioning.

POSITIONING

You can control the placement of elements on the page with the CSS position property.

Static positioning is the default. All elements on the page that are in the flow have a position value of static.

Relative positioned elements are in the flow of the page but you can shift their position by using the top, right, bottom and left offset properties as well as by establishing a stacking order with z-index. The element is positioned in relationship to itself, so its position is calculated based on where it would be located on the page if the CSS wasn't telling it to move. Changing the offset values of a relatively positioned element does not affect the position of other elements on the page.

Absolute positioning takes an element out of the flow completely. The position of an absolute-positioned element is based on the closest non-static positioned parent element. If the direct parent element is not positioned, then the absolute positioned element will search outward to the page's base element until it finds an ancestor that is positioned, or reaches the base <html> element, which would make its position relative to the page itself. If the direct parent is positioned, then the absolutely-positioned element will be positioned with the parent element as the base for the offset values.

Fixed positioning is akin to absolute positioning, except that the base element is always the viewport itself. Fixed elements don't move, even when the rest of the page elements scroll.

A Side-View: Positioning in 3-D

One fascinating aspect of positioned elements is their place in the 3-D space of the page. Yes, it's true—as with the fateful discovery by Christopher Columbus (or a Chinese admiral, depending on who's doing the telling), a browser page is not actually flat, limited by two dimensions, but rather has infinite layers in the third dimension (**Figure 4.1**).

Positioned elements are placed on layers and moved above the flow. They can actually be stacked on top of each other by establishing their `z-index`, which is based on the z-axis of the three-dimensional grid. Z-index values with smaller numbers are farther away from the user in space, while those with larger numbers are closer. If not established, then the z-index stacking order should be determined by the source order in the markup.

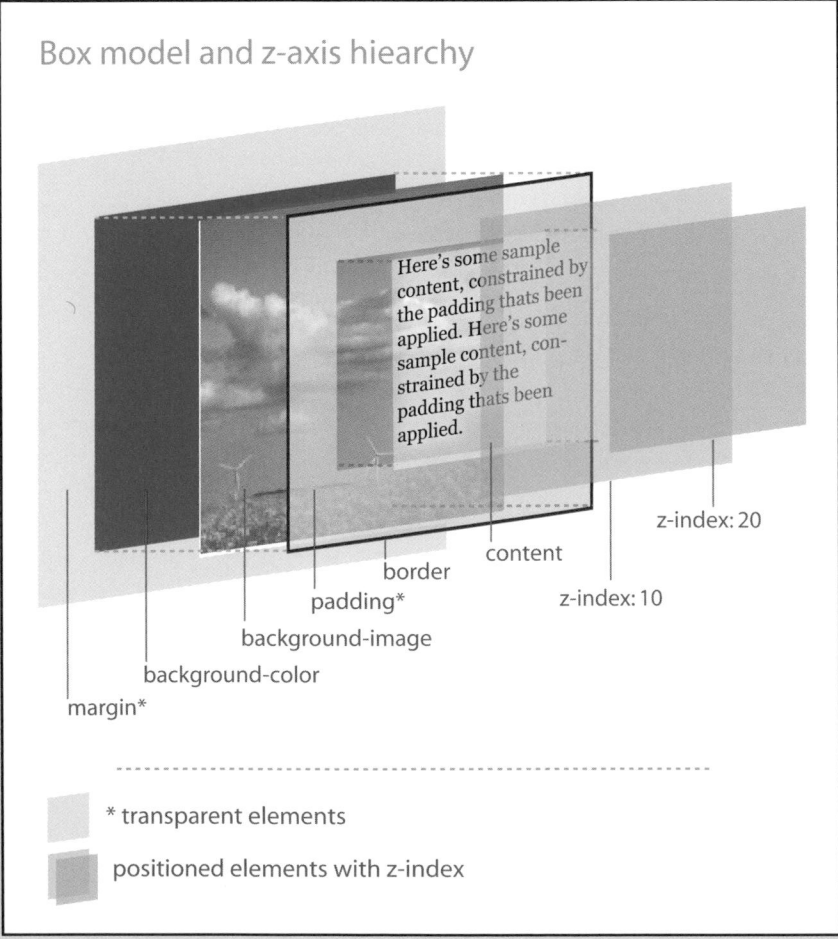

Figure 4.1 *The box model hierarchy with z-axis positioned elements.*

A Broken Box

According to the box model as written by the W3C, every element in HTML is composed of a rectangular box consisting of multiple concentric layers (**Figure 4.2**):

- The **content** itself, defined by the four edges of the content box.

- The **padding** around the content, which surrounds the content edge. If the padding value is 0, then the padding edge is the same as the content edge.

- The **border**, which surrounds both the content and padding. If the border value is 0, then the border edge is the same as the padding edge.

- The **margin** outside of the border. If the margin value is 0, then the margin edge is the same as the border edge.

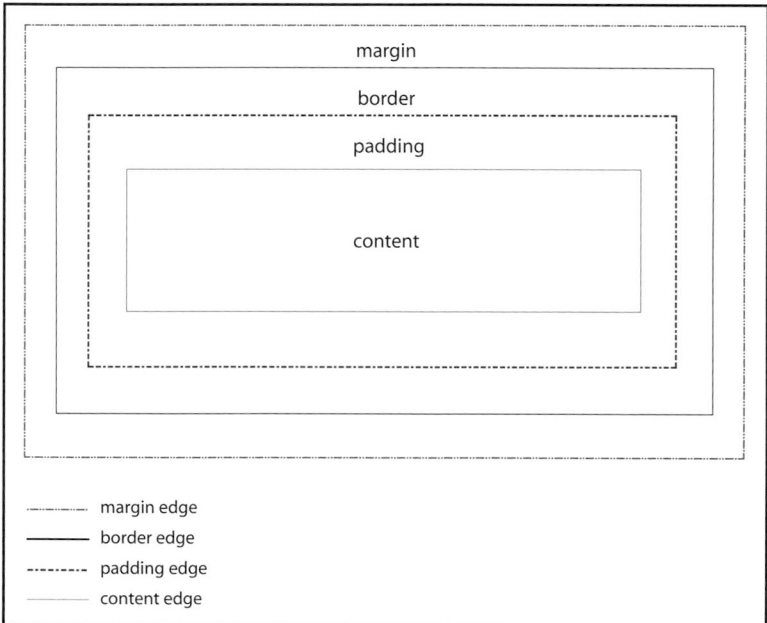

Figure 4.2 *The components of the element box.*

A BOXED SET OF PROBLEMS

The box model as written is a great idea. But for great ideas to work well, everybody has to adhere to the rules (or understand them the same way). Most browsers calculate the size of the box according to the W3C specification, where the width of the box is calculated using the content box as the base.

For example, for this code:

```
#keysersoze {
border: 2px solid black;
margin: 5px;
padding: 10px;
width: 200px;
}
```

Most browsers would calculate the width as

```
2px+10px+200px+10px+2px=224px
```

However, Microsoft Internet Explorer 6, 7 and 8 in quirks mode and lower versions of IE in any mode, calculate the width by including the border and padding in the width of the content: a width of 200px would actually equal 2px+10px+176px+10px+2px=200px (**Figure 4.3**).

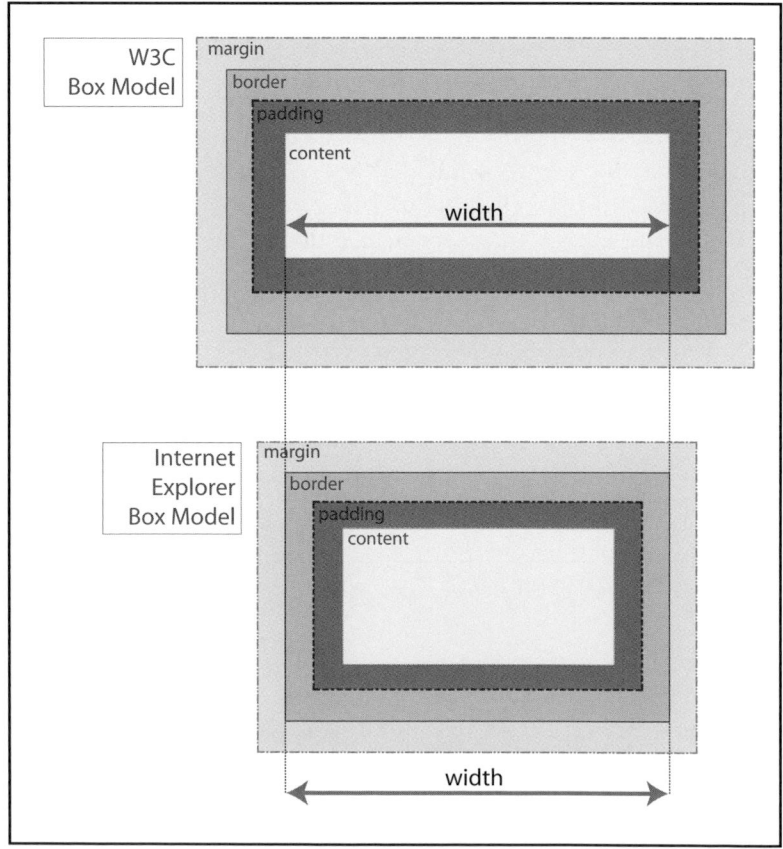

Figure 4.3 *Different interpretations of the box model.*

Whoa—that's a significant difference! Obviously, this can cause problems.

A COMPLEMENT OF SOLUTIONS

If you are lucky, you might never have to deal with IE's broken box model. Fewer and fewer people are using IE6 and earlier, so there's light at the end of the tunnel. But if your pages do have to work in older browsers, here are some tips that will help.

Stay in standards mode

Use the HTML 4.01 strict or any of the XHTML doctypes, as described in Chapter 3.

Margin and padding workarounds

Be proactive in your styling:

- Avoid declaring the margin and padding on the same item.
- Avoid declaring either the margin or the padding on an item where you have declared a width.
- Apply the padding or margin to the parent element, instead of the element to which you want the padding to apply. The visual outcome will be the same, but you will avoid the headache of having to try to fix an element box that is dramatically smaller than you intended.

Employ a CSS reset

Instituting a full reset will allow you to deliberately set values for the padding and margins of all of the critical elements on the page, and help you avoid issues based on incorrect box model interpretations.

If you don't want to go whole-hog and do a full reset for most of the elements in the document, you can do a partial reset to establish the margins and padding for divs.

IE Hacks We Can Live With

While developers lamented IE's limited capacity to render selectors, they soon learned to capitalize on it with ways to serve alternate styles to browsers based on the properties the browsers support.

I'm not a fan of CSS hacks, but there are times when they effectively solve cross-browser issues. When employing hacks, the goal is to use effective, visible solutions that validate. Here are some of the least complicated methods:

Underscore Hack

IE6 and lower understand properties that are preceded by an underscore or hyphen while other browsers will ignore them. The jury is out on whether or not this is true to the CSS specification, but these declarations will not validate, so use with care.

Example:

```
#content {width: 268px; _width: 260px;}
```

Star HTML Hack

The star HTML hack works because IE6 and lower act as if the HTML element was the child of a higher parent element, while other browsers only accept HTML as the parent element of the page. Therefore, the older IEs will accept a declaration with * html at the beginning of it, while the rest of the browsers will not. These declarations will validate.

Example:

```
* html p {font-size: 1.2em;}
```

Child Hack

In versions IE6 and below, the child selector is not supported, while all other browsers will recognize and render child selector declarations. Leverage this by writing the first declaration for IE and then overriding it with a second declaration for the rest of the browsers.

```
#nav {width: 30em;}
html > body #nav {width: 32em;}
```

Conditional Comments

Conditional comments used in the HTML markup are interpreted by IE only, and are ignored by other browsers because they are cached in comment tags.

For example, you could serve an IE-specific stylesheet via a conditional statement with this code:

```
<!--[if IE6]>
<link href="ie6boxfix.css" rel="stylesheet">
<![endif]-->
```

Conditional comments do validate.

You can find more information on the syntax for conditional statements in the Resources section.

hasLayout (hasIssues)

Now that we have gotten past IE's broken box model, let's tackle hasLayout. Many of the bugs that exist in IE7 and earlier versions of IE are a result of the hasLayout model. Once you have ruled out the broken box model as the culprit for your issue, it's time to see if the element has a layout problem.

HASWHAT?

In versions of IE7 and lower, hasLayout is a quality that is assigned to an element to give it the ability to render itself, sizing and arranging its own contents (including child elements), as opposed to inheriting its rendering properties from an ancestor element.

While you may be thinking that not that many people use IE7 (or even IE6), think again. According to some web browser usage statistics, as many as 30% of users are still using IE7 and below in early 2010, so the numbers are significant enough to justify having a better understanding of this particular aspect of IE and how it affects elements on the page.

Some of the characteristics of an element having layout are:

- The element is treated as a block element for formatting purposes.

- The element sizes and positions itself, and its children.

- The element is constrained to a rectangular shape. In other words, it can't flow around other elements (such as text does around floated images).

- Margins between parent and children elements do not collapse correctly when an element hasLayout.

- Parent elements will not "shrink to fit" their hasLayout children. They will expand to full width even when a smaller width is defined.

What is Shrink-to-Fit?

You have already seen "shrink to fit" or "shrink-wrapping" in action: by default, a display block shrinks to the size of its declared width and height unless otherwise specified. This is normal behavior. When shrink-wrapping does not occur as expected, it could be an indicator that your element is talking a walk on the buggy side.

If need be, you can force shrink-wrapping by applying these properties to an element: `float: left` or `right`, `display: inline-block` or `table`, and `position: absolute`.

Many of the bugs you may encounter in IE are due to an element *not* having layout. In fact, one of the main uses of giving elements layout is to solve dimensional bugs! For the most part, having layout causes an element to act as a potentially more stable, independent entity incurring fewer browser bugs. However, sometimes having layout causes an element to behave weirdly.

I CAN HASLAYOUT?

Many block-level elements and elements with default heights already have layout assigned to them, including <html>, <body>, <table>, <tr>, <td>, <textarea>, <legend>, and <fieldset>. Additionally, floated elements, inline-block elements, inline elements such as <hr>, <img>, <input>, <button>, <select>, and absolutely-positioned elements also have layout by default. Note the absence of the <div> element from the list: <div> does *not* have layout by default.

If you are dealing with an element that doesn't have layout already assigned to it, certain CSS properties will trigger layout in IE, changing the IE hasLayout flag from false to true, thereby giving the element layout.

For example, the following properties and values will give an element layout:

- float: left, float: right
- display: inline-block
- overflow: hidden, overflow: auto, overflow: scroll
- position: absolute, position: fixed (IE7)
- height (any value other than auto)
- min-height (any value other than auto in IE7 only)
- width (any value other than auto)
- min-width (any value other than auto in IE7 only)
- zoom (any value other than normal)

note
zoom *is a Microsoft proprietary property.*

Can I *not* hasLayout?

While you cannot remove layout from any element that has layout by default, you can unflag an element that previously had layout triggered by overriding the CSS property that set the hasLayout property later in the CSS cascade. The later ruleset will undo hasLayout if there are no other conflicting properties that give layout later in the CSS (or with greater specificity)

The following values can override previous properties that have set hasLayout:

- width: auto, height: auto
- max-width: none, max-height: none (IE7)
- position: static
- float: none
- overflow: visible (IE7)
- zoom: normal (MS proprietary property)

A BLANKET HASLAYOUT APPLICATION

You can apply hasLayout to the main container and allow it to cascade down to all of the children. This is a good way to proactively code to avoid any potential issues from not having layout in IE6 and 7.

```
#container {overflow: hidden; }
* html #container {height: 0;}
```

IE7 will act on the first set of styles, ignoring the star HTML hack declaration, whereas IE6 and below will take the height declaration, treat it as a min-height, and resize the page's elements accordingly.

note
The first line clears floats in modern browsers and gives layout in IE7 and the second line gives layout in IE6.

Quick hasLayout Activation

To turn on hasLayout in a pinch, here are some tips:

- For IE7, use display: inline-block.
- For IE6 and lower, use the **height** property, unless it conflicts with another important property like **overflow: hidden**. The values 0, 1px, and 1% work similarly.

Flaky Floats

Floats are true champs of CSS. Designers use them for everything from positioning images on a page, to making lists horizontal, to creating complex page layouts. However, their very ubiquity means that they are also often the source of problems.

HOW FLOATS WORK

The float property is used to move elements on the page to either the far left or far right of the containing element. Floating an element takes it out of the flow of the document, pushes it to the farthest edge of its containing element, and forces the other elements to wrap around it unless otherwise specified. Once floated, an element acts like a block, even if it is an inline element by definition.

The values for float are left, right, inherit, and none (default).

To send an element to the far left of its containing element, apply float: left (**Figure 4.4**).

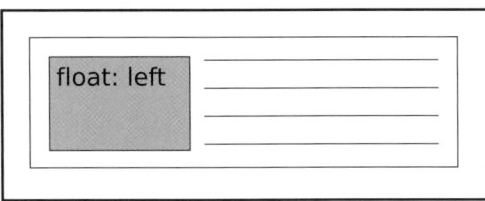

Figure 4.4 *An element floated left.*

To send an element to the far right of its containing element, apply float: right (**Figure 4.5**).

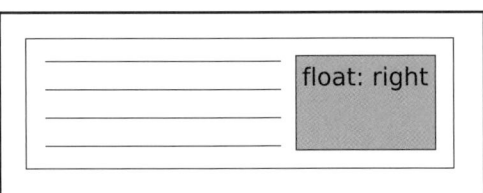

Figure 4.5 *An element floated right.*

To have an element exhibit the same floating behavior as its parent element, apply float: inherit.

When two elements with combined widths that are smaller than their container are floated next to each other, they will stack horizontally and be aligned by their tops (**Figure 4.6**).

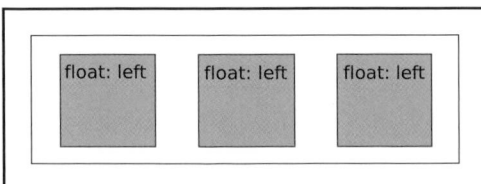

Figure 4.6 *Multiple elements floated left.*

If there is not enough room for them to display next to each other, then the following floated element(s) will be pushed down to the next line (**Figure 4.7**).

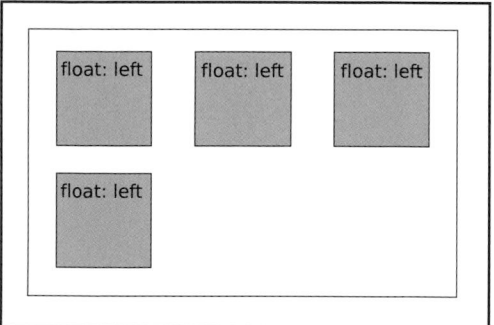

Figure 4.7 *Multiple elements floated left. The last element is pushed to the next line.*

In order to help the browser render the floated element better, it is always best to provide a value for the width of a floated element. Images are the one exception.

CONTAINING FLOATS

One of the first float issues that novice developers encounter is what happens when you enclose one or more floats in a container.

Because a floated element is taken out of the normal flow of the document, the element that contains only floated children has no content to provide height. The parent element "collapses": in essence, it doesn't take up any dimension around the floated elements (**Figure 4.8**).

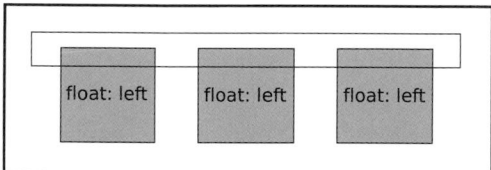

Figure 4.8 *Collapsed parent element containing floats.*

This isn't a problem if you know that this is the standard behavior, but if you were expecting the element to expand to contain the float, it could be a nasty shock. For the parent element to not collapse, you need is to clear the floats.

There are several ways to clear floats: by floating the parent element, by using a form of the "easy clear" method, or by using the "simple clear" (overflow) method.

Floating the parent

Floating the parent element itself is known as "float nearly everything" or FnE. It's a simple solution, because a floated element always grows to be at least as tall as its tallest floated child, and it doesn't require any additional markup. However, you may then have to make other adjustments in the styles to accommodate the parent element being floated.

```
<div id="notablequotes">
   <img src="kujan.jpg" alt="Agent Kujan" class="floatleft">
   <p class="floatleft">First day on the job, you know what I learned?
➥How to spot a murderer. Let's say you arrest three guys for the
➥same killing. You put them all in jail overnight. The next
➥morning, whoever's sleeping is your man. You see, if you're
➥guilty, you know you're caught, you get some rest, you let your
➥guard down.</p>
</div>
#notablequotes {
border: 1px solid #999;
float: left;
padding: 30px;
width: 550px;
}

.floatleft {
border: 1px solid #333;
float: left;
margin-right: 30px;
}
```

Easy clear

If you have an inline or block level element following a floated element and you don't want the inline or block element to either wrap around or stack next to the floated element, you need to apply the clear property to the inline or block element. The clear property has meaning only for block-level elements and floated elements that behave like block elements.

Apply clear: left to clear an element that has been floated left (**Figure 4.9**).

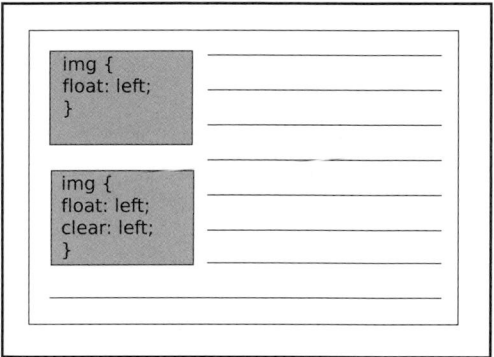

Figure 4.9 *Two elements floated left. The second element is clearing the first float.*

Apply clear: right to clear an element that has been floated right.

Apply clear: both to a subsequent element to ensure that the previous floated elements are cleared on both sides (**Figure 4.10**).

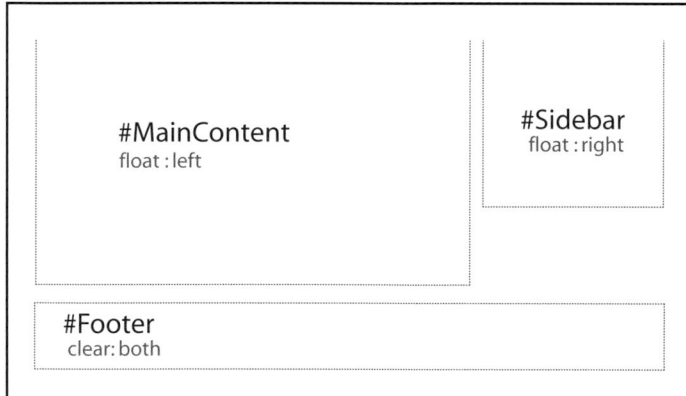

Figure 4.10 *The footer element clears both floats.*

You can use clear: inherit to apply the same clear value to a child element as its parent, while clear: none is the default value.

With the "easy clear" method, you create an entity with the generated content property and then apply the clear property to it. You style the entity to take up no space and disappear. On the page, it's invisible but it forces your floated element to clear.

The traditional easy-clear is usually structured as follows:

```css
.clearfix {display: inline-block;}
.clearfix:after {
    clear: both;
    content: ".";
    display: block;
    font-size: 0;
    height: 0;
    visibility: hidden;
}
```

There is also a variation on the first easy-clear method that employs a space instead of a period. With this method, you don't have to be concerned with trying to hide a generated character.

```css
.clearfix {display: inline-block;}
.clearfix:after {
    clear: both;
    content: " ";
    display: block;
    font-size: 0;
    height: 0;
    visibility: hidden;
}
```

This code is useful for the standard browsers, but you will need a different clearing method for IE 6/7. The simplest easy-clear for those browsers is to trigger hasLayout by assigning height or another property that gives layout, but this wreaks havoc in browsers other than IE 6/7, so you should use it with conditional comments:

```html
<!--[if lte IE7]>
<style type="text/css">
#photogallery {height: 1%;}
</style>
<![endif]-->
```

Simple clear (using overflow)

The "simple clear" method is aptly named as it uses only the overflow property to clear the float.

The overflow property tells the browser how to render the contents of an element's box when that content is larger than the dimensions (height and width) of the element. If you think of an element box as a window, you can easily visualize how the overflow property works and hides (or clips) pieces of content.

The default is overflow: visible, which allows the content to be rendered regardless of the element box's dimensions. Interestingly enough, while the content is shown outside of the parameters of the box, it does not affect the flow of the page (**Figure 4.11**).

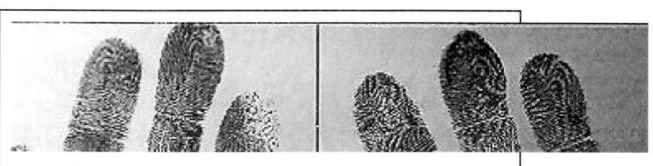

Figure 4.11
An element with overflow: visible.

Lorem ipsum dolor sit amet, consectetur adipiscing elit. Donec nec orci id mi adipiscing facilisis. Ut erat orci, fermentum ultrices ultrices et, luctus eu lectus.

Nulla euismod enim a nisi laoreet interdum id quis sapien. Aliquam erat volutpat. Donec in elit metus, sed semper massa. Nullam tristique eleifend est, ac congue est molestie semper. Nam aliquet auctor mattis. Aliquam non urna diam, vitae ullamcorper nisl.

Vivamus vitae arcu vel tellus pretium dapibus ac vel lacus. Integer faucibus ligula id justo lacinia ultricies. Donec vel diam id sem mollis facilisis. Proin venenatis rutrum vehicula. Morbi eget mi lacinia mi malesuada gravida. Suspendisse eros libero, tincidunt a rhoncus a, tincidunt eu erat.

Pellentesque sit amet nunc augue, ac rhoncus odio. Mauris sed ante ipsum.ultricies est, dignissim rhoncus odio urna id nibh.

Apply overflow: hidden when you want the content in the element box to disappear if it extends past the boundaries of the box. This property is particularly useful in maintaining control of page layouts where an overflow could throw the rest of the page elements out of alignment (**Figure 4.12** on the next page).

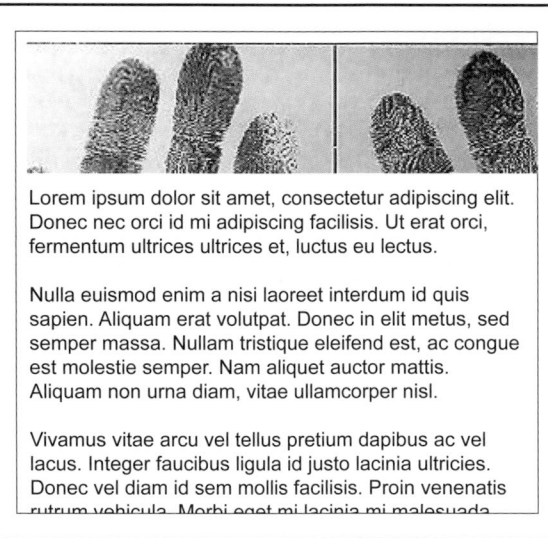

Figure 4.12 *An element with* overflow: hidden.

With overflow: scroll, the browser creates scrollbars to let the user view the content of the element while maintaining the specified dimensions. Both the horizontal and vertical scrollbars will display, whether or not they are needed (**Figure 4.13**).

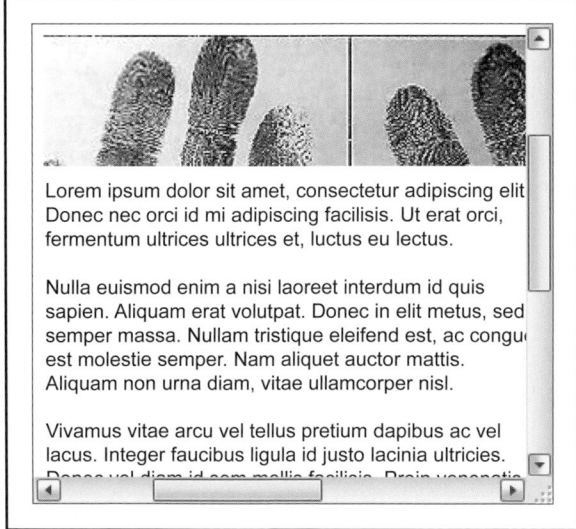

Figure 4.13 *An element with* overflow: scroll.

Finally, overflow: auto lets the browser determine whether scrollbars are needed, and will only create them if and where necessary (**Figure 4.14** and **4.15**).

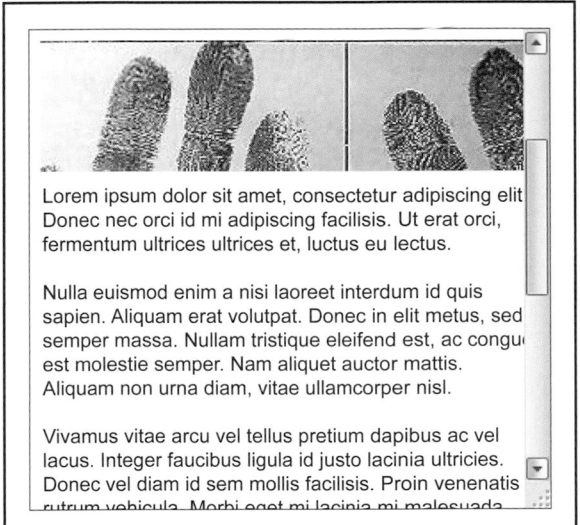
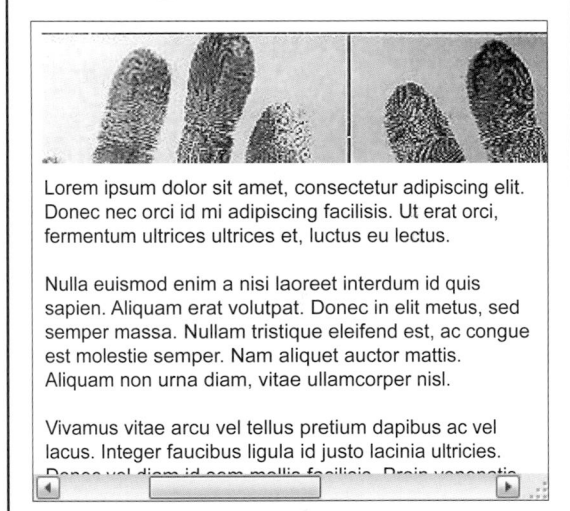

Figure 4.14 *and* **4.15** *An element with* overflow: auto.

With the simple-clear method, you apply the overflow property to the parent container, preventing it from collapsing around its floated children.

```
div.container {
border: 1px solid #000000;
overflow: hidden;
width: 998px;
}

div.left {
width: 75%;
float: left;
}

div.right {
width: 24%;
float: right;
}
```

 **note**
You can also use
overflow: auto;

For the purpose of clearing floats, there isn't a lot of difference between overflow: hidden and overflow: auto: they work by containing the float and hiding anything past the established width.

The display Property

In CSS, the display property can be used to establish the display of an element as inline, block, inline-block, list-item, run-in, compact, table or none (and some other less well known and supported values). This property can override the default value of an element and effectively change its behavior.

Through years of bug-fighting, this pearl of wisdom has emerged as a simple solution to many IE float bugs: display: inline. If all else fails add display: inline to your page and see if your problem disappears.

To learn more about the characteristics and uses of display, please refer to the Resources section.

"WE HAVE A FLOAT DOWN!"

Even though floats are champs in the world of CSS, IE's older rendering engine still manages to bully and push them around. Don't worry—we have the means to stand up to those typical IE float bugs and show them who's boss.

Float drop

Float drop or pushdown happens when the float contains an item bigger than its specified width. Current browsers render the item past the confines of the float without having it affect the layout. However, old IE will try to contain the item by expanding the float, which usually also alters the layout (**Figure 4.16**).

It's the overflow property to the rescue in this case. Applying overflow: hidden to the container's styles will hide or clip the oversized element, thereby maintaining the layout.

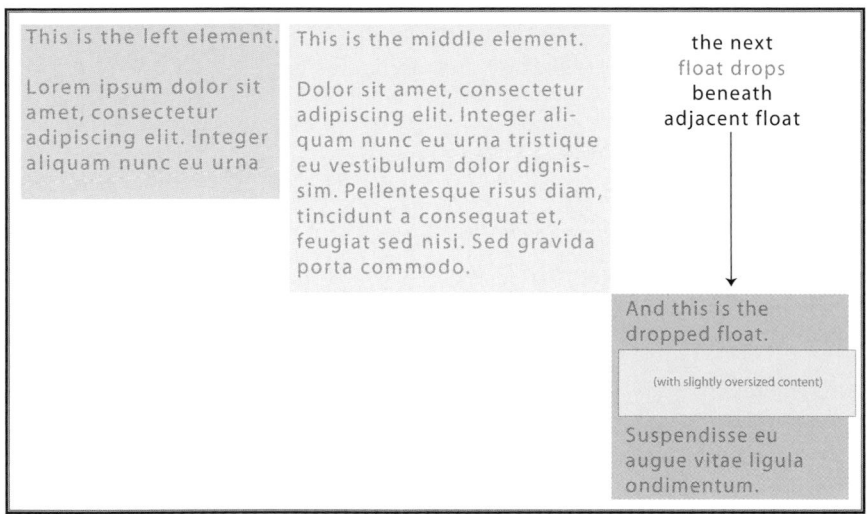

Figure 4.16 *Example of float drop.*

```
#maincontent {
float: left;
margin: 10px;
overflow: hidden;
padding: 10px;
width: 650px;
}
```

Float stepdown

Under most circumstances, when you float elements, they will stack according to the float specification. However, not in IE6: when a series of floated elements are contained in a series of block level elements that are not floated, in IE6 the floated elements may end up in a step-down effect (**Figure 4.17**).

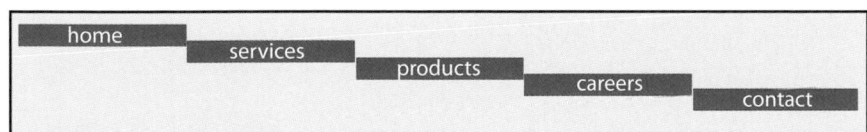

Figure 4.17 *Example of float stepdown.*

You can fix this problem in one of two ways.

- You can employ FnE by floating the parent elements.

```
#navigation {
list-style-type: none;
margin: 0;
padding: 0;
width: 700px;
}

  #navigation li {float: left;}
  #navigation li a {
  border-right: 1px solid #BC4622;
  background-color: #ddd;
  display: block;
  float: left;
  padding: 2px;
  text-decoration: none;
  width: 100px;
  }
```

- You can also change the element's display value to display: inline:

```
#navigation {
font-size: 1.1em;
list-style-type: none;
margin: 0;
padding: 0;
width: 700px;
}

  #navigation li {display: inline;}
  #navigation li a {
  border-right: 1px solid #BC4622;
  background-color: #ddd;
  display: block;
  float: left;
  padding: 2px;
  text-decoration: none;
  width: 100px;
  }
```

Misbehaving Lists

After floats, lists are another key component of CSS page layouts. But unsurprisingly, IE6 keeps us on our toes with rendering lists that won't listen to reason.

SCRATCHING WHITE SPACE FROM LISTS

IE6 and down has a weird habit of adding extra white space to list items. When you apply display:block to links within a list, IE6 and lower incorrectly add white space. So whether you are employing a horizontal or vertical list, the results will be the same in IE: unwanted extra space (**Figure 4.18**).

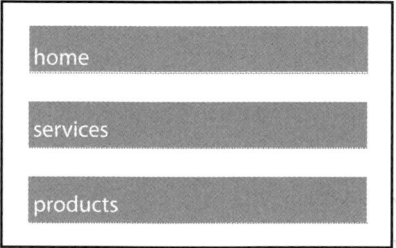

Figure 4.18 *Where does the extra white space come from?*

Here are a couple of ways to solve the problem.

Old-school markup solution

It's not sexy, but it is effective. Eliminating the actual white space in the code will take care of the problem in a pinch.

So, you would change this code:

```
<ul class="nysfinesttaxiservice">
<li><a href="#">take emeralds</a></li>
<li><a href="#">take money</a></li>
<li><a href="#">set car on fire</a></li>
</ul>
```

To this:

```
<ul class="nysfinesttaxiservice">
 <li><a href="#">take emeralds</a></li><li><a href="#">take money
➥</a></li><li><a href="#">set car on fire</a></li>
</ul>
```

And, yes, as strange as it seems, it does work.

Solutions with style

If you start off with your styles like the below, you are going to find yourself with an embarrassment of white space riches:

```css
#navigation {
list-style-type: none;
margin: 0;
padding: 0;
width: 200px;
}
```

```css
#navigation li a {
background-color: #ddd;
display: block;
margin: 0;
padding: 0;
text-decoration: none;
}
```

To pull everything back into place, you have a plethora of options:

1. Set the width of the anchor elements

```css
#navigation {
list-style-type: none;
margin: 0;
padding: 0;
width: 200px;
}
```

```css
#navigation li a {
background-color: #ddd;
display: block;
margin: 0;
padding: 0;
text-decoration: none;
width: 200px;
}
```

2. Change the display of the anchor elements

```css
#navigation {
list-style-type: none;
margin: 0;
```

```
padding: 0;
width: 200px;
}

#navigation li a {
background-color: #ddd;
display: inline-block;
margin: 0;
padding: 0;
text-decoration: none;
width: 200px;
}
```

note
*You could also
use simply*
display: inline;.

3. Change the height of the anchor elements

```
#navigation {
list-style-type: none;
margin: 0;
padding: 0;
width: 200px;
}

#navigation li a {
background-color: #ddd;
display: block;
height: 1em;
margin: 0;
padding: 0;
text-decoration: none;
}
```

note
*You can change the
size of the height to
suit your needs.*

4. Float the links

Floating the links within the list items will remove the extra white space, but may not work for your design if you've applied a background color to the links.

```
#navigation {
list-style-type: none;
margin: 0;
padding: 0;
width: 200px;
} ➡
```

```
#navigation li a {
float: left;
clear: left;
background-color: #ddd;
display: block;
margin: 0;
padding: 0;
text-decoration: none;
}
```

5. Apply a bottom border to the list items (*not* the anchor element)

```
#navigation {
list-style-type: none;
margin: 0;
padding: 0;
width: 200px;
}

#navigation li {border-bottom: 1px solid #112233;}
#navigation li a {
background-color: #ddd;
display: block;
margin: 0;
padding: 0;
text-decoration: none;
}
```

Any of the above solutions will yield the desired result: a white space–free list (**Figure 4.19**).

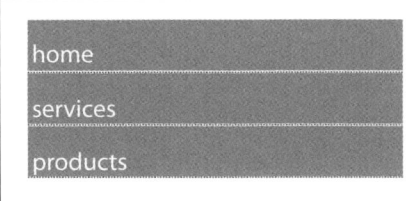

Figure 4.19 *Extra white space: fixed!*

Margins and Errors

As you know, margins are the transparent area around the borders of an element box that maintains space between that box and other elements.

When the margins of two elements meet, the correct behavior according to the box model is that the margins collapse. The term "collapse" sounds much more ominous than it is. What happens is that the browser determines the larger of the two joining margins, and instead of adding the two margins together to determine the distance between the two elements, the browser adjusts the margin height or width to equal the larger of the two measurements. The value of the largest margin is honored while the other margin "collapses" to zero. If either margin measurement value is negative, the browser adds the values and combines them to form a single margin.

You can see this best in the case of paragraphs (**Figure 4.20**).

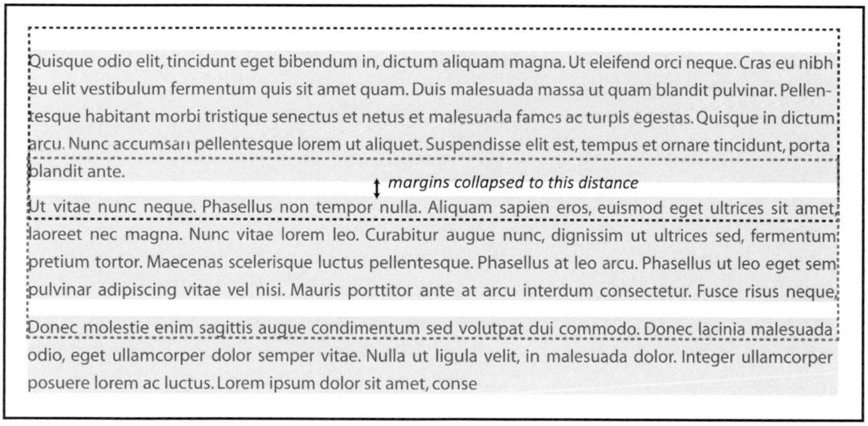

Figure 4.20 *Paragraphs with collapsed margins*

Knowing about collapsing margins is important for the instances when margins start acting funny and exhibiting behavior that you *don't* want.

NEGATIVE MARGINS

Interestingly, margins can have negative values along with positive values. As you may have suspected, negative values work the opposite of positive values. While positive values push the element box away from the margin position indicated, a negative value will pull the box toward the position. This moves the box itself around on the page, and can be used as a method of positioning for page layouts.

If either a top or left margin is given a negative value, the element box will be pulled in that direction. If either a right or bottom margin is given a negative margin, it will pull the adjacent element towards the main element box, creating an overlap. Many developers use this characteristic of negative margins to fix spots where an element's spacing seems a little off and needs tweaking (**Figure 4.21**).

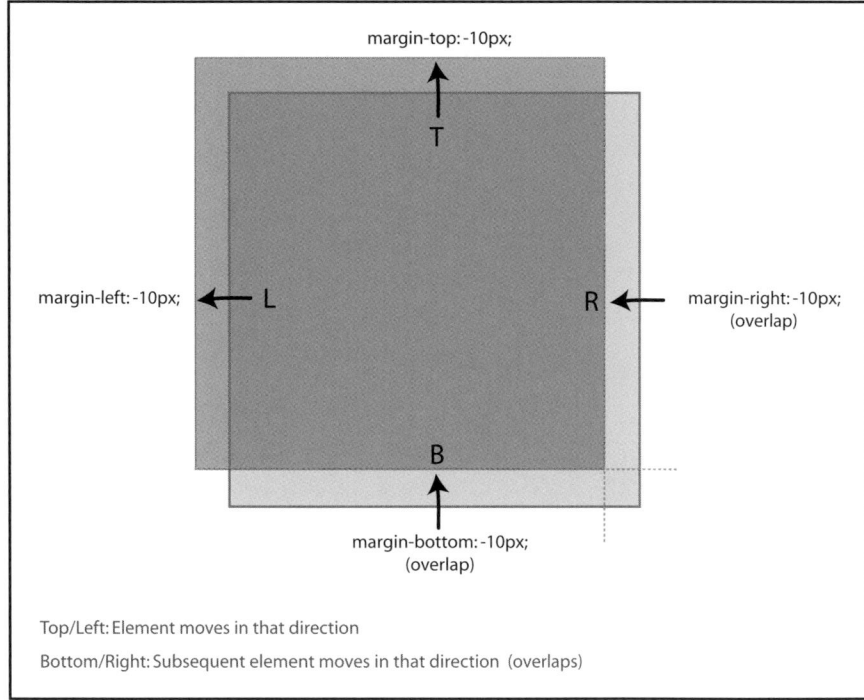

Figure border labels:

margin-top: -10px;

T

margin-left: -10px;   L   R   margin-right: -10px;
(overlap)

B

margin-bottom: -10px;
(overlap)

Top/Left: Element moves in that direction

Bottom/Right: Subsequent element moves in that direction (overlaps)

Figure 4.21 *Negative margin behavior*

UNWANTED SPACE

The following margin bugs either give too much space or take it away. Let's see how we can set things straight.

3 pixel text jog bug

You have a floated element and you detect that the text that is floating next to it is somehow pushed away by 3px. It's the 3 pixel text jog bug (**Figure 4.22**).

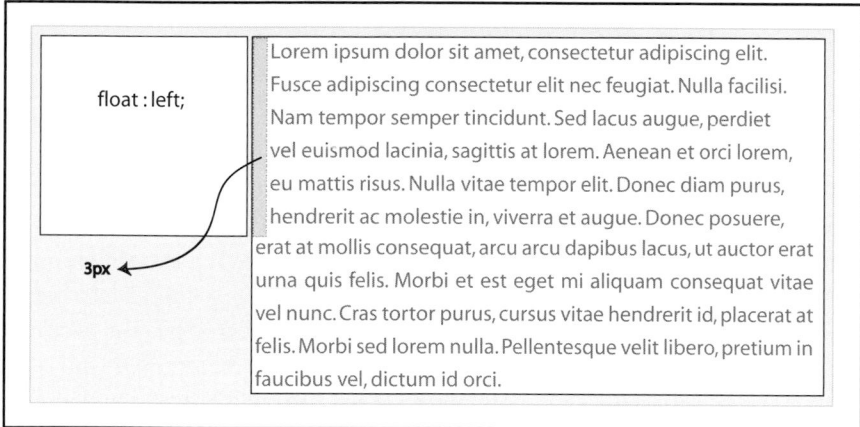

Figure 4.22 *3px Text Jog Bug*

Fortunately, there are a couple of ways to solve this issue:

You can use the float nearly everything method (FnE) and float the parent element. This will eliminate the behavior. Using the FnE example from earlier:

```
<div id="memorablequotes">
   <img src="verbal.jpg" alt="Verbal" class="floatleft">
   <p>&quot;Who is Keyser Soze? He is supposed to be Turkish. Some
   ➥say his father was German. Nobody believed he was real....That
   ➥was his power. The greatest trick the Devil ever pulled was
   ➥convincing the world he didn't exist. And like that, poof. He's
   ➥gone.&quot;</p>
</div>
#memorablequotes {
border: 1px solid #999999;
float: left;
padding: 30px;
width: 450px;
margin: 0 auto;
}

.floatleft {
border: 1px solid #333;
float: left;
}

p {float: left;}
```

You could also set a `width` or `height` on the affected element to eliminate the behavior.

```
* html #memorablequotes p {float: left; height: 0;}
```

Double margin float bug

The double margin bug in IE6 occurs on the first floated element that has a margin value set on the same side as the float on a line. The margin becomes twice the intended size! For example, if you had an element floated left and with `margin-left: 10px`, the 10px would actually render as 20px. The peculiarity of this bug is that it only occurs when the float and margin are on the same side—margins on the other side of the float will not be doubled (**Figure 4.23**).

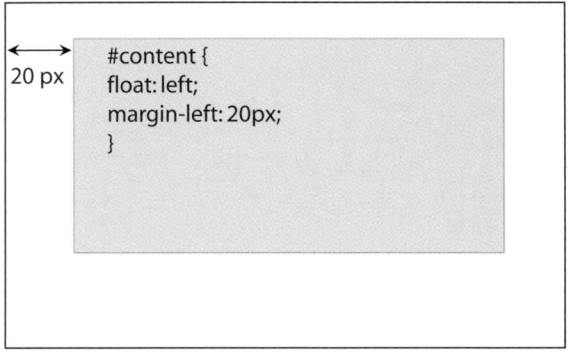
Compliant Browsers

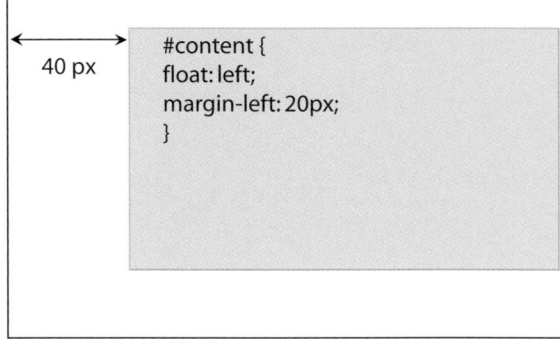
IE6 and lower

Figure 4.23 *Example of the double margin float bug.*

This bug is responsible for many of the layout problems that developers experience in IE6 and below. The additional pixels will cause one of your columns to have insufficient space available for it based on the given widths, and you'll get float drop.

The fix is to set `display: inline` on the floating elements. Remember that we are only affecting the display characteristics with this property; the elements will remain block-level.

```
#navigation {
display: inline;
float: left;
margin-left: 10px;
width: 200px;
}
```

Bottom margin bug

If you have a floated parent element that also has floated children in it, you may experience the bottom margin bug in which the bottom margin is ignored by the parent and collapses in IE7 and earlier browsers (**Figure 4.24**).

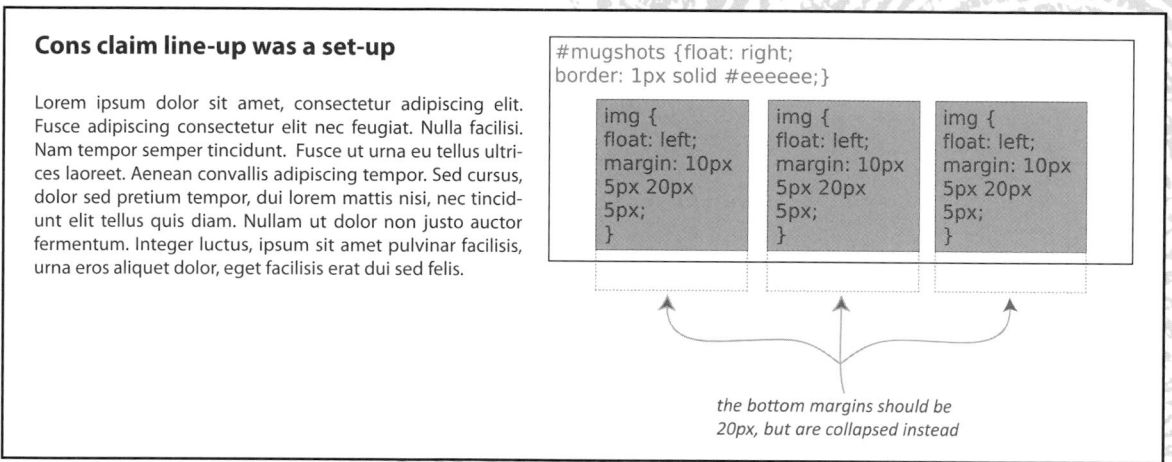

Figure 4.24 *Example of the bottom margin float bug.*

The fix is easy: rather than getting the space you want from the margin of the children elements, establish the space by setting padding for the parent element.

Disappearing Acts

The peekaboo bug and the guillotine bug are probably the two most infamous IE6/7 bugs. Fortunately, there are solid fixes for both of them.

PEEKABOO BUG

You've worked hard to layout and code your page—it's only fair that you want your users to actually see it, right? Well, IE6 seems to have a sense of humor, adding a little Houdini spice into the mix.

The peekaboo bug causes floated elements or text inside of a container next to floated elements to disappear—most often when the page is resized, and sometimes seemingly at random (**Figure 4.25** on the next page).

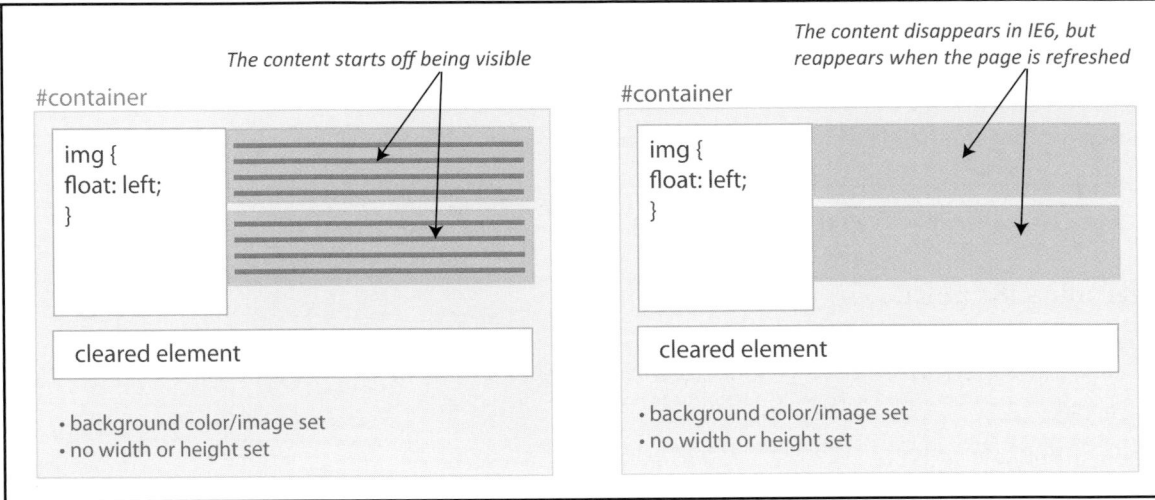

Figure 4.25 *Example of the peekaboo float bug in action.*

Here is a stripped-down example of the code that will create the peekaboo sleight of hand:

```
<h1>The Usual Suspects</h1>
<div id="container">
   <p id="floater">
   Q: Who are the ususal suspects?<br>
   A: Dean Keaton, Michael McManus, Fred Fenster, Todd Hockney, Roger
   ➥ 'Verbal' Kint
   </p>
   <p>Q: Who disappeared without a trace?</p>
   <div class="clearer"></div>
   <p>A: Ha! We're not going to give you the spoiler!</p>
</div>
...
#container {
border: 1px solid #000;
background-color: #eee;
}

#floater {
background-color: #dec;
float: left;
width: 35%;
}
```

```
.clearer {
clear: both;
}
```

Manifold fixes

It may seem like magic, but each of these solutions will help solve your "now you see it, now you don't" problem.

Determine the position

Applying position:relative to the disappearing element will keep it visible for everyone using IE6. For IE7 users, add min-width: 0 as well.

```
#container {
border: 1px solid #000;
background-color: #eee;
}

#floater {
background-color: #dec;
float: left;
width: 35%;
position: relative;  /* peekaboo bug fix for IE6 */
min-width: 0;  /* peekaboo bug fix for IE7 */
}

.clearer {
clear: both;
}
```

Trigger hasLayout

Giving layout to the parent container with any of the properties that trigger hasLayout will also keep the content from disappearing:

- float: left, float: right
- display: inline-block, display: block
- overflow: hidden, overflow: auto, overflow: scroll
- position: absolute, position: fixed (IE7)
- height (any value other than auto)
- min-height (any value other than auto in IE7 only)
- width (any value other than auto)

note

zoom *is a Microsoft proprietary property.*

- min-width (any value other than auto in IE7 only)

- zoom (any value other than normal)

Establish line-height

Setting the line-height on the main container will cascade down to the descendants and keep all of the content in plain sight.

```
#container {
border: 1px solid #000;
background-color: #eee;
line-height: 1em;
}

#floater {
background-color: #dec;
float: left;
width: 35%;
}

.clearer {
clear: both;
}
```

Presto! All fixed.

GUILLOTINE BUG

The guillotine bug is one of the oddest IE bugs. As with any good mystery, all of the parts have to be in place: a parent container element, a floated element inside of that container that is not cleared, links inside the parent container in non-floated content after the float, and finally, style rules for those links that change certain link properties on hover. The result? Not murder, no, but hovering over the links causes part of the floated element inside of the parent container to get cut off and become inaccessible (**Figure 4.26**).

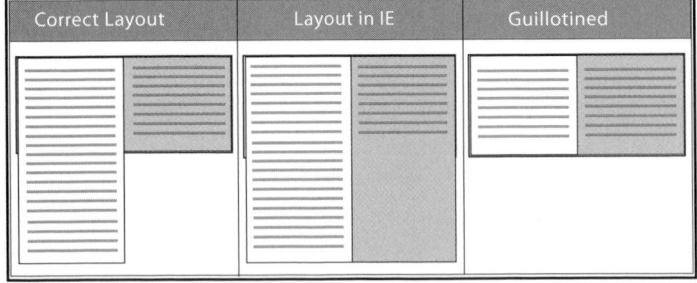

Figure 4.26
Example of the guillotine bug.

Clear solutions

The most popular fixes involve adding a cleared element either inside of the container or outside and after the container.

By adding an element

Add an element, such as a <div>, that has the clear property assigned to it:

```
<div id="container">
   <div id="left">
   <p>To a cop the explanation is never that complicated. It's always
   ➡simple. There's no mystery to the street, no arch criminal behind
   ➡it all. If you got a dead body and you think his brother did it,
   ➡you're gonna find out you're right.</p>
   </div>
   <div id="right">
   <p>This is a <a href="#">reset link</a> here.</p>
   <p>This is another <a href="#">reset link</a> here.</p>
   <p>This is a <a href="#">trigger link</a><br></p>
   </div>
   <div class="clear"></div>
</div>
...
#container {
background-color: #88eeaa;
border: 1px solid #44bb66;
width: 800px;}

#left {
border: 1px dotted #aa3355;
float: left;
width: 200px;
}

#container a:hover {
background: #FFFFCC;
padding: 5px;
text-style: italic;
border-bottom: #0000FF 1px solid;
}

.clear {clear: both;}
```

Easy clear

You can also use the easy-clear method, by adding a .clearfix class to the elements that contain the uncleared float:

```
.clearfix {display: inline-block;}
.clearfix:after {
clear: both;
content: " ";

display: block;
font-size: 0;
height: 0;
visibility: hidden;
}
...
<div id="right" class="clearfix">
    <p>This is a <a href="#">reset link</a> here.</p>
    <p>This is another <a href="#">reset link</a> here.</p>
    <p>This is a <a href="#">trigger link</a><br></p>
</div>
```

note

the generated content is a space.

By using easy clear, you get the parent element to completely contain the children elements and stabilize them.

Alternate solutions

Giving all of the containers a height using the star HTML hack also does the trick.

```
* html div {height: 1%;}

#container {
background-color: #88eeaa;
border: 1px solid #44bb66;
width: 800px;}

#left {
border: 1px dotted #aa3355;
float: left;
width: 200px;
}
```

```css
#container a:hover {
background: #FFFFCC;
padding: 5px;
text-style: italic;
border-bottom: #0000FF 1px solid;
}
```

A final solution is to wrap the content outside of the float in another div container and give it a width, which eliminates the quirky behavior.

```html
<div id="right">
   <p>This is a <a href="#">reset link</a> here.</p>
   <p>This is another <a href="#">reset link</a> here.</p>
   <p>This is a <a href="#">trigger link</a><br></p>
</div>
...
#right {width: 400px;}
```

Your page will stay intact, and heads *won't* roll from tragic IE outcomes.

Fonts Gone Wrong

Way back in the equivalent of the Mesozoic era of the web (which was only about 10 years ago), web developers used `<font size=x></font>` to change the font size on the page (and worked with only 6 sizes!). Now that we are in the modern epoch of CSS, evolutionary progress has brought us many more options.

However, with the power of options also comes the responsibility to be mindful of potential issues. As a suspect, typography rarely reaches the level of murder, but if done incorrectly, a change in font size can break the design of the page for users who need a larger text size.

While your pages don't need to be pixel-perfect in every browser, consistency is still a goal. Let's take a look at the different ways you can control fonts on your page and also what to do if they turn out differently cross-browser.

AN ASSORTMENT OF SIZES

There are still absolute or fixed sizes based on either pixels or points as in the days of yore. However, there are now multiple relative sizing options as well, using keywords, em, percentages, or ex.

Fixed (absolute) sizes

Pixels are usually the first choice for developers when they want a lot of control over how the page looks. The advantage of pixels is that they are more consistent across screens, browsers, and operating systems. However, the main complaint about pixels is that in IE6 and below users cannot easily resize them.

Points should really only be used for print CSS if at all. The point unit related to the defacto printed point sizes. They are best avoided for screen use.

Size keywords

Keywords are actually very consistent across browsers and platforms. The font-size keyword values are xx-small, x-small, small, medium, large, x-large, and xx-large as well as relative keywords smaller and larger.

While the standard keywords (small, medium, large) don't lend themselves to scaling, the relative ones do. You could create pages with scalable text using a fixed keyword as the base, and establishing the other font-sizes on the page with the relative keywords.

Relative sizes

Relative-sized on-screen text allows the user to easily adjust the size of all of the page text.

An important thing to remember when using relative font-sizing: unless specified otherwise, with a few exceptions, an element will inherit the font size of its parent. This means that you have to be particularly aware of nesting elements and how the font sizes may change because of how the elements are nested.

Ems are a measurement based on the height of a font and the width of the letter 'M' in the same font. In terms of scalability and correspondingly, accessibility, ems are the perfect choice. They are also resizeable in IE and cascade well.

Ems aren't just for fonts. Savvy developers will also use ems as a unit of measurement for layout elements and spacing to keep the scale of the entire page consistent.

Percentage font-sizing is another relative method, based on the default size of the font. For example, 100% is equivalent to the current font size. 200% is twice as large. Percentage font-sizing also cascades well.

How Big Is an Em?

1em is equivalent to capital M in the the current font size; 2em is twice as large, and so on.

Below is an extremely useful coversion table that lists the corresponding values between pixels, points, ems and percentages:

Font Size Conversion			
Points	**Pixels**	**Ems**	**Percent**
6pt	8px	0.5em	50%
7pt	9px	0.55em	55%
7.5pt	10px	0.625em	62.5%
8pt	11px	0.7em	70%
9pt	12px	0.75em	75%
10pt	13px	0.8em	80%
10.5pt	14px	0.875em	87.5%
11pt	15px	0.95em	95%
12pt	16px	1em	100%
13pt	17px	1.05em	105%
13.5pt	18px	1.125em	112.5%
14pt	19px	1.2em	120%
14.5pt	20px	1.25em	125%
15pt	21px	1.3em	130%
16pt	22px	1.4em	140%
17pt	23px	1.45em	145%
18pt	24px	1.5em	150%
20pt	26px	1.6em	160%
22pt	29px	1.8em	180%
24pt	32px	2em	200%
26pt	35px	2.2em	220%
27pt	36px	2.25em	225%
28pt	37px	2.3em	230%
29pt	38px	2.35em	235%
30pt	40px	2.45em	245%
32pt	42px	2.55em	255%
34pt	45px	2.75em	275%
36pt	48px	3em	300%

Note that the numbers are approximate and may vary depending on font, browser and operating system.

Yet another relative unit of measurement is the **ex**. An ex is based on the height of the letter 'x' in the current font. Very few developers use ex at present: ems are much more widely employed.

TYPOGRAPHY TIPS

Generally speaking, use relative font sizes as opposed to absolute: they are better for usability and accessibility (users can scale their text as need be) and cross-browser consistency.

But the world of CSS is rarely simple: while you might hope you could just apply an em or percentage-based font value for the page and be able to go on about your business, there are many inconsistencies in browser font-rendering due to differences in established base values of the different font families in the user agent style sheets.

Thus, there is a little additional thinking you should do in general when coding the fonts for the page. We've already discussed the whys of relative sizing, but there are some further considerations to incorporate.

Techniques for scaling

The one disadvantage with ems and percentages is all of the calculations that you have to do to make sure that you are establishing the correct sizes for all of the elements. You can avoid the math but still get the benefit of relative font sizing by using a pixel size as the base, and then using relative font sizing for all of the other elements (either by ems or percentages).

For example, you could establish the base font size to be 10 pixels, and then scale up the elements relative to that base.

```
body {font-size: 10px}
p, li {font-size: 1.2em}
h1 {font-size: 2em;}
```

The best thing about this: easy math! Usability, accessibility, and bug-free functionality are bonus features.

Test the scale

After devising your font sizes for your pages, you should test your pages to be sure that the sizes all work together as expected.

A well-designed page will flow with the resize, while a poorly designed page will have overlapping elements that cause the page to be less readable or even illegible as the page size and zoom change. Reset the font size and page zoom to their default values in all your browsers before testing to be sure you are getting accurate results, and use real-world combinations of text sizing and page zooming in all of the major browsers to determine that the text remains readable in every context. Increasing the font size twice should not break the layout.

TEXT SIZE BUG

Despite all of the advantages of using ems to establish your font sizes in the page, IE6 still manages to shift the rules on rendering them. The text size bug comes about when the font size of the body is set to 1em. When a user uses the text size feature of the browser, the rest of the sizes are hugely out of proportion (**Figure 4.27**).

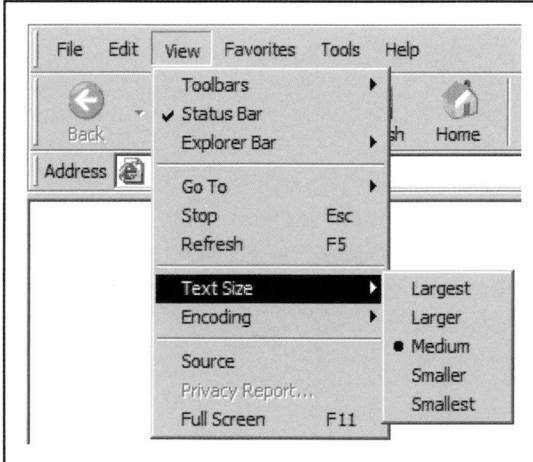

Figure 4.27 *Text resizing feature in IE6.*

Usually this will be due to a font size set this way:

```
body {font-size:1em;}
```

The fix is easy. By changing the font size to 100%, the problem is solved:
```
body {font-size:100%;}
```

The solution is unconventional, but effective. By replacing the ems with percentage, we still have the usability of relative fonts but side-step the resizing bug. A few tips when using this solution:

- Stick with percentages 100% and over. Lower numbers will cause Opera (of all browsers) to render incorrectly.

- Avoid using keywords to set the font size of other elements. Your values should stay with ems or percentages.

Remember that line-height goes hand-in-hand with font-size, so the best practice is to establish a properly scaling line-height as well. The recommendation is this: once you have established the font-size at 100%, then establish the line-height with ems, taking into consideration the corresponding size in pixels. Using the example above, you would have this:

```
body {
font-size:100%;
line-height: 1.125em;
}
```

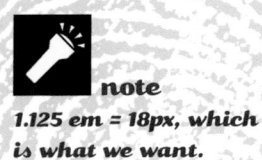

note

1.125 em = 18px, which is what we want.

This set-up at the very beginning of your document will cascade down to all of the elements and create visual consistency throughout your page.

Planning for the Future

You have seen the lineup of known felons. But there are some new kids on the block that you should also know about: CSS3 properties. Many of these burgeoning properties are actually the new good guys, making time-honored challenges such as drop-shadows, importing fonts, rounded corners, column sizing, and multiple background images easy. But even heroes have an Achilles heel. Unsurprisingly, the weak spot with CSS3 is not the properties themselves, but rather their support by browsers.

At present, the browsers that support most of the CSS3 properties are Firefox, Safari, and Google Chrome. Opera supports many of the properties but not all (although newer versions are slated to have increased support), while Internet Explorer supports practically none of them, with the exception of some of the newer selectors.

Another issue is that the CSS3 specifications themselves are not yet finalized. Some browsers utilize the properties, but in a proprietary form. Because of this, you may have to use several versions of the same property in order for it to be rendered by different browsers. Hopefully, the specification will be solidified soon and all browsers will accept the same standard properties.

So, what can you do now? I say, boldly go forth and start to incorporate CSS3 properties into your code, but also know that for true cross-browser compatibility, you will have to employ alternate solutions.

Learn more about CSS3

Want to get on the CSS3 train? Here are some good resources for you to familiarize yourself with the properties and which browsers support what:

- The W3C CSS3 Specifications: http://www.w3.org/TR/css3-roadmap/
- CSS3 info: http://www.css3.info/
- CSS3 Property Support table at Quirksmode.org: http://www.quirksmode.org/css/contents.html

A Positive ID

Looking at face after face, trying to remember who exactly did the crime, how it went down and each character's modus operandi can take a lot out you. The work of a CSS detective is not all glitz and glamour! At the end of the day, however, it is worth it to know that you have the tools to catch bugs before they become delinquent and cause even bigger problems later.

Here is a quick and dirty wrap-up of the allies, miscreants, and solutions that we gave the once-over to in this chapter.

PROPERTIES

Here are the properties mentioned in this chapter and the bug fixes for which they play a part:

Dimensions (height and width)

`height: 1%, min-height, width, min-width, line-height`

- Easy clear
- Give layout
- Fixes the peekaboo bug
- Fixes the guillotine bug

note
Remember that IE6 does not understand `min-height` *or* `min-width`.

Display changes

display: inline

- Fixes the double margin float bug
- Fixes multiple float problems

display: inline-block

- Forces shrink wrapping
- Gives layout

Overflow changes

overflow: hidden, overflow: auto

- Contains floats
- Fixes float drop and overly wide floated columns

Padding and margin changes

padding instead of margin

- Fixes the bottom margin bug
- Fixes the double margin bug

Positioning

position: relative

- Fixes the peekaboo bug

Clear

clear: left, right or both

- Fixes the guillotine bug

Generated Content (for IE8 and up)

:after

- Contains floats
- Fixes the guillotine bug

Font size

font-size

- Fixes the text size bug

TECHNIQUES

These techniques and solutions are achieved using these properties or practices:

Broken box model fix

- Stay in standards mode
- Margin and padding workarounds
- CSS reset

Acceptable IE hacks

- Star HTML hack
- Underscore hack
- Child hack
- Conditional comments

Giving layout

- `float: left`, `float: right`
- `display: inline-block`, `display: block`
- `overflow: hidden`, `overflow: auto`, `overflow: scroll`
- `position: absolute`, `position: fixed` (IE7)
- `height` (any value other than `auto`)
- `min-height` (any value other than `auto`, not IE6)
- `width` (any value other than `auto`)
- `min-width` (any value other than `auto`, not IE6)
- `zoom` (any value other than `normal`, Microsoft proprietary property)

Removing layout

- `width: auto`, `height: auto`
- `max-width: none`, `max-height: none` (IE7)
- `position: static`
- `float: none`
- `overflow: visible` (IE7)
- `zoom: normal` (Microsoft proprietary property)

Force shrink-wrapping

- `display: inline`
- `display: inline-block`
- `display: table`

Preventing problems with floats

- `float: left,` `float: right` (FnE)
- `overflow: hidden,` `overflow: auto,` `overflow: scroll`
- `display: inline`
- `line-height: 0;`
- `width, height`
- `:after` (easy clear)

List white space fix

- `float: left,` `float: right` (FnE)
- `width, height`
- `display: inline or inline-block`
- `width`
- `border-bottom`

Margins and space issues

- `float: left,` `float: right` (FnE)
- `width, height`
- `margin, padding` (on parent element)

QUICK-FIX LIST

One of these rules may be the fix you need. If you are pressed for time or just want a quick fix without thinking about theory or strategy, here are some styles you can apply and see if they solve your problem:

- `position: relative;`
- `display: inline;`
- `display: inline-block;`
- `margin: 0;`
- `padding: 0;`
- `overflow: hidden;`

The Game's Afoot!

YOU'VE MADE IT THROUGH THE RIGORS OF YOUR APPRENTICESHIP, and now you want to hone your training through real-world application, right? Well, my friend, say no more: your time has come! Now we are going to roll up our sleeves and get into the nitty-gritty of some classic cases of code gone wrong.

EACH CHAPTER WILL PRESENT YOU WITH AN OVERVIEW OF THE CASE, and then we will visit the crime scene by taking a look at screenshots of the intended site, and of the site with the problems. Then you'll get to review the complete code for the page, down to the last detail. Once you see all of the evidence, we will employ the tools of the CSS detective—from validation to code elimination—to find the guilty parties and solve the case.

SO PAY CLOSE ATTENTION TO THE DETAILS AND REMEMBER YOUR training. By the end of the section, I am confident that you will be able to crack any CSS mystery that crosses your path.

5

The Case of
the Devilish Details

IN THIS CASE, WE'LL SEE HOW A HARRIED HARRY
Terry tarries and finds that the devil indeed is in
the details.

123

The Crime Scene

Renée Lilldeh of FarfallaEffect Design is suffering from an embarrassment of good fortune. A blossoming in business has prompted an expanded office, a move to bigger quarters, and a website redesign. But exhausted by the demands of clients, new-business pitches, employee training, and settling into a new space, she and her staff have handed the initial website development to their newest intern, Harry Terry.

Passionate about design and front-end coding, Harry is eager to impress, but also still a little unsure of his skills. He's come to the CSS Detective for help with a coding mystery that currently stumps him. Follow along and see if you can spot where Harry's code went wrong.

INITIAL SNAPSHOTS

Harry shares the original design comp of the FarfallaEffect home page with us (**Figure 5.1**).

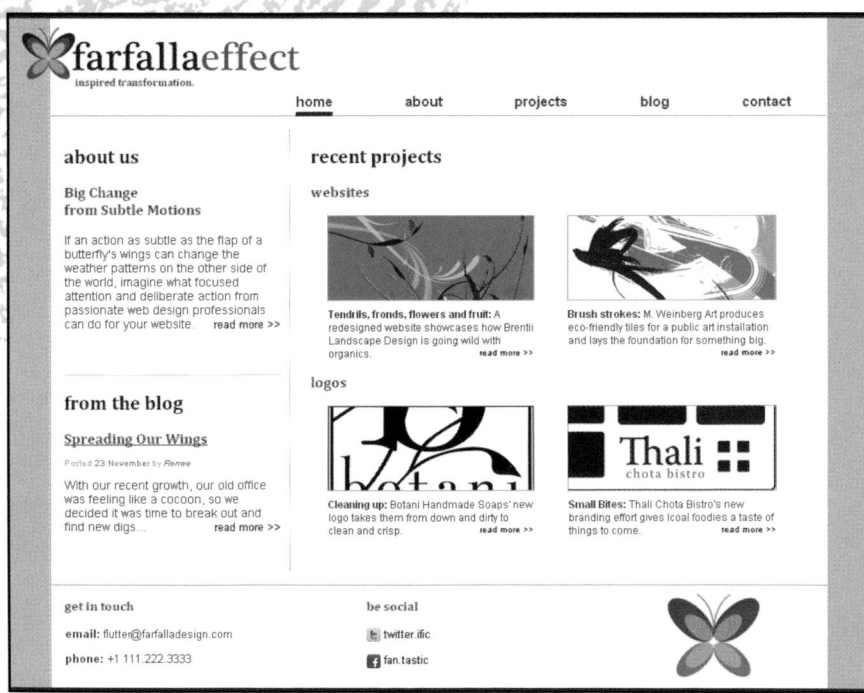

Figure 5.1 *FarfallaEffect's home-page design comp*

However, Harry's late-night coding endeavors have left him with this (**Figure 5.2**):

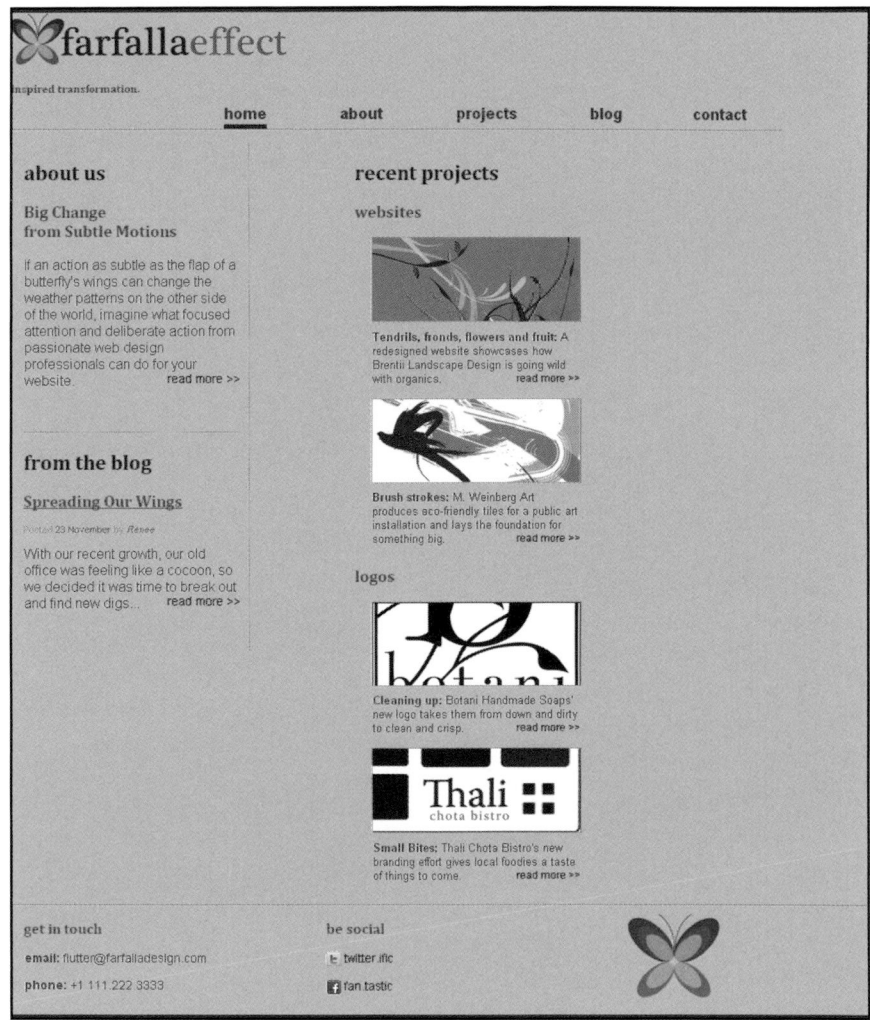

Figure 5.2 *Harry's version of the FarfallaEffect home page*

Follow the Evidence

Harry is a closet procrastinator. He waited until the 11th hour to start on the coding, thinking it would be easy, given the simplicity of the design. But the developed page is due this afternoon, and his fatigue from late-night hours and growing anxiety leave him unable to decipher the cause of the problems in the page.

IDENTIFYING SUSPICIOUS CHARACTERS

I listen carefully to Harry, who, despite his fatigue, is talking a mile a minute, pausing only long enough to burn his mouth with too-hot coffee. The first thing I wonder is whether he has validated the page. As you know, validation is one of the most important tools in our detective toolkit, because it's so useful for showing the small but important details that one can miss— especially when in a hurry. Validating both markup and CSS should be the first practice in solving any coding mystery.

MUG SHOTS

Harry's page code seems benign on first glance. He is using an HTML 4.01 strict doctype, and he has the correct syntax for the style tag. But something is askew:

```
<!DOCTYPE HTML PUBLIC "-//W3C//DTD HTML 4.01//EN"
➡ "http://www.w3.org/TR/html4/strict.dtd">
<html>
<head>
   <title>FarfallaEffect Design</title>
<meta http-equiv="Content-Type" content="text/html; charset=utf-8">
<style type="text/css">
body {
background-color: #ffcc66;
border-top: 5px solid #C0272D;
border-bottom: 5px solid #C0272D;
color: #444444;
font-family: Arial, "Trebuchet MS", sans-serif;
font-size: 1em;
margin: 0;
padding: 0;
}

h1, h2, h3 {font-family: Cambria, serif;}

h2 {color: #96222A;}

#logo {
position: relative
top: 0;
left: -33px;
}
```

```
#tagline {
color: #BF4B1D;
font-size: .8em;
margin: -13px 0 0 28;
}

h3, #blogteaser h3 a {color: #D85623;}

container {
background-color: #ffffff;
border-left: 1px solid #aaaaaa;
font-size: .9em;
margin: 0 auto;
padding: 10px 1px 0 1px;
text-align: left;
width: 900px;
}

    #container h1 {
    color: #ffffff;
    display: none;
    font-size: 1px;
    margin: 0;
    }

#navigation {
border-bottom: 1px solid #aaaaaa;
font-size: 1.1em;
margin: 5px 0 15px 0;
padding: 0 0 6px 0;
text-align: right;
width: 899px;
}

    #navigation li {
    display: inline;
    list-style-type: none;
    }

    #navigation a {
    color: #BC4622;
    font-weight: bold;
    margin: 0 40px;
```

```
text-decoration: none;
}

li.current a, #navigation a:hover {
border-bottom: 5px solid #C0272D;
font-weight: bold;
padding-bottom: 2px;
}

#mainbody {
border-right: 1px dotted #aaaaaa;
float: left;
margin-bottom: 15px;
padding: 0 10px 30px 15px;
width: 250px;
}

#introcontent {
margin-bottom: 50px;
}

.readmore a {
color: #990022;
float: right;
font-size: .9em;
text-decoration: none;
}

#blogteaser {
border-top: 1px dotted #aaaaaa;
margin-top: 10px;
}

.postinfo {
color: #aaaaaa;
font-size: .70em;
line-height: .5em;
}

    .postinfo a {
    color: #777777;
    text-decoration: none;
    } ➡
```

```
#recentprojects {
float: right;
margin: 0 0 10px 0;
width: 600px;
}
   #recentprojects h3 {clear: both;}

   #recentprojects img {border: 1px solid
   ➥#aaaaaa;}

   dl.projects {
   float: lefr;
   margin: 0 10px 10px 10px;
   text-align: center;
   width: 260px;
   }

   dl.projects dd {
   font-size: .8em;
   margin: 0;
   padding: 5px 10px;
   text-align: left;
   }

#footer {
clear: both;
border-top: 1px solid #aaaaaa;
font-size: .9em;
overflow: hidden;
padding: 0 0 0 15px;
}

   #footer div {
   float: left;
   margin: 0;
   padding: 0 0 10px 0;
   }

   #contactinfo, #sociallinks {width: 350px;}

   #sociallinks img {
   border: 0;
   vertical-align: middle;
   }
```

```
   #sociallinks a {
   color: #990022;
   text-decoration: none;
   }

  #footerlogo {text-align: center;}

     #footerlogo img {margin-top: 10px;}
</style>
</head>

<body>

<div id="container">
   <div id="logo">
      <img src="logo_farfallaeffect_serif_alt.png"
      ➥alt="logo">
   </div>

   <h1>farfalle design</h1>
   <h2 id="tagline">inspired
   ➥transformation.</h2>

   <ul id="navigation">
      <li class="current"><a href="#">home
      ➥</a></li>
      <li><a href="#">about</a></li>
      <li><a href="#">projects</a></li>
      <li><a href="#">blog</a></li>
      <li><a href="#">contact</a></li>
   </ul>

   <div id="mainbody">
      <div id="introcontent">
      <h2>about us</h2>
      <h3>Big Change<br>
      <span class="">from Subtle Motions</span>
      </h3>
      <p>If an action as subtle as the flap
      ➥of a butterfly's wings can change
      ➥the weather patterns on the other
      ➥side of the world, imagine what
      ➥focused attention and deliberate
      ➥action from passionate web design
```

```
➥professionals can do for your website.
➥<span class="readmore"><a href="#">
➥read more &gt;&gt;</a></span></p>
</div><!--end introcontent -->

<div id="blogteaser">
<h2>from the blog</h2>
<h3><a href="#">Spreading Our Wings
➥</a></h3>
<p class="postinfo">Posted <a href="#">
➥23 November</a> by <cite>
➥<a href="#">Renee</a></cite></p>
<p>With our recent growth, our old
➥office was feeling like a cocoon, so
➥we decided it was time to break out
➥and find new digs...
<span class="readmore"><a href="#">
➥read more &gt;&gt;</a></span></p>
</div><!--end blogteaser -->
</div><!--end mainbody -->

<div id="recentprojects">
   <h2>recent projects</h2>
   <h3>websites</h3>
   <dl class="projects">
      <dt><img src="example1-1.gif" alt="">
      ➥</dt>
      <dd><strong>Tendrils, fronds, flowers
      ➥and fruit:</strong> A redesigned
      ➥website showcases how Brentii
      ➥Landscape Design is going wild with
      ➥organics.
      <span class="readmore"><a href="#">
      ➥read more &gt;&gt;</a></span></dd>
   </dl>
   <dl class="projects">
      <dt><img src="example1-2.gif" alt="">
      ➥</dt>
      <dd><strong>Brush strokes:</strong>
      ➥M. Weinberg Art produces eco-
      ➥friendly tiles for a public art
      ➥installation and lays the
      ➥foundation for something big.
```

```
      <span class="readmore"><a href="#">
      ➥read more &gt;&gt;</a></span></dd>
   </dl>

   <h3>logos</h3>
   <dl class="projects">
      <dt><img src="example1-3.gif" alt="">
      ➥</dt>
      <dd><strong>Cleaning up:</strong>
      ➥Botani Handmade Soaps' new logo
      ➥takes them from down and dirty to
      ➥clean and crisp.
      <span class="readmore"><a href="#">
      ➥read more &gt;&gt;</a></span></dd>
   </dl>
   <dl class="projects">
      <dt><img src="example1-4.gif" alt="">
      ➥</dt>
      <dd><strong>Small Bites:</strong>
      ➥Thali Chota Bistro's new branding
      ➥effort gives local foodies a taste
      ➥of things to come.
      <span class="readmore"><a href="#">
      ➥read more &gt;&gt;</a></span></dd>
   </dl>
</div><!--end recentprojects-->

<div id="footer">
   <div id="contactinfo">
      <h3>get in touch</h3>
      <p><strong>email:</strong>
      ➥flutter@farfalladesign.com</p>
      <p><strong>phone:</strong>
      ➥+1 111.222.3333</p>
   </div><!--end contactinfo-->

   <div id="sociallinks">
      <h3>be social</h3>
      <p><a href="#"><img src="twitter_16.png"
      ➥alt=""></a> <a href="#">twitter.ific
      ➥</a></p> ➥
```

```
            <p><a href="#"><img src="facebook_16.png"
          ➥alt=""></a> <a href="#">fan.tastic
          ➥</a></p>
        </div><!--end sociallinks-->

        <div id="footerlogo">
          <img src="farfalle_bf.png" alt="logo"
        </div><!--end footerlogo-->
      </div><!--end footer-->
    </div><!--end container-->
  </body>
</html>
```

The Evidence Never Lies

Our initial review of the HTML page code indicated that the markup is well structured, and a routine validation produced no errors. Harry grins with self-satisfied relief.

The CSS validation results, however, are another story (**Figure 5.3**):

```
W3C CSS Validator results for TextArea (CSS level 2.1)
Sorry! We found the following errors (3)

18  #logo  Value Error : position attempt to find a semicolon before
    ➥the property name. Add it.
25  #tagline  Value Error : margin only 0 can be a length. You must
    ➥put a unit after your number : -13px 0 0 28
119  dl.projects  Value Error : float lefr is not a float value : lefr
```

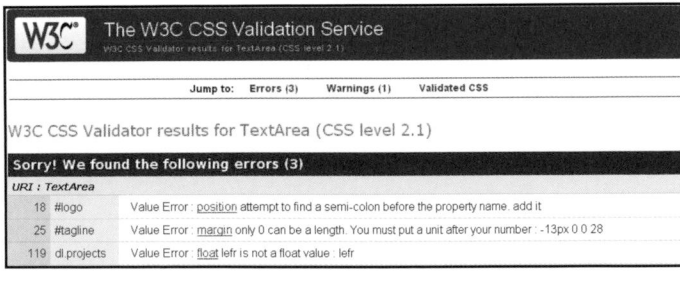

Figure 5.3
FarfallaEffect's page-validation results

CONFIRMING SUSPICIONS AND NAMING THE CULPRIT

My first hunch was correct: Harry's knowledge of HTML and CSS is solid, but he missed some minutia that made the difference between the page he was shooting for and the one he was getting.

Upon reviewing the validation results, it's clear that we need to make the following fixes:

1. The logo is out of position because Harry forgot the semicolon at the end of the following declaration:

```
#logo {
position: relative;
top: 0;
left: -33px;
}
```

2. The tagline is slightly off because Harry forgot the unit of measurement after the value:

```
#tagline {
color: #BF4B1D;
font-size: .8em;
margin: -13px 0 0 28px;
}
```

3. The list items aren't floating to the left because of a misspelling:

```
dl.projects {
float: left;
margin: 0 10px 10px 10px;
text-align: center;
width: 260px;
}
```

note
Left was originally written as lefr.

Once these changes are incorporated, the validation results produce no errors, but the look of the page shows that something is still amiss (**Figure 5.4** on the next page).

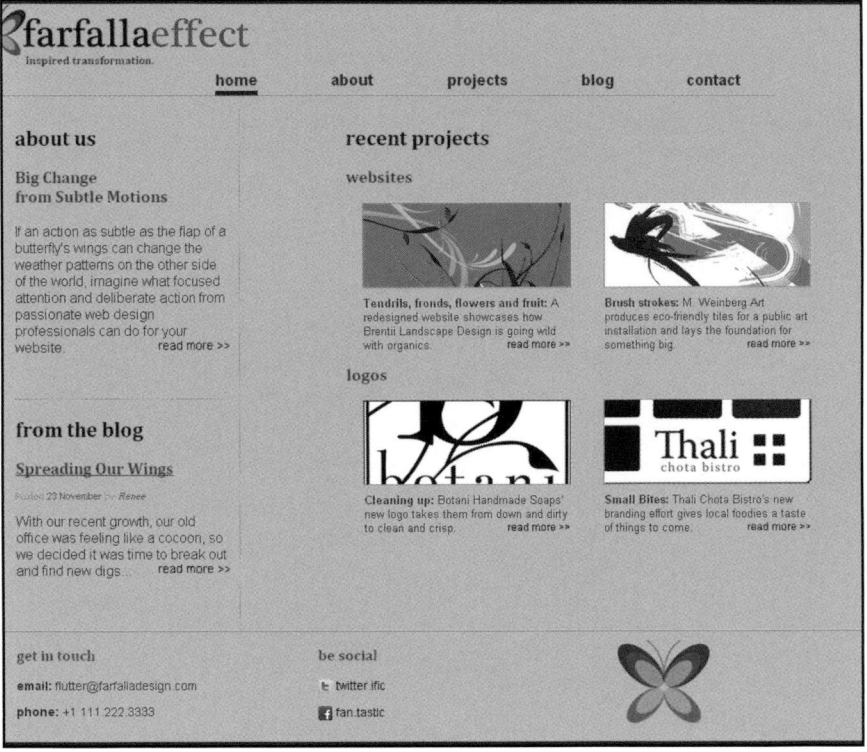

Figure 5.4 *Page after validation errors were fixed*

The logo is still not where it's supposed to be and didn't the main body area have a white background in the original design spec? There is something wrong with the styles that control the main body of the page. Let's go back to the styles to see what small detail could elude *both* the validator and Harry's tired eyes.

Did you spot it yet? If not, go back to the code and read it through from the top, keeping in mind that the problem will probably be with a selector that controls the main section of the page. Also remember that it may be a simple detail that makes the difference.

Aha! Something just isn't quite right about the selector created for the `<div id="container">`, is it? In typical Harry Terry fashion, he forgot to put a # in front of the `container` selector. Thus, none of the `#container` styles show up: the middle alignment from the margins, the background color and the border, and the font size as well. If you found it, then bravo! Your apprenticeship has already served you well!

Here is the fix:

```
#container {
background-color: #ffffff;
border-left: 1px solid #aaaaaa;
font-size: .9em;
margin: 0 auto;
padding: 10px 1px 0 1px;
text-align: left;
width: 900px;
}
```

With the addition of the # sign, voilà! The main container shows up as expected, the logo and tagline finally fall into place properly (**Figure 5.5**) and the relative text sizes all render as desired (**Figure 5.6**).

Figure 5.5 *FarfallaEffect Design's logo in place*

about us

Big Change from Subtle Motions

If an action as subtle as the flap of a butterfly's wings can change the weather patterns on the other side of the world, imagine what focused attention and deliberate action from passionate web design professionals can do for your website.   read more >>

from the blog

Spreading Our Wings

Posted 23 November by *Renee*

With our recent growth, our old office was feeling like a cocoon, so we decided it was time to break out and find new digs...   read more >>

recent projects

websites

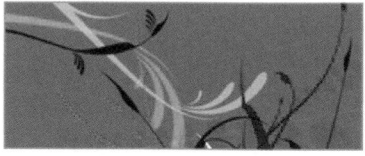

Tendrils, fronds, flowers and fruit: A redesigned website showcases how Brentii Landscape Design is going wild with organics.   read more >>

logos

Cleaning up: Botani Handmade Soaps' new logo takes them from down and dirty to clean and crisp.   read more >>

Figure 5.6 *Relative text sizes are fine and dandy.*

Case Closed!

With these simple fixes, Harry is up and running again and on top of the world. I commend him on his clean markup, but warn him to make sure to give himself more time, remember the little details, and to validate before panicking. He thanks us both profusely, and leaves to finish his preparation for the big presentation—and his inevitable promotion.

Harry's problems were simple ones, but also small and detail-oriented. They could be easily missed by the untrained eye or without a reasonable dose of patience. Obviously, the validators are invaluable for finding the sorts of problems that a human can easily miss, but there are some problems that even the validator will overlook that a keen eye won't. After validating, a great place to start is with the basics: spelling, punctuation, and proper syntax. Often, something as small as a missing period can make a huge difference.

In addition to validating and starting with the basics, remember to start searching for the culprit at the top of the document and work your way down. Many of Harry's problems were in the top third of the CSS code, but had large effects on the way the page appeared.

Finally, using a process of elimination to focus on the elements that are out of place will most often take you straight to the heart of the problem.

Our first case together was a success. However, I suspect that our problems may get more complicated.

6

The Case of the Mistaken Identity

IN THIS CASE, WE'LL ANSWER THE AGE-OLD question "What's in a name?" and see just how important it is to know exactly who's who.

The Crime Scene

Zimma Studios, while great at designing websites, does not have the resources to do any major programming. They hire Bob Cobb to do both the front-end and back-end development for their client's foodie blog and community, EateryJunkie.com. Bob is mainly a back-end developer who specializes in Java and doesn't really deal with HTML and CSS much anymore unless he has to. Ironically, he is a bit of a know-it-all despite being a little rusty.

During the development process, Bob has run into problems. He swallows his pride and discreetly turns to the CSS Detective for a fresh set of eyes and solutions to his layout problems.

INITIAL SNAPSHOTS

Like many back-end programmers, Bob is less interested in the design and more compelled by how the functionality will be achieved. However, he knows that he does need to make the site look like the design given to him (**Figure 6.1**). But from the results of his first attempt, you can see why he seeks assistance (**Figure 6.2**).

Follow the Evidence

I notice that Bob avoids eye contact, so I guess he is a bit ruffled by having to ask for help. He hides his discomfort with bluster: "I've been doing stuff on the web for years," he says smugly, "probably way before you got started with it. Once you learn HTML and CSS, there's really not a lot more to it. That's why I got into the back end."

IDENTIFYING SUSPECTS

Bob's demeanor tells me that while he may know actual programming well, he's overconfident about his CSS coding. I suspect that he didn't validate because he didn't think he needed to.

Figure 6.1 *The EateryJunkie design comp*

Figure 6.2 *Not quite what we are shooting for*

MUG SHOTS

I'm not surprised that as a developer, Bob has gone for using a strict doctype.
A preliminary review of the code shows this:

```
<!DOCTYPE html PUBLIC "-//W3C//DTD XHTML 1.0 Strict//EN"
 "http://www.w3.org/TR/xhtml1/DTD/xhtml1-strict.dtd">
<html xmlns="http://www.w3.org/1999/xhtml" xml:lang="en" lang="en">
```

```
<head>
<meta http-equiv="Content-Type"
content="text/html; charset=utf-8" />
<title>EateryJunkie - Get your eatery on!
➥ </title>
<link rel="shortcut icon" type="image/x-icon"
➥ href="eatery_junkie.ico" />
<style type="text/css">
body {
background-color: #D1000E;
color: #535353;
font: .95em/1em Arial, sans-serif;
margin: 0;
}

h2, h3, h4, #sitenav {
font-face: Courier New, monospace;}

a {
color: #F2F2F2;
text-decoration: none;
}

a:hover {
text-decoration: underline;}

a img {
border: none;}

ul {
list-style-type: none;}

input {
margin: 0 5px 5px 0;}

.styled {
font-style: italic;}

.morelink {
text-align: right;}

#pagehead, #sitenav li, #pagebody,
➥ #recentposts, #recentcomments,
➥ #recenttweets, #sideimage, #feed,
➥ #subscription, #community, #recipe, #social {
```

```
border-bottom: 2px solid #FFF4ED;}
#sitesearch, #postlist, #subscription p,
➥ #subscription form, #community p.members,
➥ #community ul, #recipe ul, #pagefoot {
text-align: center;}
#recentscolumn, #blogessentials {
font-size: .75em;}

#pagewrapper {
background-color: #FFF;
border-top: 1px solid #FFF4ED;
border-right: 2px solid #FFF4ED;
border-bottom: 1px solid #FFF4ED;
border-left: 2px solid #FFF4ED;
margin: 0 auto;
width: 979px;
}

    #pagewrapper div {
    over-flow: hidden;}

#pagehead {
background: transparent url(bg_head.jpg)
➥ 178px 0 no-repeat;}
    #pagehead h1 {
    background: #F9ECD4 url(logo_eateryjunkie.png)
    ➥ middle middle no-repeat;
    border-right: 2px solid #FFF4ED;
    float: left;
    height:200px;
    margin: 0;
    text-indent: -9999px;
    width:189px;
    }

    #pagehead a {
    display: block;
    height: 100%;
    width: 100%;
    }

    #sitenav {
    background-color: #CC0000;
    border-left: 2px solid #FFF4ED;
```

```
float: right;
margin: 0;
padding: 0;
height: 200px;
width: 250px;
}

   #sitenav li {
   font-size: 1.1em;
   font-weight: bold;
   line-height: 1.7em;
   padding-left: 8px;
   height: 15%;
   width: 100%;
   }

      #sitenav li.about {
      background-color: #660000;}
      #sitenav li.reviews {
      background-color: #9E0F13;}
      #sitenav li.recipes {
      background-color: #BE0E10;}
      #sitenav li.community {
      background-color: #D1000E;}
      #sitenav li.contact {
      background-color: #E82C0C;}
      #sitenav li.last {
      border-bottom: none;}
   #sitenav a {
   color: #FFF4ED;}

      #sitenav a:hover {
      font-style: italic;
      text-decoration: none;
      }

#searchsite {
background-color: #482C21;
border-top: 2px solid #FFF4ED;
clear: right;
float: right;
height: 40px;
margin: -42px 0 0 0;
```

```
width: 250px;
   }

      #searchsite p {
      margin: 8px 0 0 0;}
#pagebody {
background: transparent url(bg_fauxcolumns.gif)
➥0 0 repeat-y;
clear: both;}
   #contentcolumn {
   float: left;
   line-height: 1.4em;
   margin: 0;
   width: 477px;}

         #contentcolumn a {
         color: #7E5E45; }

         #contentcolumn .morelink {
         font-size: .8em;}

   #featuredpost {
   padding: 0 15px 0;}

      #featuredpost h2 {
      background: #FFF url(title_latestpost.png)
      ➥0 0 no-repeat;
      height: 44px;
      text-indent: -9999px;
      width: 137px;
      }

      #featuredpost h3 {
      border-bottom: 1px dotted #A15825;
      font-face: Georgia, serif;
      line-height: 1.3em;
      }

      #featuredpost p a {
      text-decoration: underline;}
      #postinfo, #imagecaption {
      font-size: .7em;}
      #blogphoto {
      border: 1px solid #7E5E45; ➥
```

```
margin: 5px auto;
padding: 5px;
width: 400px;
}

#catstags {
background-color: #F9ECD4;
border: 2px solid #edd0b2;
font-size: .76em;
line-height: .75em;
padding: 2px 8px;
}

#catstags p {
margin: 10px 0;
padding: 0;
}

#recentscolumn {
background-color: #7E5E45;
color: #FFF4ED;
float: left;
width: 250px;
margin: 0;
}

#recentscolumn a {
color: #FFF;}

#recentscolumn ul {
margin: 10px 15px 10px;
padding: 0;
}

#recentscolumn li {
margin: 0 0 .8em 0;}

#recentscolumn h3 {
color: #FFF4ED;
margin: 0;
}

h3.posts {
background: transparent url
➥(title_recentpost.png) 0 0 no-repeat;
```

```
height: 35px;
text-indent: -9999px;
width: 113px;
}

h3.comment {
background: transparent url
➥(title_recentcomment.png) 0 0
➥no-repeat;
height: 29px;
text-indent: -9999px;
width: 131px;
}

h3.tweet {
background: transparent url
➥(title_recenttweet.png) 0 0 no-repeat;
height: 28px;
text-indent: -9999px;
width: 107px;
}

h3.pic {
background: transparent url
➥(title_recentpic.png) 0 0 no-repeat;
height: 36px;
text-indent: -9999px;
width: 93px;
}

#recentposts, #recentcomments,
➥#recenttweets, #recentpics {
padding: 8px 10px;
}

#recentpics {}

#recentpics ul {
margin: 10px auto 10px;
over-flow: auto;
width: 156px;
}

#recentpics li {
float: left;
```

```
        margin: 0;
        width: 74px;
        }

        #recentpics img {
        border: 2px solid #FFF4ED;
        margin: 0;
        }

        #recentpics li.left {
        margin-right: 8px;}

        #recentpics li.top {
        margin-bottom: 4px;}

#blogessentials {
background-color: #482C21;
color: #FFF4ED;
float: left;
line-height: 1.2em;
margin: 0 0 0 2px;
width: 250px;
}

    #feed, #subscription, #social, #recipe,
    ➥#community, #blogroll {
    padding: 8px 10px;
    }

    #blogessentials img {
    margin-right: 5px;
    valign: middle;
    }

    #blogessentials p {
    margin-top: 0;}

    #blogessentials ul {
    margin: 0;
    padding: 0;
    }

        #blogessentials li {
        line-height: 2em;
        padding: 0 0 0 12px;
        }
```

```
#blogessentials h4 {
color: #FFF4ED;
margin: 0;
}

    h4.feed {
    background: transparent url
    ➥(title_junkiefeed.png) 0 0 no-repeat;
    height: 32px;
    text-indent: -9999px;
    width: 101px;
    }

    h4.subscription {
    background: transparent url
    ➥(title_junkiesubscribe.png) 0 0
    ➥no-repeat;
    height: 32px;
    text-indent: -9999px;
    width: 147px;
    }

    h4.community {
    background: transparent url
    ➥(title_junkiecommunity.png) 0 0
    ➥no-repeat;
    height: 33px;
    text-indent: -9999px;
    width: 123px;
    }

    h4.recipe {
    background: transparent url
    ➥(title_junkierecipe.png) 0 0
    ➥no-repeat;
    height: 32px;
    text-indent: -9999px;
    width: 97px;
    }

    h4.social {
    background: transparent url
    ➥(title_junkiesocial.png) 0 0
    ➥no-repeat; ➥
```

```
height: 32px;
text-indent: -9999px;
width: 98px;
}

h4.blogroll {
background: transparent url
➥ (title_junkieblogs.png) 0 0 no-repeat;
height: 32px;
text-indent: -9999px;
width: 114px;
}

#sideimage {
background: url(img_side.jpg) no-repeat
➥ 0px 0;
height: 375px;
width: 250px;
}

#feed p {
margin: 5px 0;
padding: 0 12px;
}

#community {}
    #community ul {
    margin: 5px auto 10px;
    over-flow: hidden;
    width: 225px;
    }

    #community li {
    float: left;
    margin: 0 8px 0 0;
    padding: 0;
    width: 50px;
    }

    #community img {
    border: 1px solid #FFF4ED;
    margin: 0;
    width: 48px;
    }
```

```
        #community li.right {
        margin-right: 0;}
        #community li.top {
        margin-bottom: 4px;}
#pagefoot {
background-color: #999;
clear: both;
font-size: .70em;
line-height: 1.1em;
padding: 8px 0;
}

/* IE6 compensation */
* html #pagehead {height: 1%;}
* html #sitenav {width: 242px;}
* html #sitesearch {height: 44px;}
* html #community li {margin: 0 7px 0 0;}
* html #sociallinks img {margin-bottom: 5px;}

</style>
</head>
<body>
<div id="pagewrapper">
    <div id="pagehead">
        <h1><a href="#">Eatery<span
class="styled">Junkie</span></a></h1>
        <ul id="sitenav">
            <li class="about"><a href="#">about
            ➥ </a></li>
            <li class="reviews">
            ➥ <a href="#">reviews</a></li>
            <li class="recipes"><a
            href="#">recipes</a></li>
            <li class="community">
            ➥ <a href="#">community</a></li>
            <li class="contact last">
            ➥ <a href="#">contact</a></li>
        </ul>
        <div id="sitesearch">
            <form id="search" action="post">
```

```
    <p><input type="text" size="23"
    ➥class="textinput" />
    ➥<input type="submit" value="search"
    ➥class="submit"/></p>
    </form>
    </div><!-- end sitesearch -->
  </div><!-- end pagehead -->
<div id="pagebody">
  <div id="contentcolumn">
    <div id="featuredpost">
      <h2 class="latestpost">Latest Post
      ➥</h2>
      <h3><a href="#">We like it raw (and
      ➥cooked, and everything in-between)
      ➥</a></h3>
      <div class="blogphoto">
      ➥<img src="main_blogphoto.jpg"
      ➥alt="" />
      <p class="imagecaption">Raw foods
      ➥goodness abounds at Cafe
      ➥Gratitude.</p>
      </div>
      <p>Two years ago, my friend
      ➥<a href="#">Ambalinn</a> toyed with
      ➥the idea of going completely raw,
      ➥In solidarity and out of curiosity,
      ➥I decided to try it myself for one
      ➥month. My friend adapted and
      ➥blossomed into a gourmet rawist
      ➥seemingly overnight. In stark
      ➥contrast, I found that my partial
      ➥interest and demanding work
      ➥schedule meant that I ate a lot of
      ➥salads (when not sampling my
      ➥friend's amazing and delicious
      ➥concoctions, which wasn't often
      ➥enough). At the end of the month, I
      ➥went back to eating cooked foods,
      ➥as I missed the warmth as well as
      ➥the comfort of making things that
      ➥were familiar.</p>
```

```
      <p>However, the endeavor did leave me
      ➥with a deeper appreciation for raw
      ➥foods and with an expanded
      ➥repertoire of food preparation
      ➥techniques (you wouldn't think that
      ➥"massaging" greens would make them
      ➥taste better, but it does). Now
      ➥when I am out in my travels,
      ➥sampling eateries all around the
      ➥world, I can't help but stop in at
      ➥raw restaurants and see what they
      ➥have up their sleeves.</p>
      <p>A recent trip to San Francisco
      ➥gave me the opportunity to try out
      ➥<a href="#">Cafe Gratitude</a>.
      ➥I have their (un)cookbook,
      ➥<a href="#">I Am Grateful</a>,
      ➥and I have been loving most of the
      ➥recipes from it, especially the
      ➥desserts. I ordered the "I Am
      ➥Abundant" sampler platter to try a
      ➥little of everything: sprouted
      ➥almond hummus, Asian kale-sea
      ➥vegetable salad, hemp-seed pesto
      ➥crostini, spicy cashew nacho cheese
      ➥with flax chips, olive tapenade,
      ➥buckwheat crackers, spring roll,
      ➥and mini house soup.</p>
      <p> Before I give my impressions, I
      ➥must confess to having a bad habit
      ➥of comparing all raw foods with
      ➥those of Ms. Ambalinn, as she has
      ➥developed a style that is flavorful
      ➥without "cheating" (relying on
      ➥fats, oils, and overspicing), and
      ➥instead produces simple
      ➥combinations with basic ingredients
      ➥to let the flavors of the food
      ➥itself sing through the dish.</p>
```

```
<p>Having said that, here was my take
➥on Cafe Gratitude: overall, each
➥item was good, but did seem to be
➥much stronger flavor-wise than
➥necessary. That didn't stop me from
➥finishing everything, though, and
➥it certainly did not stop me from
➥ordering dessert. Ah, dessert. I
➥went with the pear-ginger
➥"cheesecake," which was so
➥incredibly delicious that I still
➥think about it to this day.</p>
<p>So, if you are in the Bay Area and
➥are curious about raw foods, make
➥an effort to stop by Cafe
➥Gratitude. You will be pleased that
➥you did.</p>
<p class="postinfo">Posted <a href="#">
➥18 June</a> by <cite><a href="#">
➥Bonita</a></cite></p>
    <div id="catstags">
    <p>filed under: <a href="#">reviews
➥</a></p>
    <p>tagged with: <a href="#">raw
➥foods</a>, <a href="#">restaurants
➥</a>, <a href="#">San Francisco
➥</a>, <a href="#">healthy eating
➥</a></p>
    <p>comments: <a href="#">(10)</a></p>
    </div><!-- end catstags -->
    <p class="morelink"><a href="#">
➥previous posts &gt;&gt;</a></p>
    </div><!-- end featuredpost -->
</div><!-- end contentcolumn -->
<div id="recentscolumn">
    <div id="recentposts">
    <h3 class="posts">recent posts</h3>
    <ul id="postlist">
        <li><a href="#">What goes on at
➥Vintner's Grill, stays...</a></li>
        <li><a href="#">Brenda's breakfast
➥breakdance</a></li>
```

```
        <li><a href="#">Amsterdam was
➥cold, but the poffertjes were
➥warm and crisp</a></li>
        <li><a href="#">Me, you, and the
➥exotic spiced halibut</a></li>
        <li><a href="#">Sweet potato
➥biscuits and other products of
➥garden bounty</a></li>
        <li><a href="#">On a lark at
➥Meadowlark</a></li>
    </ul>
    <p class="morelink"><a href="#">
➥More posts &gt;</a></p>
    </div><!-- end recentposts -->
    <div id="recentcomments">
    <h3 class="comment">recent comments</h3>
    <ul id="commentlist">
        <li><a href="#">Natalie</a>
➥commented on<br />
        <a href="#">We like it raw (and
➥cooked, and everything in
➥between)</a> March 1</li>
        <li><a href="#">Amber</a>
➥commented on<br />
        <a href="#">Brenda's breakfast
➥breakdance</a> January 19</li>
        <li><a href="#">Deloria</a>
➥commented on<br />
        <a href="#">What goes on at
➥Vintner's Grill, stays...</a>
➥January 18</li>
        <li><a href="#">Andrew</a>
➥commented on<br />
        <a href="#">Amsterdam was cold,
➥but the poffertjes were warm and
➥crisp</a> December 28</li>
        <li><a href="#">Christine</a>
➥commented on<br />
        <a href="#">Me, you, and the exotic
➥spiced halibut</a> December 5</li>
    </ul>
```

```
<p class="morelink"><a href="#">
➥More comments &gt;</a></p>
</div><!-- end recentposts -->
<div id="recenttweets">
<h3 class="tweet">recent tweets</h3>
<ul id="tweetlist">
   <li>OH: "it's like a little man
   ➥with a sweet potato outfit is
   ➥breakdancing on my tongue!" with
   ➥@tungstenrs <a href="#">on 21
   ➥January</a></li>
   <li>Ahhh. Finally sitting down to
   ➥a nice dinner at Michael's. Still
   ➥my favorite place in town.
   ➥<a href="#">17 January</a></li>
   <li>The Winds never disappoints:
   ➥pear poached in spiced red wine
   ➥with mascarpone and almond
   ➥shortbead. Very pleased.
   ➥@drjartnsoul @luddlj <a href="#">
   ➥23 December</a></li>
   <li>Back in the homeland. Hello
   ➥Winds, Jeet, Sunrise, and finally
   ➥after many years, Auberge. I can't
   ➥wait to eat you! <a href="#">
   ➥20 December</a></li>
   <li>@lipstickvegan has made more
   ➥raw chocolate truffles! thank
   ➥heavens for foodie friends.
   ➥<a href="#">November 23</a></li>
   <li>Ft. Meyers had some nice
   ➥surprises: Cibo and Crave.
   ➥Definitely worth the trip, and
   ➥next door to each other!
   ➥@ciboftmeyers @craveftmeyers
   ➥<a href="#">November 9</a></li>
</ul>
<p class="morelink"><a href="#">
➥More tweets &gt;</a></p>
</div><!-- end recenttweets -->

<div id="recentpics">
<h3 class="pic">recent pics</h3>
<ul id="photobadge">
   <li class="left top"><img src=
   ➥"th_vintnergrill.jpg" alt="" /></li>
   <li class="top"><img src="
   ➥th_poffertjes.jpg" alt="" /></li>
   <li class="left top"><img src=
   ➥"th_empanadasplace.jpg" alt="" />
   ➥</li>
   <li class="top"><img src=
   ➥"th_amberstorte.jpg" alt="" /></li>
   <li class="left top"><img src=
   ➥"th_rawlv.jpg" alt="" /></li>
   <li class="top"><img src=
   ➥"th_dupain.jpg" alt="" /></li>
   <li class="left"><img src=
   ➥"th_rawchocolate.jpg" alt="" />
   ➥</li>
   <li><img src="th_meadowlark.jpg"
   ➥alt="" /></li>
</ul>
<p class="morelink"><a href="#">
➥More pics &gt;</a></p>
</div><!-- end photos -->
</div><!-- end recentscolumn -->
<div id="blogessentials">
<div id="sideimage">
</div><!-- end sideimage -->
<div id="feed">
<h4 class="feed">feed<span class="styled">
➥junkie</span></h4>
<p><a href="#"><img src="rss-red16.gif"
➥alt="" /></a> Feed me Seymour!</p>
</div><!-- end feed -->
<div id="subscription">
   <h4 class="subscription">subscription
   ➥<span class="styled">junkie</span>
   ➥</h4> ➥
```

```html
<p>You know you've gotta have it.<br />
Don't fight it. Get your fix by
email:</p>
<form id="subscribeform" action="post">
<p><input type="text" size="16"
class="textinput" /><input
type="submit" value="subscribe"
class="subscribe"/></p>
</form>
</div><!-- end subscription -->
<div id="recipe">
<h4 class="recipe">recipe<span
class="styled">junkie</span></h4>
<ul id="recipelist">
<li><a href="#">Sweet potato
biscuits</a></li>
<li><a href="#">Tilapia Piccata
</a></li>
<li><a href="#">Cornmeal Pancakes
</a></li>
<li><a href="#">Jamaican Laktes
</a></li>
<li><a href="#">Vegan Chocolate
Pudding</a></li>
<li><a href="#">Sunny Tapenade
</a></li>
</ul>
<p class="morelink"><a href="#">
More recipes &gt;</a></p>
</div><!-- end recipe -->
<div id="community">
<h4 class="community">community<span
class="styled">junkie</span></h4>
<p class="members">Newest community
members to join!</p>
<ul id="communityphotos">
<li class="top"><img src=
"photos_community/th_mellemusic.jpg"
alt="" /><br /><a href="#">
mellemusic</a></li>
<li class="top"><img src="photos_
community/th_allaboutgeorge.jpg"
alt="" /><br /><a href="#">
george</a></li>
<li class="top"><img src=
"photos_community/th_webinista.jpg"
alt="" /><br /><a href="#">
webinista</a></li>
<li class="top right"><img src=
"photos_community/th_lynneluvah.png"
alt="" /><br /><a href="#">
lynneluvah</a></li>
<li><img src="photos_community/
th_mmoss7.jpg" alt="" /><br />
<a href="#">mmoss</a></li>
<li><img src="photos_community/
th_msjen.jpg" alt="" /><br />
<a href="#">msjen</a></li>
<li><img src="photos_community/
th_misterjt.jpg" alt="" /><br />
<a href="#">misterjt</a></li>
<li class="right"><img src="photos_
community/th_skeskali.jpg" alt="" />
<br /><a href="#">skeskali</a></li>
</ul>
<p class="morelink"><a href="#">Join
in and share! &gt;</a></p>
</div><!-- end community -->
```

```
<div id="social">
   <h4 class="social">social<span class=
➡"styled">junkie</span></h4>
   <ul id="sociallinks">
      <li><a href="#"><img src="flickr.png"
➡alt="" /></a> <a href="#">flickr
➡</a></li>
      <li><a href="#"><img src=
➡"twitter.png" alt="" /></a>
➡<a href="#">twitter</a></li>
      <li><a href="#"><img src=
➡"friendfeed.png" alt="" /></a>
➡<a href="#">friendfeed</a></li>
      <li><a href="#"><img src=
➡"facebook.png" alt="" /></a>
➡<a href="#">facebook</a></li>
      <li><a href="#"><img src=
➡"delicious.png" alt="" /></a>
➡<a href="#">delicious</a></li>
      <li><a href="#"><img src=
➡"yelp_16.png" alt="" /></a>
➡<a href="#">yelp</a></li>
      <li><a href="#"><img src="dopplr.png"
➡alt="" /></a> <a href="#">
➡dopplr</a></li>
      <li><a href="#"><img src=
➡"tripadvisor.png" alt="" /></a>
➡<a href="#">tripadvisor</a></li>
      <li><a href="#"><img src=
➡"brightkite.png" alt="" /></a>
➡<a href="#">brightkite</a></li>
      <li><a href="#"><img src="vimeo.png"
➡alt="" /></a> <a href="#">vimeo
➡</a></li>
   </ul>
</div><!-- end social -->
```

```
<div id="blogroll">
   <h4 class="blogroll">foodblog<span
➡class="styled">junkie</span></h4>
   <ul id="bloglist">
   <li><a href="#">Mango &amp; Lime</a>
➡</li>
   <li><a href="#">Serious Eats</a></li>
   <li><a href="#">Chocolate and
➡Zucchini</a></li>
   <li><a href="#">Aapplemint</a></li>
   <li><a href="#">Albion Cooks</a></li>
   <li><a href="#">The Raw Chef</a></li>
   <li><a href="#">Chez Pim</a></li>
   <li><a href="#">Confessions of a
➡Cardamom Addict</a></li>
   <li><a href="#">Food Blogga</a></li>
   <li><a href="#">Gluten-free Goddess
➡</a></li>
   <li><a href="#">Lipstick Vegan</a></li>
   </ul>
   </div><!-- end blogroll -->
   </div><!-- end blogessentials -->
</div><!-- end pagebody -->
<div id="pagefoot">
<p>copyright &copy; eateryjunkie 2010
➡&middot; powered by <a href="#">somecms</a>
➡<br />
theme design by <a href="#">zimma studios</a>
➡&middot; main photo by <a href="#">
➡billwisserphoto.com</a></p>
</div><!-- end pagefoot -->
</div><!-- end pagewrapper -->
</body>
</html>
```

The Evidence Never Lies

The XHTML validation produced no errors—I would expect no less from a developer (**Figure 6.3**):

This document was successfully checked as XHTML 1.0 Strict!

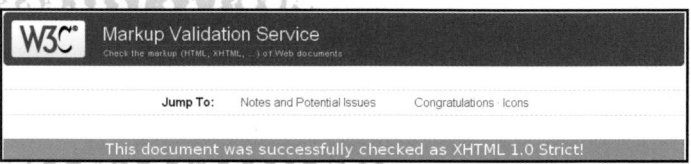

Figure 6.3
EateryJunkie's HTML validation results

In stark contrast, the CSS report was less than sterling (**Figure 6.4**):

Sorry! We found the following errors (8)

9   h2, h3, h4, #sitenav Property font-face doesn't exist :
     ➥Courier New,monospace
54   #pagewrapper div Property over-flow doesn't exist : hidden
60   #pagehead h1 Value Error : background Too many values or
     ➥values are not recognized : #f9ecd4 url(logo_eateryjunkie.png)
     ➥middle middle no-repeat
161 #featuredpost h3 Property font-face doesn't exist :
     ➥Georgia,serif
251 #recentpics ul Property over-flow doesn't exist : auto
287 #blogessentials img Property valign doesn't exist : middle
365 #community ul Property over-flow doesn't exist : hidden

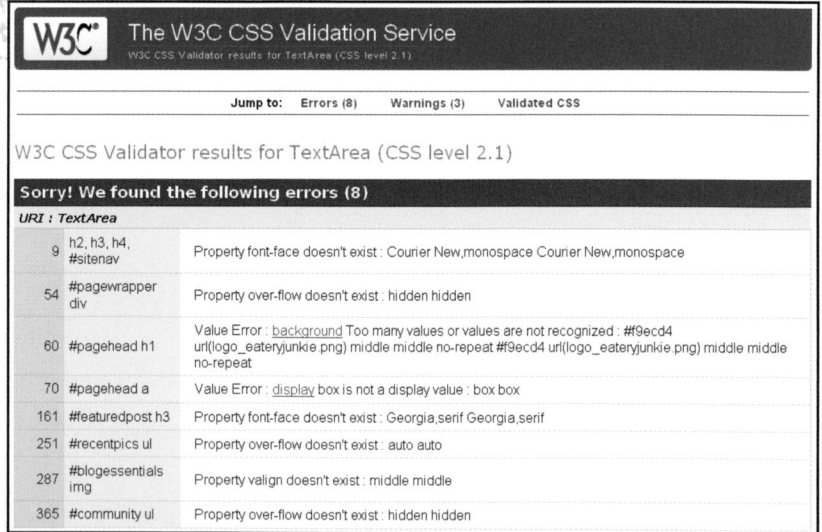

Figure 6.4 *EateryJunkie's CSS validation results*

CONFIRMING SUSPICIONS AND NAMING THE CULPRIT

My read of Bob was spot on: the CSS and design stuff was never particularly interesting to him, so he hasn't put much effort toward retaining it. Many of his errors were made because he confused HTML tag attributes with the equivalent CSS property, which he easily would have found with validating. To wit:

1. The navigation font was incorrect because he confused font-face with font-family in two instances.

   If we look at the style, we can see that the intention was for the font to show up as Courier (**Figure 6.5**):

```
h2, h3, h4, #sitenav {
font-face: Courier New, monospace;}
```

Figure 6.5
Nice enough navigation, but not exactly the style we wanted

In order to let the style express itself, we need to make a simple change:

```
h2, h3, h4, #sitenav {
font-family: Courier New, monospace;}
```

Similarly, the blog-post title is supposed to be in Georgia, or at least with a serif font, but instead we have this:

```
#featuredpost h3 {
border-bottom: 1px dotted #A15825;
font-face: Georgia, serif;
line-height: 1.3em;
}
```

And here's the rendered product (**Figure 6.6**):

We like it raw (and cooked, and everything in-between)

Figure 6.6 *A simple case of an unintended non-serif font*

So we definitely need to make this change to get some satisfaction:

```
#featuredpost h3 {
border-bottom: 1px dotted #A15825;
font-family: Georgia, serif;
line-height: 1.3em;
}
```

2. Bob rightfully employed a clearing technique for all of the floated divs. However, by misstating the overflow property as over-flow, the uncontained floating divs break the design (**Figure 6.7**) and also cause some spacing and layout issues (**Figures 6.8** and **6.9**).

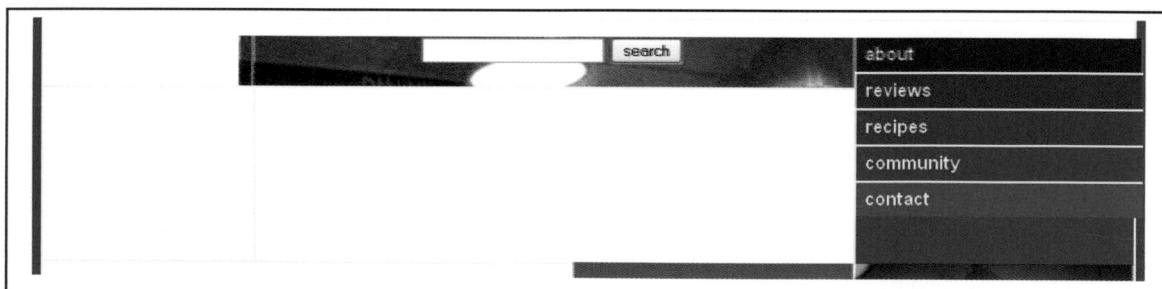

Figure 6.7 *Uncontained floats break the page head.*

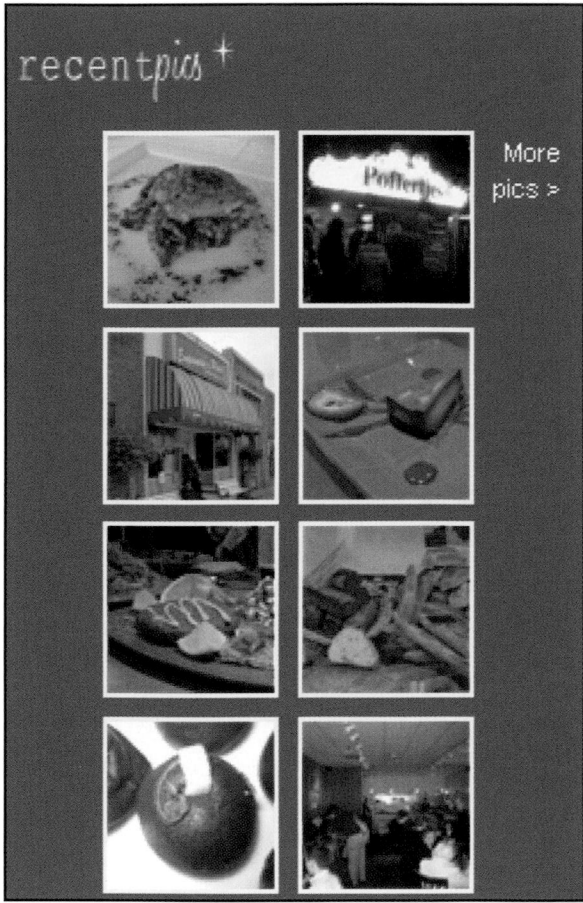

Figure 6.8 *Uncontained floats cause text misplacement.*

Figure 6.9 *Where's the page background for the faux columns?*

All of these problems are fixed simply by changing over-flow to overflow:

```
#pagewrapper div {
overflow: hidden;}

...
```

```
#recentpics ul {
margin: 10px auto 10px;
overflow: auto;
width: 156px;
}
...
#community ul {
margin: 5px auto 10px;
overflow: hidden;
width: 225px;
}
```

With all of these changes, the page is looking a lot better, but there's still room for improvement (**Figure 6.10** on the next page).

The final fixes from the CSS validation results help tremendously.

3. The page logo wasn't showing up because Bob used middle instead of center in the style declaration (**Figure 6.11** on the next page).

But this is easily changed:

```
#pagehead h1 {
background: #F9ECD4 url(logo_eateryjunkie.png) center center
➥no-repeat;
border-right: 2px solid #FFF4ED;
float: left;
height:200px;
margin: 0;
text-indent: -9999px;
width: 189px;
}
```

4. The RSS button wasn't lining up with the text because Bob used valign instead of vertical-align (**Figure 6.12**):

Figure 6.12 *The RSS button is out of alignment.*

Say no more: we quickly change it to the correct property:

```
#blogessentials img {
margin-right: 5px;
vertical-align: middle;
}
```

Figure 6.10 *Things are falling into place.*

Figure 6.11 *EateryJunkie's logo is missing.*

Once we fix these problems, we re-validate the CSS and produce a report with no errors. However, the head of the page still has issues (**Figure 6.13**), as do parts of the main content area (**Figures 6.14** and **6.15**).

Figure 6.13 *Search is still out of place.*

Figure 6.14 *The image and caption styling is missing.*

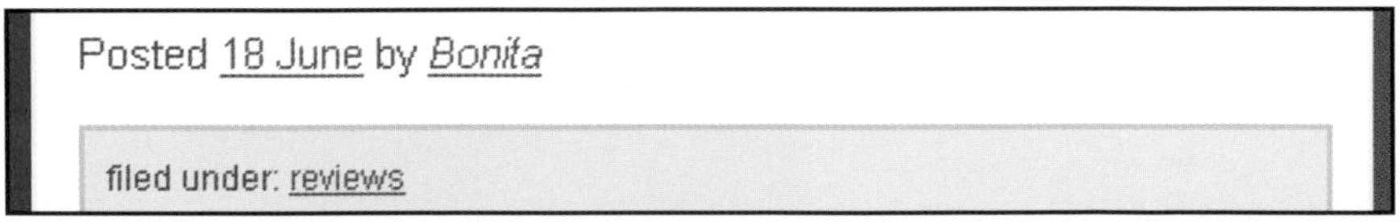

Figure 6.15 *The styling for the "posted by" information is missing as well.*

So far, Bob has consistently let what he thinks he knows get in the way of using correct code. Let's bear this in mind while looking at areas where he may have mistakenly named one thing for another.

What do you think we found? You guessed it:

1. The search-box div was out of place because he specified `<div id="sitesearch">` in the markup, but referred to it as `#searchsite` in the CSS in two instances:

```
#searchsite {
background-color: #482C21;
border-top: 2px solid #FFF4ED;
clear: right;
float: right;
height: 40px;
margin: -42px 0 0 0;
width: 250px;
}
```

```
  #searchsite p {
  margin: 8px 0 0 0;}
```

   Changing the div id to #sitesearch puts the box and the paragraph in it right into place.

2. Neither the post date line nor the image caption were getting their styling and the caption the smaller text because he confused `#postinfo`, `#imagecaption` for `.postinfo`, `.imagecaption`:

```
#postinfo, #imagecaption {
font-size: .7em;
}
```

   Changing them to `.postinfo, .imagecaption` gets those styles to render.

3. Finally, the main blog-post photo didn't get the border styling for the same reason: he confused `#blogphoto` for `.blogphoto`.

```
#blogphoto {
border: 1px solid #7E5E45;
margin: 5px auto;
padding: 5px;
width: 400px;
}
```

   A simple swap of . for #, making it `.blogphoto`, does the trick.

With these problems fixed, the page is now where it needs to be, but there was one last thing that I wanted to warn Bob about. Did you notice it? This part of the code caught my eye—first the markup:

```
<div id="feed">
  <h4 class="feed">feed<span class="styled">junkie</span></h4>
...
```

Then the CSS:

```
h4.feed {
background: url(title_junkiefeed.png) no-repeat;
height:32px;
text-indent: -9999px;
width: 101px;
}
```

You probably remember that an id should be a unique identifier and used only once in a document. Because the true forbidden practice is to have two ids with the same name, having an id and a class value the same is *technically* allowable.

However, as a general principle, the best practice is to keep your values different from one another. It's easier to keep track of which element you are targeting with your styles, and makes for cleaner markup as well.

Although he remained impassive throughout the process, I sense that Bob is actually pleased and relieved that we have found all of the culprits in his code. His page is back to looking exactly like the design spec, and now he can get to the part he enjoys the most: developing the back end.

Case Closed!

It just goes to show you that it's important to keep up with the CSS properties and specifications. No matter how long you've been doing it, there's a chance you've simply gotten something wrong. It takes less time to validate and look up a property than to spin your wheels just because you think (or hope) that you are right.

Furthermore, as in the previous case, while we could rely heavily on the CSS validation results to point the way to the problems, you also need to have an idea of the range of items that could turn out to be issues. Keeping close track of who's who in terms of id and class names, as well as HTML attributes versus CSS properties, will prevent you from mistaking one for the other.

Finally, you saw the importance of clearing floats in order to make sure a floated layout doesn't break in action. The overflow: hidden (or auto) property is a great technique and easy to apply to elements.

Another set of culprits found and summarily dealt with. On to the next case!

7

The Case of the Single White Space

IN THIS CASE, WE'LL SEE HOW IMPORTANT IT IS TO be clear about exactly what you want in your rendered page, and how a seemingly benign single space can wreak havoc with a layout.

The Crime Scene

Nena Stefani's jewelry business is really taking off. A self-proclaimed "Jane of all trades" and lover of all things creative, Nena learned web design and development in order to create her own website. However, she is stymied by the spacing problems that her page is giving her. She brings her code to the CSS Detective for help in identifying the sources of slightly off placement and spacing.

INITIAL SNAPSHOTS

Nena's design is clean and simple, and does a good job of incorporating all the features she needs, including links to the social media that have helped her build a name for herself (**Figure 7.1**).

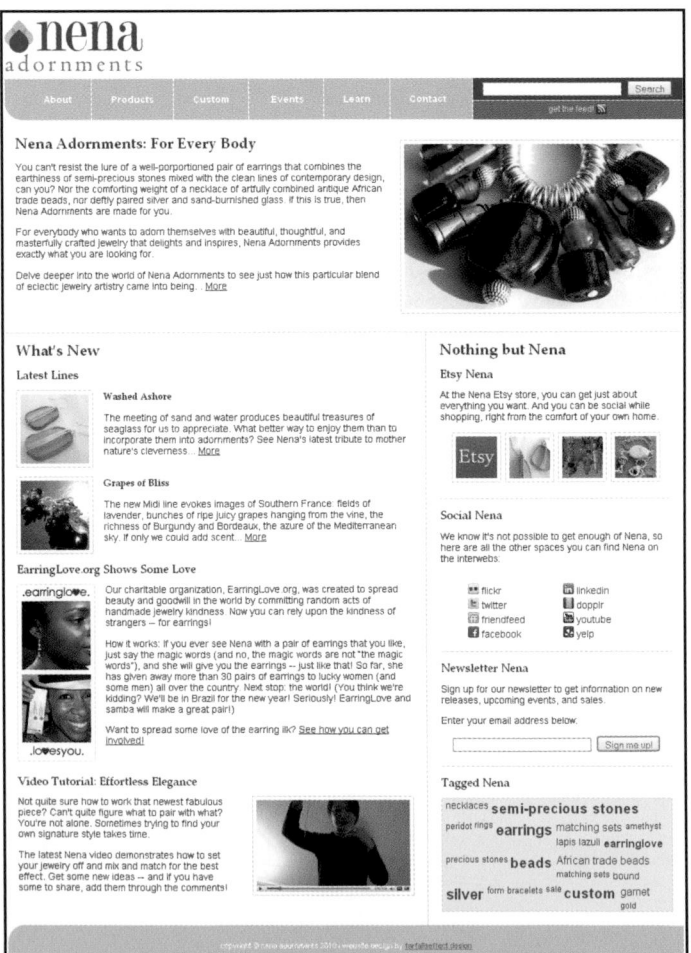

Figure 7.1
Nena Adornments design comp

Unfortunately, Nena's knowledge gaps have her stalled here (**Figure 7.2**).

Figure 7.2
Nena's slightly off rendition

Follow the Evidence

Nena loves the challenge of learning new things that will enable her to express her limitless creativity. However, she tends to learn only the basics until she is pushed to increase her knowledge, an inclination that is proving to be the case with her CSS.

IDENTIFYING SUSPECTS

A big handmade arts show is coming up soon, and Nena planned on launching her website in time for it. All of her print collateral has the web address listed, and she wants to be sure that all of her marketing pieces are properly in place so that she can continue to grow her business. However, with her website development progress stalled, she worries that she won't launch in time for the event.

What do you think my first inquiry is? Of course: check to see if she has validated her code. She assures me that as a novice developer, she relies heavily on both the HTML and CSS validators, and neither returned any errors. This fact has only heightened her level of frustration. "I can't figure out what in the world could be wrong with it," she says angrily. "There's nothing wrong with the code!"

MUG SHOTS

I have to admit I was impressed that Nena has given herself the small challenge of using XHTML and wants to adhere to standards-based design. While her initial document structure looks legitimate, I'm still skeptical as to her claim, so I validate the code myself just to rule out invalid code as the culprit in my own mind.

```
<!DOCTYPE html PUBLIC "-//W3C//DTD XHTML 1.0 Transitional//EN"
➡ "http://www.w3.org/TR/xhtml1/DTD/xhtml1-transitional.dtd">
<html xmlns="http://www.w3.org/1999/xhtml" xml:lang="en" lang="en">
<head>
<title>Nena Adornments</title>
<meta http-equiv="Content-Type" content="text/html; charset=utf-8" />
<link rel="shortcut icon" type="image/x-icon" href="nena.ico" />
<style type="text/css">
body {
background-color: #fff;
color: #444;
font: 1em/1em Arial, sans-serif;
}

h1, h2, h3, h4 {
font-family: "Palatino Linotype", Georgia, "Times New Roman", serif;}
```

```
h1 {
background: transparent url(logo_
nenaadornments_updated.png) no-repeat 0 0;
height: 79px;
width: 223px;
text-indent: -9999px;
}

    h1 a {
    display: block;
    height: 100%;
    width: 100%;
    }

h2 {
margin: 15px 0 20px 0;
padding: 0;}

h3 {
clear: both;
margin: 15px 0;
padding: 0;}

a {
color: #2A4D94;}

a img {
border: none;}

ul {
list-style-type: none;}

#latestlines img, #etsyphotobadge img {
border: 1px solid #ddd;
padding: 5px;
}

img.right {
border: 1px solid #ddd;
float: right;
margin-left: 20px;
padding: 5px;
}
```

```
.clearfix {display: inline-block;}
.clearfix:after {
    clear: both;
    content: ".";
    display: block;
    font-size: 0;
    height: 0;
    visibility: hidden;
}

#wrapper {
font-size: .9em;
margin: 10px auto 0;
width: 990px;
}

#navigation {
background: transparent url(bg_navigation.jpg)
➡left top no-repeat;
margin: 10px 0 0 0;
width: 992px;
overflow: hidden;
}

    #mainnav {
    background-color: #cdcdcf;
    height: 59px;
    line-height: 4.2em;
    margin: 0 0 10px 20px;
    text-align: center;
    width: 664px;
    float: left;
    display: inline;
    }

        #mainnav li {
        border-right: 1px solid #fff;
        display: inline;
        padding: 1.6em 1.95em;
        } ➡
```

```
#mainnav li.last {
border-right: none;}

#mainnav li a {
color: #fff;
font-weight: bold;
text-decoration: none;
}

#mainnav li a:hover {
text-decoration: underline;}

#search {
background-color: #2A4D94;
border-left: 1px solid #fff;
height: 29px;
padding: 3px 0 0 0;
width: 307px;
float: right;
}

    input.textinput {
    border: 1px solid #999;
    margin: 0 8px 0 0;
    }

    input.submit {
    color: #777;
    font-size: .9em;
    height: 24px;
    }

#feed {
background-color: #678184;
border-top: 1px solid #fff;
border-left: 1px solid #fff;
clear: right;
color: #eee;
float: right;
font-size: .85em;
height: 27px;
line-height: 1.8em;
width: 307px;
}
```

```
    #feed img
    {vertical-align: middle;}

  #feed, #tagcloudtags, #earringlovephotos,
  ↪#etsyphotobadge, #footer, form
  {text-align: center;}

#maincontent, #etsy, #social, #newsletter
{border-bottom: 1px solid #ddd;}

#maincontent {
margin: 0;
padding: 0 0 45px 15px;
clear: both;
}

    img.main {
    margin-top: -30px;}

#newfeatures {
float: left;
padding: 0 5px 10px 15px;
width: 580px;
}

    #newfeatures h4 {
    line-height: .5em;
    margin-top: 5px;
    }

    dl, dd, dt {
    float: left;}

        dl {
        margin: 0 0 10px 0;}

        dd {
        margin: 0 0 0 15px;
        width: 450px;
        }

    #earringlovephotos {
    border: 1px solid #eee;
```

```css
float: left;
margin: 0 15px 20px 0;
padding: 1px;
width: 110px;
}

    li.spaced img {
    margin-top: 4px;}

#sidebar {
border-left: 1px solid #ddd;
float: right;
margin: 0 0 0 5px;
padding: 0 15px 0 20px;
width: 340px;
}

    #etsy, #sociallinks, #newsletter {
    padding-bottom: 20px;}

    #etsyphotobadge {
    margin: 0 auto;
}

    #etsyphotobadge li {
    padding: 0 1px;
    display: inline;}

    #social {
    overflow: hidden;
    padding: 0 0 0 0;
    }

    * html #social {height: 1%;}

    #social ul{
    float: left;
    width: 100px;}

    #social ul li {
    line-height: 20px;}

    #social ul a {
    text-decoration: none;}
```

```css
#social ul a:hover, #tagcloud a:hover {
    text-decoration: underline;}

#tagcloudtags {
border: 1px solid #ddd;
background-color: #eee;
margin: 0 0 20px 0;
padding: 0 5px 0;}

#tagcloud li {
float: left;
padding: 0 .3em 0 0;}

#tagcloud a {
line-height: 1.5em;
text-decoration: none;
}

.tclevel1 {font-size: .8em; font-weight: 200;}
.tclevel2 {font-size: .9em; font-weight: 300;}
.tclevel3 {font-size: 1em; font-weight: 400;}
.tclevel4 {font-size: 1.1em; font-weight: 500;}
.tclevel5 {font-size: 1.2em; font-weight: 600;}
.tclevel6 {font-size: 1.3em; font-weight: 700;}
.tclevel7 {font-size: 1.4em; font-weight: 800;}
.tclevel8 {font-size: 1.5em; font-weight: 900;}

#footer {
background: url(bg_footer.jpg) no-repeat;
clear: both;
color: #fff;
font-size: .75em;
height: 59px;
line-height: 5.5em;
width: 990px;
}

    #footer a {
    color: #777;}
</style>
</head> ➡
```

```
<body>
<div id="wrapper">

<div id="head">
   <h1><a href="#">Nena Adornments</a></h1>
</div><!-- end head -->

<div id="navigation">
   <ul id="mainnav">
   <li><a href="#">About</a></li>
   <li><a href="#">Products</a></li>
   <li><a href="#">Custom</a></li>
   <li><a href="#">Events</a></li>
   <li><a href="#">Learn</a></li>
   <li class="last"><a href="#">Contact</a></li>
   </ul>

   <form id="search" action="post">
      <input type="text" size="30"
      ➥class="textinput" /><input type="submit"
      ➥value="Search" class="submit"/>
   </form>

   <p id="feed">get the feed! <a href="#">
   ➥<img src="rss-blue16.png" alt="" /></a></p>
</div><!-- end navigation -->

<div id="maincontent">
   <h2>Nena Adornments: For Every Body</h2>
   <img class="right main"
   ➥src="necklace_bigbrown.jpg"
   ➥alt="Earth and Sky Necklace" />
   <p>You can't resist the lure of a well-
   porportioned pair of earrings that combines
   ➥the earthiness of semi-precious stones
   ➥mixed with the clean lines of contemporary
   ➥design, can you? Nor the comforting weight
   ➥of a necklace of artfully combined antique
   ➥African trade beads, nor deftly paired silver
   ➥and sand-burnished glass. If this is true,
   ➥then Nena Adornments are made for you.</p>
   <p>For everybody who wants to adorn them
   ➥selves with beautiful, thoughtful, and
   ➥masterfully crafted jewelry that delights
```

```
   ➥and inspires, Nena Adornments provides
   ➥exactly what you are looking for.</p>
   <p>Delve deeper into the world of Nena
   ➥Adornments to see just how this
   ➥particular blend of eclectic jewelry
   ➥artistry came into being... <a href="#">
   ➥More</a></p>
</div><!-- end maincontent -->

<div id="newfeatures">
   <h2>What's New </h2>

   <div id="latestlines">
      <h3>Latest Lines</h3>

      <dl>
      <dt><img src="sm_earrings_greenglass.jpg"
      ➥alt="" /></dt>
      <dd><h4>Washed Ashore</h4>
      <p>The meeting of sand and water
      ➥produces beautiful treasures of
      ➥seaglass for us to appreciate. What
      ➥better way to enjoy them than to
      ➥incorporate them into adornments? See
      ➥Nena's latest tribute to mother
      ➥nature's cleverness... <a href="#">
      ➥More</a></p>
      </dd>
      </dl>

      <dl>
      <dt><img src="sm_earrings_grapesofbliss.jpg"
      ➥alt="" /></dt>
      <dd><h4>Grapes of Bliss</h4>
      <p>The new Midi line evokes images of
      ➥Southern France: fields of lavender,
      ➥bunches of ripe juicy grapes hanging
      ➥from the vine, the richness of Burgundy
      ➥and Bordeaux, the azure of the
      ➥Mediterranean sky. If only we could
      ➥add scent... <a href="#">More</a></p>
      </dd>
      </dl>
   </div><!-- end latestlines -->
```

```
<div id="orgnews">
   <h3>EarringLove.org Shows Some Love</h3>
   <ul id="earringlovephotos">
   <li><img src="logo_earringlove.png"
➥alt="" /></li>
   <li><img src="earringlove2.jpg" alt="" />
➥</li>
   <li class="spaced"><img src=
➥"earringlove1.jpg" alt="" /></li>
   <li><img src="logo_earringlovesyou.png"
➥alt="" /></li>
   </ul>

   <p>Our charitable organization,
➥EarringLove.org, was created to spread
➥beauty and goodwill in the world by
➥committing random acts of handmade
➥jewelry kindness. Now you can rely
➥upon the kindness of strangers -- for
➥earrings!</p>
   <p>How it works: if you ever see Nena
➥with a pair of earrings that you like,
➥just say the magic words (and no, the
➥magic words are not &ldquo;the magic
➥words&rdquo;), and she will give you
➥the earrings -- just like that! So
➥far, she has given away more than 30
➥pairs of earrings to lucky women (and
➥some men) all over the country. Next
➥stop: the world! (You think we're
➥kidding? We'll be in Brazil for the
➥new year! Seriously! EarringLove and
➥samba will make a great pair!)</p>
   <p>Want to spread some love of the
➥earring ilk? <a href="#">See how you
➥can get involved!</a></p>
</div><!-- end orgnews -->

<div id="multimedia">
   <h3>Video Tutorial: Effortless Elegance
➥</h3>
   <img src="video.jpg" class="right"
➥alt="" />
```

```
   <p> Not quite sure how to work that
➥newest fabulous piece? Can't quite
➥figure what to pair with what? You're
➥not alone. Sometimes trying to find
➥your own signature style takes time.</p>
   <p>The latest Nena video demonstrates
➥how to set your jewelry off and mix
➥and match for the best effect. Get some
➥new ideas -- and if you have some to
➥share, add them through the comments!
➥</p>
</div><!-- end multimedia -->

</div><!-- end newfeatures -->

<div id="sidebar">
   <h2>Nothing but Nena</h2>

   <div id="etsy">
      <h3>Etsy Nena</h3>
      <p>At the Nena Etsy store, you can get
➥just about everything you want. And
➥you can be social while shopping,
➥right from the comfort of your own
➥home.</p>
      <ul id="etsyphotobadge">
         <li><img src="th_etsy.jpg" alt="" />
➥</li>
         <li><img src="th_tealglass.jpg"
➥alt="" /></li>
         <li><img src="th_earrings_hanging.jpg"
➥alt="" /></li>
         <li><img src="th_blueeggs.jpg" alt="" />
➥</li>
      </ul>
   </div><!-- end etsy -->

   <div id="social" class="clearfix">
      <h3>Social Nena</h3>
      <p>We know it's not possible to get
➥enough of Nena, so here are all the
➥other spaces you can find Nena on the
➥interwebs:</p>
      <ul> ➥
```

```
<li class="col1"><a href="#">
➥<img src="flickr_16.png"
➥alt="link to Nena on flickr" /></a>
➥<a href="#">flickr</a></li>
<li class="col1"><a href="#">
➥<img src="twitter_16.png"
➥alt="link to Nena on twitter" />
➥</a> <a href="#">twitter</a></li>
<li class="col1"><a href="#">
➥<img src="friendfeed_16.png"
➥alt="link to Nena on friendfeed" />
➥</a> <a href="#">friendfeed</a></li>
<li class="col1"><a href="#">
➥<img src="facebook_16.png"
➥alt="link to Nena on facebook" />
➥</a> <a href="#">facebook</a></li>
</ul>
<ul
<li class="col2"><a href="#">
➥<img src="linkedin_16.png"
➥alt="link to Nena on linkedin" />
➥</a> <a href="#">linkedin</a></li>
<li class="col2"><a href="#">
➥<img src="dopplr_16.png"
➥alt="link to Nena on dopplr" />
➥</a> <a href="#">dopplr</a></li>
<li class="col2"><a href="#">
➥<img src="youtube_16.png"
➥alt="link to Nena on youtube" />
➥</a> <a href="#">youtube</a></li>
<li class="col2"><a href="#">
➥<img src="yelp_16.png"
➥alt="link to Nena on yelp" /></a>
➥<a href="#">yelp</a></li>
</ul>
</div><!-- end sociallinks -->

<div id="newsletter">
<h3>Newsletter Nena</h3>
<p>Sign up for our newsletter to get
➥information on new releases, upcoming
➥events, and sales.</p>
```

```
<p>Enter your email address below:</p>
<form action="post">
<input type="text" size="30" class=
➥"textinput" /><input type="submit"
➥value="Sign me up!" class="submit" />
</form>
</div><!-- end newsletter -->

<div id="tagcloud">
<h3>Tagged Nena</h3>
<ul id="tagcloudtags" class="clearfix">
<li class="tclevel3"><a href="#">
➥necklaces</a></li>
<li class="tclevel7"><a href="#">
➥semi-precious stones</a></li>
<li class="tclevel2"><a href="#">
➥peridot</a></li>
<li class="tclevel1"><a href="#">
➥rings</a></li>
<li class="tclevel8"><a href="#">
➥earrings</a></li>
<li class="tclevel4"><a href="#">
➥matching sets</a></li>
<li class="tclevel2"><a href="#">
➥amethyst</a></li>
<li class="tclevel3"><a href="#">
➥lapis lazuli</a></li>
<li class="tclevel5"><a href="#">
➥earringlove</a></li>
<li class="tclevel2"><a href="#">
➥precious stones</a></li>
<li class="tclevel7"><a href="#">
➥beads</a></li>
<li class="tclevel4"><a href="#">
➥African trade beads</a></li>
<li class="tclevel1"><a href="#">
➥matching sets</a></li>
<li class="tclevel3"><a href="#">
➥bound</a></li>
<li class="tclevel8"><a href="#">
➥silver</a></li>
<li class="tclevel2"><a href="#">
➥form</a></li>
```

```
        <li class="tclevel2"><a href="#">bracelets</a></li>
        <li class="tclevel1"><a href="#">sale</a></li>
        <li class="tclevel7"><a href="#">custom</a></li>
        <li class="tclevel4"><a href="#">garnet</a></li>
        <li class="tclevel1"><a href="#">gold</a></li>
      </ul>
    </div><!-- end tagcloud -->
  </div><!-- end sidebar -->

<div id="footer">
   copyright &copy; nena adornments 2010 | website design by <a href="#">
   ➡farfallaeffect design</a>
</div><!-- end footer -->

</div><!-- end wrapper -->
</body>
</html>
```

The Evidence Never Lies

To my eye, both Nena's XHTML and CSS looked really solid from the standpoint of well-formed markup, and the validation results confirmed this as well. And, true to Nena's emphatic testimony, neither validation produced any errors.

"I may not know *everything* about coding," Nena admitted, "but what I do know, I know well."

Here is the validation report for the XHTML markup (**Figure 7.3**).

```
This document was successfully checked as XHTML 1.0 Transitional!
```

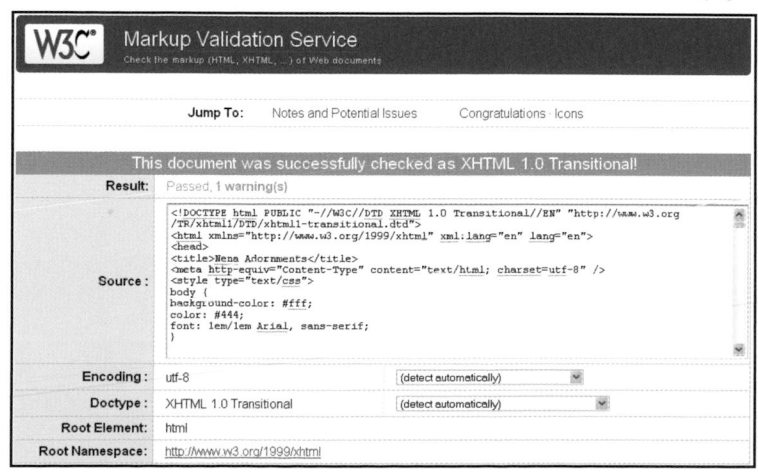

Figure 7.3 *Nena Adornments' XHTML validation results*

And here is the report for the CSS (**Figure 7.4**).

Congratulations! No Error Found.

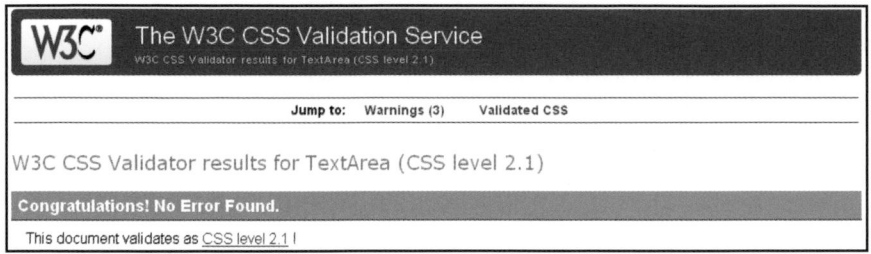

Figure 7.4 *Nena Adornments' CSS validation results*

CONFIRMING SUSPICIONS AND NAMING THE CULPRIT

The case was turning out to be a little trickier than I had expected. Obviously, the validators weren't going to shine any light on the problems, so now we have to roll up our sleeves and take a much closer look at the code.

Has anything jumped out at you? One item that caught my eye was the absence of margins and padding on some of the layout elements that were having spacing problems. Nena was conscientious about using margins and padding where she needed a value. However, she may not have known (or remembered) that the browser will supply its own values for margins and padding on an element if the author does not.

Here's what I suggest for our first approach to fixing Nena's spacing problems. Let's make the lack of margins and padding explicit where they currently are not, starting with the most glaringly obvious problems.

Right at the top of the page, the search and RSS feed boxes aren't at all where they are supposed to be, and the alignment for the links in the navigation bar seems to be a little off, doesn't it (**Figure 7.5**)?

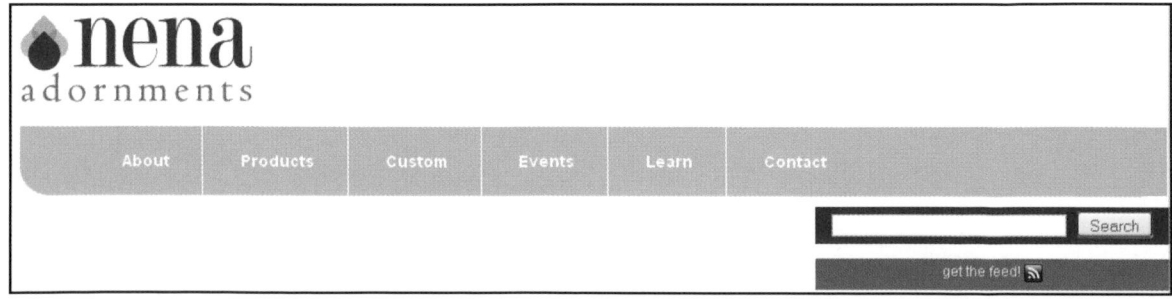

Figure 7.5 *Nena Adornments' problem RSS feed box and navigation bar*

Both #search and #feed are floated right, and #mainnav is floated left. There should be enough room for both of them, so I suspect this misplacement is due to float drop caused by one element being wider than it should be.

An examination of the #mainnav styles confirms my suspicions. While there are multiple style declarations for the #mainnav element, and even margin values, the padding values are conspicuously absent. Remember that browsers give ordered and unordered lists padding by default, and that the padding may differ from browser to browser.

```
#mainnav {
background-color: #cdcdcf;
height: 59px;
line-height: 4.2em;
margin: 0 0 10px 20px;
text-align: center;
width: 664px;
float: left;
display: inline;
}
```

As a fix, let's set the padding to 0 to effect the desired change:

```
#mainnav {
background-color: #cdcdcf;
height: 59px;
line-height: 4.2em;
margin: 0 0 10px 20px;
padding: 0;
text-align: center;
width: 664px;
float: left;
display: inline;
}
```

Aha! This takes care of the float drop issue (**Figure 7.6**).

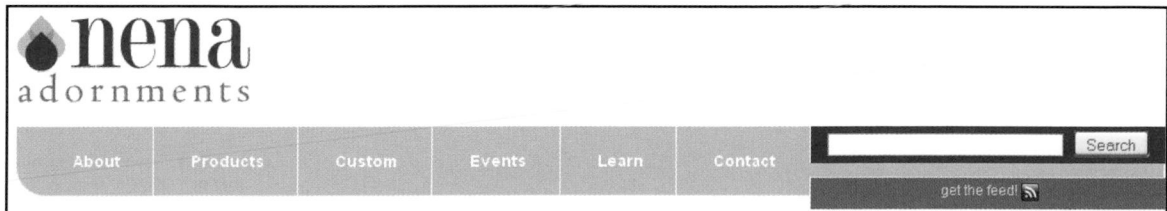

Figure 7.6 *Tremendous improvement, but still work to be done*

I think we are on to something here, don't you? Let's see if we can use the same approach with the out-of-place RSS box.

In the styles for the #feed element, this is what Nena has:

```
#feed {
background-color: #678184;
border-top: 1px solid #fff;
border-left: 1px solid #fff;
clear: right;
color: #eee;
float: right;
font-size: .85em;
height: 27px;
line-height: 1.8em;
width: 307px;
}
```

Hmmm. Do you see any margin or padding values declared? Nope, I don't either. From this code alone, you would think that everything would be fine, but often when using positioning on elements, it is better to err on the side of caution and explicitly declare the element's margin, at the very least. Margin is particularly relevant in this situation because the problem has to do with the box's relationship with the elements around it, as opposed to the elements inside of it (which would lend itself more to looking at the padding). Just a small addition should do the trick:

```
#feed {
background-color: #678184;
border-top: 1px solid #fff;
border-left: 1px solid #fff;
clear: right;
color: #eee;
float: right;
font-size: .85em;
height: 27px;
line-height: 1.8em;
margin: 0;
width: 307px;
}
```

Eureka! This seems to put the RSS box in the place that Nena intended (**Figure 7.7**).

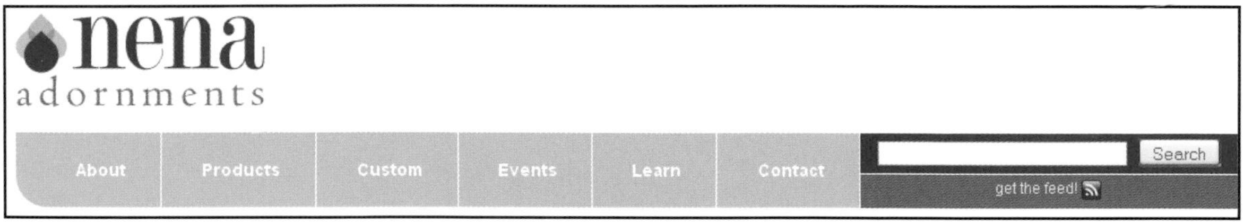

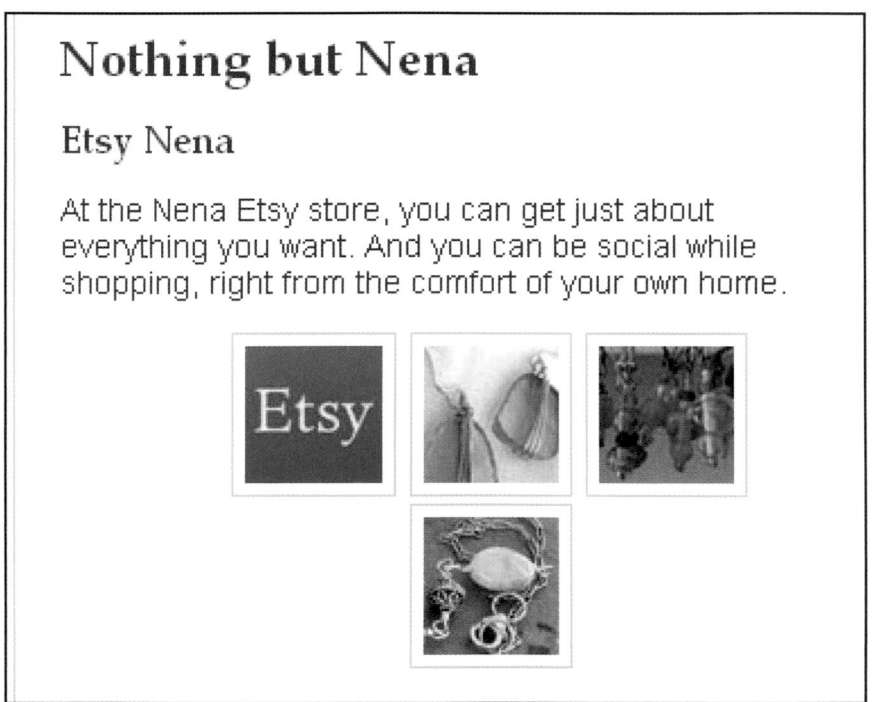

Figure 7.7 *The RSS feed bar is in its proper place, and the navigation is much-improved.*

Now, on to the out-of-place photos in the sidebar (**Figure 7.8**).

Figure 7.8 *Off-kilter Etsy photo badge*

Heartened that my hunch about the margin and padding has paid off so far, I suggest we continue looking in the styles of the area in question for absent explicit margin and padding declarations. Here's what we find:

```
#etsyphotobadge {
margin: 0 auto;}
```

Yep, again there is no explicit margin or padding on an unordered list. Because the problem seems to be more about size than the box's relationship with the elements around it, I decide to make it clear that no padding is wanted within that element box:

```
#etsyphotobadge {
margin: 0 auto;
padding: 0;
}
```

This fix did the trick (**Figure 7.9**)!

Nothing but Nena

Etsy Nena

At the Nena Etsy store, you can get just about everything you want. And you can be social while shopping, right from the comfort of your own home.

 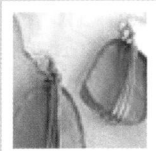  

Figure 7.9
Fixed Etsy photos!

We're pulling into the home stretch, but my client, with her discerning design eye, sees that we are not quite there yet.

Nena points out that the spacing is still off on the page itself, notably on the top of the page with the logo (**Figure 7.10**), and then at the bottom of the page with the footer (**Figure 7.11**), and the alignment of the navigation links isn't quite right.

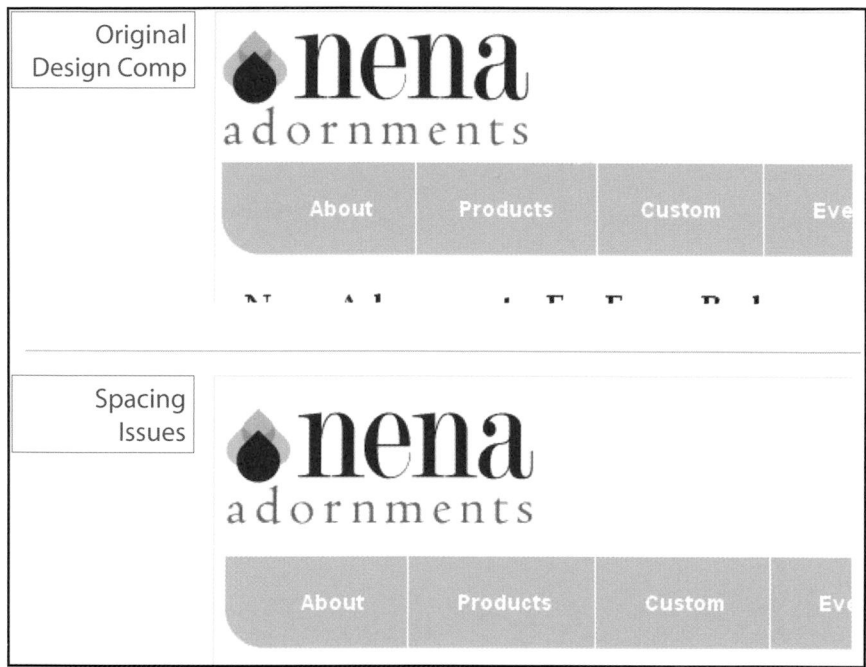

Figure 7.10 *Too much between the logo and the top of the page and nav bar*

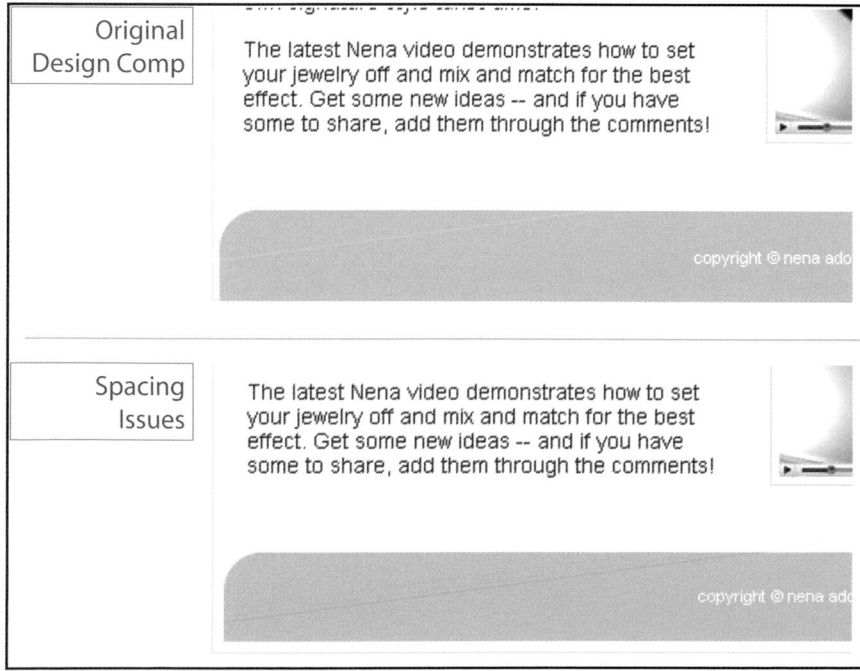

Figure 7.11 *Hey! That space isn't supposed to be there!*

These points warrant a final look at the CSS, and a potential delving into the HTML markup.

What do you think we will find when we look at the code once again? You guessed it: right in front of our faces, the declarations for body are missing an explicit margin value. Let's put it in now:

```
body {
background-color: #fff;
color: #444;
font: 1em/1em Arial, sans-serif;
margin: 0;
}
```

Nena smiles. The footer is flush with the bottom of the page, just as she intended in her original design.

As for the extra space for the header, similarly, we make this addition:

```
h1 {
background: transparent url(logo_nenaadornments_updated.png) no-
repeat 0 0;
height: 79px;
margin: 0;
width: 223px;
text-indent: -9999px;
}
```

Now the site logo is the proper amount of space from the top.

The last mystery to solve is that of the navigation links (**Figure 7.12**).

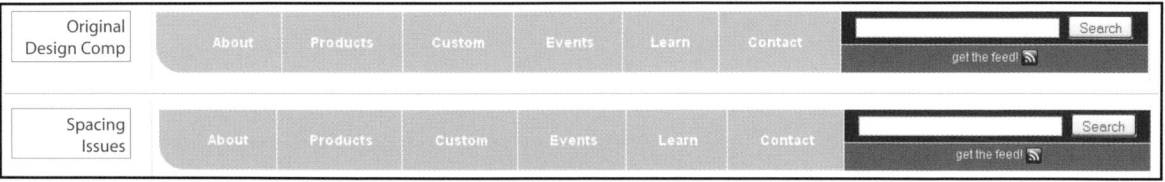

Figure 7.12 *Just slightly off, but enough to notice the difference.*

This issue is especially puzzling, given that we have already fixed the spacing styles for the #mainnav section. What else could cause the spacing to be off? Then the answer comes to me: the list white-space bug! I go to the HTML code to see if I am correct, and sure enough, we find this:

```
<ul id="mainnav">
<li><a href="#">About</a></li>
<li><a href="#">Products</a></li>
<li><a href="#">Custom</a></li>
<li><a href="#">Events</a></li>
<li><a href="#">Learn</a></li>
<li class="last"><a href="#">Contact</a></li>
</ul>
```

I was hoping that the newer versions of browsers wouldn't still have this problem, but apparently they still do. The speediest fix is inelegant but effective: remove all the white space from in-between the list items. To wit:

```
<ul id="mainnav">
<li><a href="#">About</a></li><li><a href="#">Products</a></
li><li>
➥<a href="#">Custom</a></li><li><a href="#">Events</a></li><li>
➥<a href="#">Learn</a></li><li class="last"><a href="#">Contact
➥</a></li>
</ul>
```

Once this is done, Nena and I celebrate—the page is completely fixed, and it looks exactly the way she wanted it to.

Case Closed!

Nena's case wasn't as cut and dried as finding misspellings and incorrect punctuation. With no validation errors, we have to understand more of the issues that cause spacing errors. You can begin to see just how insidious the browser's default styles can be and how important it is to make explicit the values that you need—particularly when it comes to margins, which affect the relationship of an element with its neighbors; and padding, which often affects an element's rendered size.

Additionally, we uncovered a surprise problem of the list white-space bug, which seems insignificant but can have unwanted effects on your page design.

In terms of process, if there are no validation errors, look for fixes in the CSS first. As always, start from the top of the page and with the most heinous problem, and then work your way down. Remember to solve only one problem at a time and see how that fix may affect anything else on the page. Once you can see the change in the fixed area, then you can move on to the next problem area.

Finally, after you have made all of the fixes that you can to the CSS declarations, look for any remaining issues in the markup itself.

Well done—another rousing success! But a CSS Detective's work is never done. Now, on to The Case of the Mistaken Identity!

8

The Case of the Float with a Mind of Its Own

IN THIS CASE, WE'LL SEE HOW TO TAME A HEADSTRONG float by gently yet firmly persuading it to get back in line.

The Crime Scene

Celebrated author Raymond Jay has finally capitulated. Because of pressure from his growing readership, his agents, and even his family, he is getting a website built to launch his web presence. Like some of his baby-boomer brethren, he uses technology only when necessary and thus is a late adopter. For example, he uses Microsoft Internet Explorer 6 as his browser, because he doesn't trust upgrading and downloading applications from the web. Needless to say, Raymond is tentative about the web as a tool for self-promotion.

Luckily for him, his daughter, Diona—a bit of a renaissance woman with a background in fine arts, design, and architecture—has recently taken up web development and is creating the site for him. But because she is new to the web development game, she doesn't have experience with solving old-school IE bugs. Imagine her horror when she sees her design is completely broken in both IE6 and IE7!

INITIAL SNAPSHOTS

Diona's design focuses on providing the user with the information she believes is most important to Raymond Jay's audience. It looks great in the modern browsers Mozilla Firefox, IE8, and Opera (**Figure 8.1**). But you can imagine Diona's frustration when she saw her page in IE7 (**Figure 8.2**). And to add insult to injury, it looks even worse in her dad's favorite browser, IE6 (**Figure 8.3**).

Follow the Evidence

Diona builds sites using CSS only for layout and relies heavily on floats. However, IE is encouraging her floats to do exactly what they please, with little regard for the style instructions.

IDENTIFYING SUSPECTS

Diona respects the importance of validating the HTML and CSS, but I suspect that because the problems are showing up specifically in IE6 and IE7 she has unwittingly stumbled into a nest of nasty IE float bugs.

Mug shots

Let's take a look at the page code and see if we can identify why these floats won't listen to reason.

Figure 8.1 *The design looks the way it's supposed to in Mozilla Firefox, Microsoft Internet Explorer 8, and Opera.*

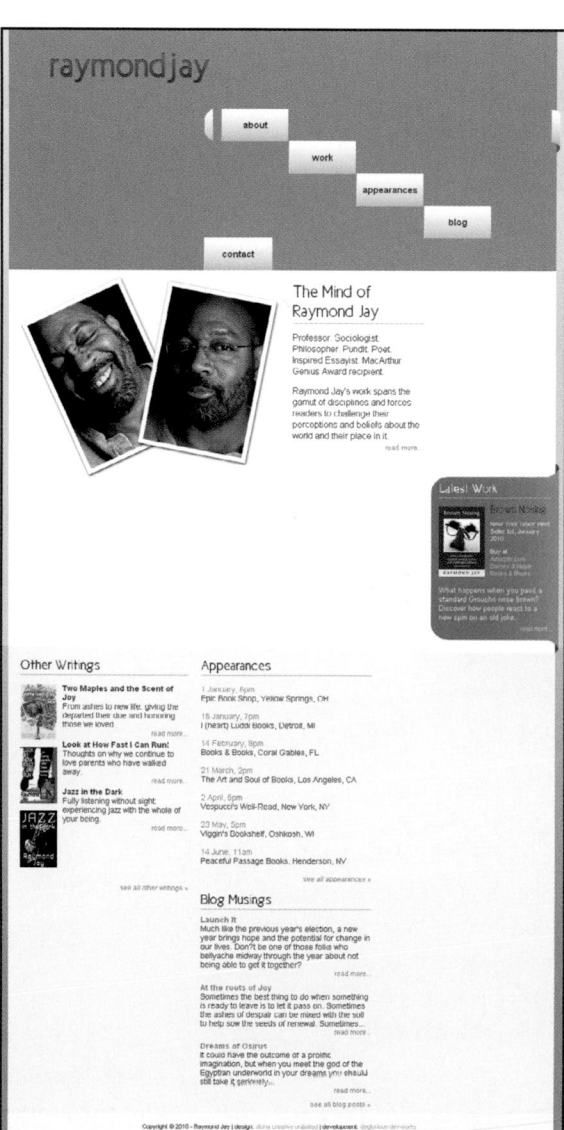

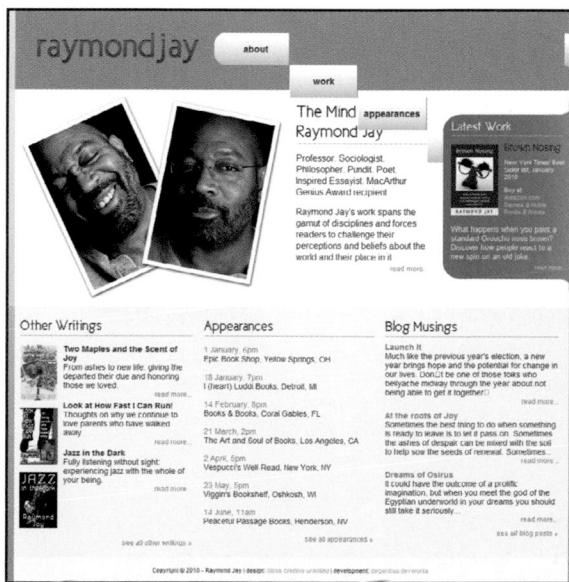

Figure 8.2 *Raymond Jay's site in IE7*

Figure 8.3 *Raymond Jay's site in IE6 (ouch!)*

```
<!DOCTYPE html PUBLIC "-//W3C//DTD XHTML 1.0
➥Strict//EN" "http://www.w3.org/TR/xhtml1/
➥DTD/xhtml1-strict.dtd">
<html xmlns="http://www.w3.org/1999/xhtml"
➥xml:lang="en" lang="en">
<head>
<meta http-equiv="Content-Type"
content="text/html; charset=utf-8" />
<title>The Mind of Raymond Jay</title>
<link rel="shortcut icon" type="image/x-icon"
➥href="raymondjay.ico" />
<style type="text/css">
/* -- reset styles -- */
html, body, div, p, span, h1, h2, h3, h4, h5,
➥h6, a, img, ul, li, form, input, hr {
margin: 0;
padding: 0;
font-size: 100%;
background: transparent;
}

body {
line-height: 1.125em;}

ul {
list-style: none;}

/* -- font faces -- */
@font-face {
font-family: 'NewCicleGordita';
src: url('New_Cicle_Gordita.eot');
src: local('New Cicle Gordita'),
local('NewCicle-Gordita'),
➥url('New_Cicle_Gordita.ttf')
➥format('truetype');
}

/* -- general page styles -- */
body, html {
background-color: #9f9a86;
color: #424031;
font: .9em Arial, sans-serif;
}
```

```
h1, h2, h3 {
color: #652a01;
font-family: 'NewCicleGordita','Trebuchet MS',
➥sans-serif;
}

h3 {
border-bottom: 1px solid #b6b18a;
padding-bottom: 4px;
}

a {
color: #9a884b;
text-decoration: none;
}

    a:hover {text-decoration: underline;}
    a img {border: none;}
    .readmore a {
    float: right;
    font-size: .85em;
    }
/* -- clearfix styles -- */
.clearfix {
display: block;
}

.clearfix:after {
content: ".";
display: block;
clear: both;
visibility: hidden;
line-height: 0;
height: 0;
}

* html .clearfix {
height: 1%;}
/* -- page layout styles -- */
#primary, #secondary, #footer {
clear: both;}
```

```
h1, p.authorphoto, #whois, #secondarycontent
➡div {
float: left;}
#primary {
background: #d6d4ca url(bg_mainbody.gif) 0 0
repeat-x;
}

   #headwrap {
   background-image:url(bg_header.gif); }
      #header {
      background-color:#9f9a86;
      margin:0 auto;
      width: 986px;
      height: 142px;
      }

         h1 {
         background: transparent url
         ➡(logo_raymondjay.gif) no-repeat 0 0;
         height: 60px;
         margin: 40px 0 0 37px;
         width: 306px;
         text-indent: -9999px;
         }

            h1 a {
            display: block;
            height: 100%;
            width: 100%;
            }

   #navcontain {
   width: 638px;
   float: right;
   position: relative;
   right: -6px;
   }

      #mainnav {
      background: transparent url
      ➡(bg_navcurve.gif) 0 0 no-repeat ;
      color: #652a01;
```

```
font-size: 1.2em;
float: left;
height: 60px;
line-height: 57px;
list-style-type: none;
margin: 40px 0 0;
padding: 0;
text-align: center;
width: 623px;
}

.end {
background: transparent url
➡(bg_navcurveend.gif) 0 0 no-repeat;
float: right;
height:76px;
width: 15px;
position: relative;
top: 40px;
margin: 0;}

   #mainnav li a {
   background: transparent url
   ➡(bg_navitems.gif) 0 0 repeat-x ;
   border-right: 1px solid #8f8766;
   border-left: 1px solid #fff;
   color: #652a01;
   display: block;
   float: left;
   font-weight: bold;
   height: 58px;
   line-height: 58px;
   padding: 0 1px;
   width: 118px;
   }

      #mainnav li.first a {
      border-left: 0;
      margin-left: 15px;
      }

      #mainnav li.last a {border-right:
      ➡0;} ➡
```

```
        #mainnav li a:hover {
        font-weight: normal;
        text-decoration: none;
        }

#primarycontent {
margin: 0 auto;
background-color:#fff;
padding: 10px 0;
width: 986px;
}

    #primarycontent h2 {
    margin: 0 0 15px 0;
    padding-bottom: 4px;
    border-bottom: 1px solid #b6b18a;
    }

    .authorphoto {
    margin: 0 0 0 10px;
    width: 471px;
    }

    #whois {
    font-size: 1.2em;
    line-height: 1.3em;
    margin:0 0 0 11px;
    padding: 10px 10px;
    width: 238px;
    }

        #whois h2 {
        font-size: 2em;
        line-height: 1.125em;
        }

        #whois p, #latestwork p {
        margin: 0 0 15px 0px;
        padding: 0;
        }

    #latestwork {
    background: url(bg_body_latestwork.gif)
    ➥repeat-y scroll center bottom;
```

```
color: #f3f1eb;
margin: 0;
width: 229px;
float: right;
position: relative;
top: 1.125em;
right: -6px;
}

    #latestwork h2 {
    background:transparent url
    ➥(bg_top_latestwork2.gif) no-repeat
    ➥scroll 0 0;
    border: 0;
    color: #fdf6f1;
    font-size: 1.7em;
    margin: 0;
    padding: 33px 0 0 15px;
    position: relative;
    top: -5px;
    }

    #lwbody {
    border-top: 1px solid #b6b18a;
    width: 200px;
    margin: auto;}

    #lwbody p {
    margin: 10px 0 0 0;
    padding: 0;}

        #lwbody p.description {
        clear: both;
        }

    #latestwork h3 {
    border-bottom: 0;
    font-size: 1.5em;
    padding: 0 0 0 10px;
    }

    #latestwork img {
    float: left;
    margin: 5px 10px 10px 0;}
```

```
#latestwork ul {
list-style-type: none;
margin: 0;
padding: 0;
}

#latestwork a {
color: #e2c9a1;}

   #promo {
   font-size: .85em;
   line-height: 1.2em;
   margin: 0 0 15px 0;
   }

p.latestend {
background: url(bg_bottom_latestwork2.gif)
➥0 0 no-repeat;
height: 50px;
position: relative;
bottom: -5px;
}

#latestwork p.readmore {
padding-right: 10px;
margin: 0;
}
```

```
#secondary {
background: transparent url(bg_bottom.gif) 0
➥0 repeat-x;
font-size: 1.1em;
}

   #secondarycontent, #footer {
   margin: 0 auto;
   width: 986px;
   }

   #secondarycontent {
   background-color: #f5f4ef;
   padding: 20px 0 10px 0;}

      #secondarycontent div {
```

```
width: 31%;
margin: 0 1%;
padding: 0;
}

#secondarycontent div div {
width: 100%;
margin: 0 0 10px 0;
padding: 0;
}
```

```
#secondarycontent h3 {
font-size: 1.75em;
margin-bottom: 10px;
}

dl, dt, dd {float: left;}
   dl {margin: 0 0 15px 0;}
   dt {
   clear: left;
   margin: 5px 0;
   width: 67px;
   }

   dd {
   margin: 5px 0 0 10px;
   width: 228px;
   }

#appearances li {
   margin: 1.125em 0;}
```

```
#footer {
background-color: #F8F7F6;
font-size: .75em;
height: 40px;
line-height: 40px;
text-align: center;
padding: 3px 0;
}

   #footer a {color: #B4AE9E;}
</style>
</head> ➥
```

```
<body>
<div id="primary">
    <div id="headwrap">
        <div class="wrap">
        <div id="header">
            <h1><a href="#">Raymond Jay</a></h1>
            <div id="navcontain">
                <ul id="mainnav">
                    <li class="about first"><a href="#">
                    ➥about</a></li>
                    <li class="work"><a href="#">work
                    ➥</a></li>
                    <li class="appearances"><a href="#">
                    ➥appearances</a></li>
                    <li class="blog"><a href="#">blog<
                    ➥/a></li>
                    <li class="contact last"><a href="#">
                    ➥contact</a></li>
                </ul>
                <div class="end"></div>
            </div>
        </div><!-- end header -->
        </div>
    </div><!-- end headwrap -->
    <div id="primarycontent" class="clearfix">
        <p class="authorphoto"><img
        ➥src="authorphoto.jpg" alt=" " /></p>
        <div id="whois">
            <h2>The Mind of Raymond Jay</h2>
            <p>Professor. Sociologist. Philosopher.
            ➥Pundit. Poet. Inspired Essayist.
            ➥MacArthur Genius Award recipient.</p>
            <p>Raymond Jay's work spans the gamut
            ➥of disciplines and forces readers
            ➥to challenge their perceptions and
            ➥beliefs about the world and their
            ➥place in it.<br />
            <span class="readmore"><a href="#">
            ➥read more...</a></span></p>
        </div><!-- end whois -->
        <div id="latestwork">
            <h2>Latest Work</h2>
            <div id="lwbody">
```

```
            <p><a href="book_brownnosing_lg.jpg">
            ➥<img src="book_brownnosing_cover
            ➥.jpg" alt="" /></a></p>
            <h3>Brown Nosing</h3>
            <div id="promo">
            <p>New York Times' Best Seller
            ➥list, January 2010</p>
            <p>Buy at</p>
                <ul>
                <li><a href="#">Amazon.com</a>
                ➥</li>
                <li><a href="#">Barnes &amp;
                Noble</a></li>
                <li><a href="#">Books &amp;
                Books</a></li>
                </ul>
            </div>
            <p class="description">What
            ➥happens when you paint a standard
            ➥Groucho nose brown? Discover how
            ➥people react to a new spin on an
            ➥old joke.</p>
            </div>
            <p class="latestend readmore">
            ➥<a href="#">read more...</a></p>
        </div><!-- end latestwork -->
    </div><!-- end primarycontent -->
</div><!-- end primary -->
<div id="secondary">
    <div id="secondarycontent"
class="clearfix">
        <div id="otherwritings">
            <h3>Other Writings</h3>
            <dl class="projects">
            <dt><a href="book_twomaplesjoy_lg.jpg">
            ➥<img src="book_twomaplesjoy.jpg"
            ➥alt="" /></a></dt>
            <dd>
            <h4>Two Maples and the Scent of Joy
            ➥</h4>
            <p>From ashes to new life: giving the
            ➥departed their due and honoring
            ➥those we loved.</p>
```

```
<p class="readmore"><a href="#">
➥ read more...</a></p>
</dd>
<dt><a href="book_lookathowfast_lg.jpg">
➥ <img src="book_lookathowfast.jpg"
➥ alt="" /></a></dt>
<dd>
<h4>Look at How Fast I Can Run!</h4>
<p>Thoughts on why we continue to
➥ love parents who have walked
➥ away.</p>
<p class="readmore"><a href="#">
➥ read more...</a></p>
</dd>
<dt><a href="book_jazzinthedark_lg.jpg">
➥ <img src="book_jazzinthedark.jpg"
➥ alt="" /></a></dt>
<dd>
<h4>Jazz in the Dark</h4>
<p>Fully listening without sight:
➥ experiencing jazz with the whole of
➥ your being.</p>
<p class="readmore"><a href="#">
➥ read more...</a></p>
</dd>
</dl>

  <p class="readmore"><a href="#">see
  ➥ all other writings &raquo;</a></p>
</div><!-- end otherwritings -->
<div id="appearances">
   <h3>Appearances</h3>
   <ul>
      <li>
      <p><a href="#">1 January, 6pm
      ➥ </a></p>
      <p>Epic Book Shop, Yellow Springs,
      ➥ OH</p>
      </li>
      <li>
      <p><a href="#">18 January, 7pm
      ➥ </a></p>
      <p>I (heart) Luddi Books, Detroit,
      ➥ MI</p>
      </li>
      <li>
      <p><a href="#">14 February, 8pm
      ➥ </a></p>
      <p>Books &amp; Books, Coral
      ➥ Gables, FL</p>
      </li>
      <li>
      <p><span class="readingdate">
      ➥ <a href="#">21 March, 2pm</a>
      ➥ </span><br />
      The Art and Soul of Books, Los
      ➥ Angeles, CA</p>
      </li>
      <li>
      <p><span class="readingdate">
      ➥ <a href="#">2 April, 5pm</a>
      ➥ </span><br />
      Vespucci's Well-Read, New York,
      ➥ NY</p>
      </li>
      <li>
      <p><span class="readingdate">
      ➥ <a href="#">23 May, 5pm</a>
      ➥ </span><br />
      Viggin's Bookshelf, Oshkosh, WI</p>
      </li>
      <li>
      <p><span class="readingdate">
      ➥ <a href="#">14 June, 11am</a>
      ➥ </span><br />
      Peaceful Passage Books, Henderson,
      ➥ NV</p>
      </li>
   </ul>
   <p class="readmore"><a href="#">
   ➥ see all appearances &raquo;</a></p>
</div><!-- end appearance -->
```

```
<div id="blogmusings">
  <h3>Blog Musings</h3>
  <div class="blogpost">
     <h4><a href="#">Launch It</a></h4>
     <p>Much like the previous year's election, a new year
     ➡brings hope and the potential for change in our lives.
     ➡Don't be one of those folks who bellyache midway through
     ➡the year about not being able to get it together...</p>
     <p class="readmore"><a href="#">read more...</a></p>
  </div>
  <div class="blogpost">
     <h4><a href="#">At the roots of Joy</a></h4>
     <p>Sometimes the best thing to do when something is ready
     ➡to leave is to let it pass on. Sometimes the ashes of
     ➡despair can be mixed with the soil to help sow the seeds
     ➡of renewal. Sometimes...</p>
     <p class="readmore"><a href="#">read more...</a></p>
  </div>
  <div class="blogpost">
  <h4><a href="#">Dreams of Osirus</a></h4>
  <p>It could have the outcome of a prolific imagination, but
  ➡when you meet the god of the Egyptian underworld in your
  ➡dreams you should still take it seriously...</p>
  <p class="readmore"><a href="#">read more...</a></p>
  </div>
  <p class="readmore clearfix"><a href="#">see all blog posts
  ➡&raquo;</a></p>
  </div><!-- end blogmusings -->
  </div><!-- end secondarycontent -->
  <div id="footer">
  <p>Copyright &copy; 2010 - Raymond Jay | design: <a href="#">
  ➡diona creative unlimited</a> | development: <a href="#">
  ➡deglorious devworks</a></p>
  </div><!-- end footer -->
</div><!-- end secondary -->
</body>
</html>
```

The Evidence Never Lies

I'd be remiss if I didn't do due diligence and double-check the validation results, so I go ahead and validate to rule out any coding mistakes. Both the HTML and CSS validation results are error free, as I expected. But then again, most IE bugs are the outcome of perfectly valid code that has been erroneously rendered by IE's "interesting" code interpretation engine.

CONFIRMING SUSPICIONS AND NAMING THE CULPRIT

It was just Diona's luck to hit three of the most common IE float bugs all in the same document. Who'da thunk it? But in comparing the pages rendered by the two older IE versions versus the modern browser, I notice our old usual suspect buddies from Chapter 4 :

1. The double margin float bug (**Figure 8.4**).

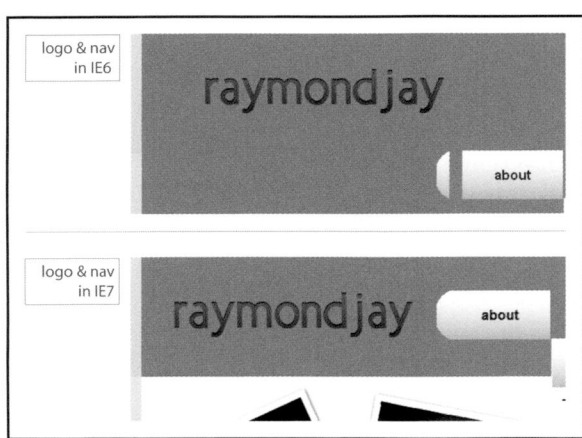

Figure 8.4 *Raymond Jay's logo is in the right place in IE7 (bottom) but not in IE6, where the double margin float bug crops up. The nav elements are also affected. That's a double bummer.*

2. The float stepdown bug (**Figure 8.5**).

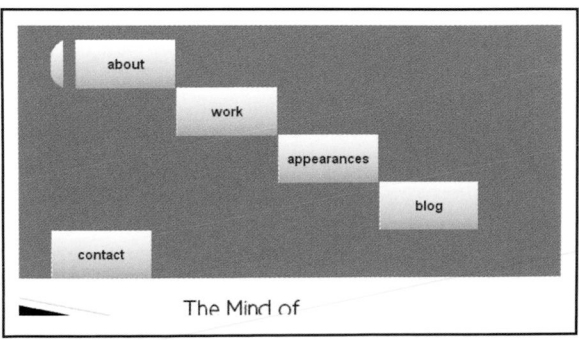

Figure 8.5 *The float stepdown bug in IE6 and IE7: quite the opposite of the stairway to heaven*

3. The float drop bug (**Figure 8.6**).

Figure 8.6 *The float drop bug in IE6*

Fortune is smiling upon us: the fixes for all these bugs are quick and easy.

So, let's get these floats in line, shall we?

First, the double margin float bug. Do you remember from your earlier training what keeps you from seeing double? That's right: apply `display: inline` to the style declaration of the errant floating element, and it will cure what ails you.

So let's add it to the logo and fix that one first:

```
h1 {
background: transparent url(logo_raymondjay.gif) no-repeat 0 0;
display: inline;
height: 60px;
margin: 40px 0 0 37px;
width: 306px;
text-indent: -9999px;
}
```

Once we do that, you can see how the logo shows up comparably in both browsers (**Figure 8.7**)

However, there are still issues in the navigation, so let's tackle those next.

Float stepdown is so dramatic and over-the-top that I almost have to do admire its pizzazz. However, just because something is entertaining doesn't mean it gets to stick around—especially when it causes major layout problems.

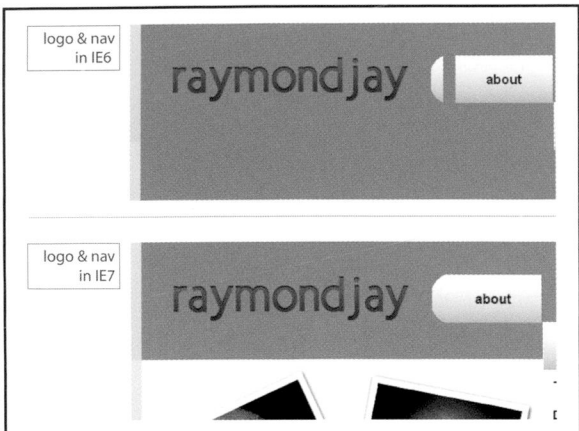

Figure 8.7 *Raymond Jay's logo in IE6: success!*

Do you have an idea for the fix? Think back to the previous example and you've got it: it's display: inline to the rescue again! Add the property to the style declaration of the containing <li> in this way:

```
#mainnav {
background: transparent url(bg_navcurve.gif) 0 0 no-repeat ;
color: #652a01;
font-size: 1.2em;
float: left;
height: 60px;
line-height: 57px;
list-style-type: none;
margin: 40px 0 0;
padding: 0;
text-align: center;
width: 623px;
}

.end {
background: transparent url(bg_navcurveend.gif) 0 0 no-repeat;
float: right;
height:76px;
width: 15px;
position: relative;
top: 40px;
margin: 0;} ⟶
```

```
#mainnav li {
display: inline;}
#mainnav li a {
background: transparent url(bg_navitems.gif) 0 0 repeat-x ;
border-right: 1px solid #8f8766;
border-left: 1px solid #fff;
color: #652a01;
display: block;
float: left;
font-weight: bold;
height: 58px;
line-height: 58px;
padding: 0 1px;
width: 118px;
}

    #mainnav li.first a {
    border-left: 0;
    margin-left: 15px;
    }
```

Now your former stepdown list items can get a new leg up on correct rendering (**Figure 8.8**).

Figure 8.8 *The navigation in IE7 as the W3C intended it—sans float stepdown*

There is still a little problem in IE6, which is another instance of the double margin float bug (**Figure 8.9**).

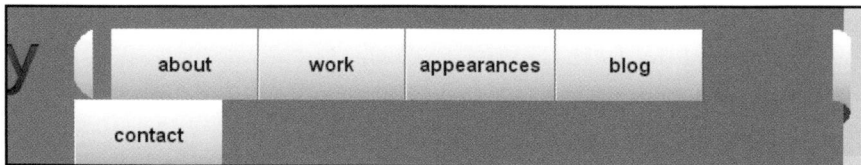

Figure 8.9 *The navigation in IE6: float stepdown due to the double margin float bug*

No problem, we just add our favorite fix again, display: inline; , which works like a charm:

```
#mainnav li.first a {
border-left: 0;
display: inline;
margin-left: 15px;
}
```

Is that the last of the double margin float bug? Somehow, my sense is "no." The float drop in the two content areas looks suspiciously like it may be a product of the double or nothing effects of the bug, especially because it is not happening in IE7.

Close examination reveals that my hunch is correct, as the author photo is farther away from the container's side in IE6 than in IE7 (**Figure 8.10** and **8.11**).

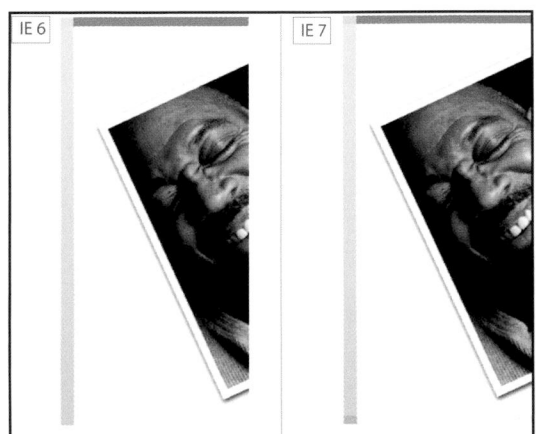

Figure 8.10 *The position of the author photo is not quite the same.*

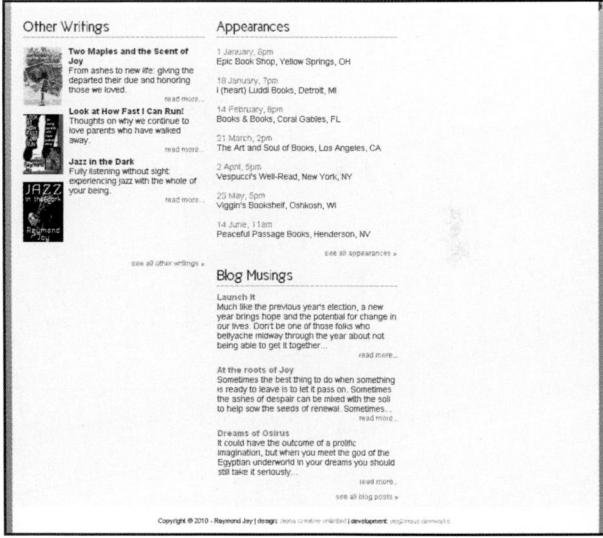

Figure 8.11 *Aha! The double margin float bug strikes again!*

I know you know the drill by now. So here's the fix:

```
.authorphoto {
display: inline;
margin: 0 0 0 10px;
width: 471px;
}
...
```

```
#secondarycontent div {
width: 31%;
margin: 0 1%;
padding: 0;
display: inline;
}
```

And last but not least, we have some definition lists in need of a firm talking to (**Figure 8.12**).

Figure 8.12 *The definitions are definitely out of line*

The <dd>s are not staying inline with the <dt>s as expected. You might be thinking, "we could use clearfix—it works great to establish clearing." True enough, but in this instance, the Swiss Army knife method of clearfix is woefully ineffective: throwing more elements in the mix won't work, but specifying the limits in the form of a height will. Yes, much like a cheeky teenager, what these floats want is structure and rules in order to feel comfortable and do what is expected of them.

```
dd {
height: 123px;
margin: 5px 0 0 10px;
width: 228px;
}
```

The result? The floated <dd>s now line up and express themselves in appropriate ways (**Figure 8.13**). All it took was a little extra definition.

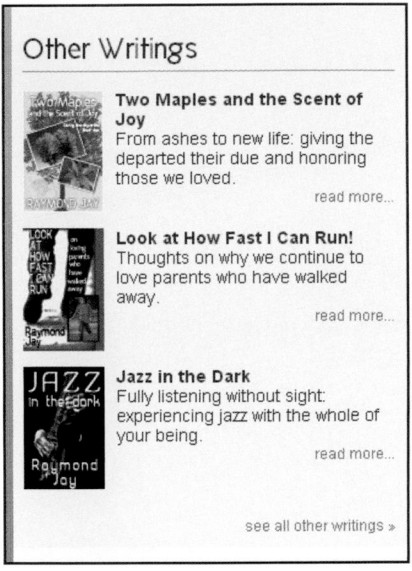

Figure 8.13 *The definitions can now do their thing—in* all *browsers.*

A final precautionary note: the instance of float stepdown, could have been avoided completely by making a slight adjustment in the code. Do you remember what the combination of factors is for float stepdown from Chapter 4? Here's a reminder: when a series of floated elements are contained in a series of block level elements that are not floated, the floated elements may end up in a stepdown effect in IE6 and IE7 and lower. The other additional piece of information is that padding on the element in question further triggers the bug.

Let's take another look at the code:

```
#mainnav {
background: transparent url(bg_navcurve.gif) 0 0 no-repeat ;
color: #652a01;
font-size: 1.2em;
float: left;
height: 60px;
line-height: 57px;
list-style-type: none;
margin: 40px 0 0;
padding: 0;
text-align: center;
width: 623px;
} ➡
```

```
.end {
background: transparent url(bg_navcurveend.gif) 0 0 no-repeat;
float: right;
height:76px;
width: 15px;
position: relative;
top: 40px;
margin: 0;}
```

```
    #mainnav li {
    display: inline;}
    #mainnav li a {
    background: transparent url(bg_navitems.gif) 0 0 repeat-x ;
    border-right: 1px solid #8f8766;
    border-left: 1px solid #fff;
    color: #652a01;
    display: block;
    float: left;
    font-weight: bold;
    height: 58px;
    line-height: 58px;
    padding: 0 1px;
    width: 118px;
    }
```

```
        #mainnav li.first a {
        border-left: 0;
        margin-left: 15px;
        display: inline;
        }
```

I suggest we do a bit of transferring many of the properties that were originally assigned to #mainnav li a to #mainnav li instead:

```
#mainnav li {
background: transparent url(bg_navitems.gif) 0 0 repeat-x ;
border-right: 1px solid #8f8766;
border-left: 1px solid #fff;
display: inline;
float: left;
font-weight: bold;
height: 58px;
```

```
line-height: 58px;
padding: 0;
width: 120px;
}

    #mainnav li.first {
    border-left: 0;
    display: inline;
    margin-left: 15px;
    }

    #mainnav li.last {
    border-right: 0;}

    #mainnav li a {
    color: #652a01;}     /* the color should stay here */

      #mainnav li a:hover {
      font-weight: normal;
      text-decoration: none;
      }
```

note

The padding isn't necessary so we can remove it and with the padding removed, the width value is 120px.

note

we now remove the border in the list.

Interestingly, it's roughly the same amount of code (maybe a little more), but it's well worth never having to worry about seeing float stepdown again.

Case Closed!

Diona proudly presented the website to her father, who, despite his initial diffidence, is starting to warm up to the idea of putting himself on the web in order to share his ideas and writing with a wider audience. He's even considering writing for major political and news blogs.

Not every client will want design integrity in IE6, but most will probably still need the site to work in IE7. In any event, it is important to recognize those shifty-eyed, sassy IE6 bugs, and code proactively against them.

Floats are wily beasts by nature (you would be too if you were always outside the flow of the page), so you need to keep in mind how sensitive they are to width, margin, padding, and border. Small changes in the size values of the element can mean the difference between a rock-solid layout and one that is broken.

Having display:inline up your sleeve for emergency bug fixing—especially in older versions of IE—usually puts you in good stead. Old standards like explicitly declaring the margin and padding for everything is helpful, and explicitly stating heights has proven useful as well. Using the overflow: hidden property works great to contain floats, but it doesn't fix every problem that you may encounter.

Ready for more IE 6/7 bug hijinks? Let's see if we can solve the next case.

9

The Case of the Browser Who Hated Me

IN THIS CASE, WE'LL SEE HOW TO DISARM
Microsoft Internet Explorer's cloak-and-dagger
bugs and quickly bring them to justice.

The Crime Scene

Just when former diplomat Guy Thenose thought he could retire with ease, an incident in the United Kingdom occurred that seemed to him to have huge potential to compromise the nation's security. His lobbying enabled him to head up a new agency to address the very serious threat: the Agency for the Prevention of Spontaneous Dancing (APoSD). Because of the whirlwind of work that accompanies pulling an organization of this import together so quickly, Guy has hired an assistant director, top Agent Single-Oh-Ten Jessica Andrew, and charged her with managing the development of their website and educating the public about the seriousness of this new threat.

As a government office, many of APoSD's primary users are still obligated to use IE 6 and 7 as their primary browsers. The APoSD site, therefore, has to be more backward-compatible than most modern sites and work perfectly in those browsers. Agent Andrew is finding that while their team is adept at forestalling major international incidents on an almost daily basis, trying to get their site to work in all browsers is a daunting task.

INITIAL SNAPSHOTS

Due to force of habit, Agent Andrew slips into my office under the cloak of darkness and in disguise. "Nice Groucho nose," I compliment her. "I almost didn't recognize you."

From a large envelope, she pulls out images of how the website was designed to look (**Figure 9.1**) and then, wincing, shows me how it looks in IE6 (**Figure 9.2**), IE7 (**Figure 9.3** on page 200), and Opera (**Figure 9.4** on page 200) onscreen. "This has to be the work of some evil mastermind," she says, glancing around furtively. "We just can't figure out why they are so different!"

Figure 9.1 *APoSD's original design as seen in Mozilla Firefox, IE8, Safari, and Google Chrome*

Figure 9.2 *APoSD's site as seen in IE6: call in the troops!*

Figure 9.3 *APoSD's site as seen in Internet Explorer 7—not horrible, but there are issues.*

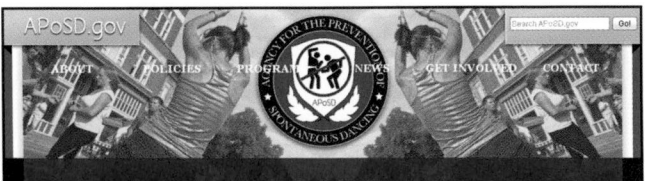

Figure 9.4 *APoSD's site navigation as seen in Opera: another indicator that something is amiss*

Follow the Evidence

None of our clients have a relaxed development schedule, and APoSD is no exception. Director Thenose and Agent Andrew will be unveiling the new website to their ultimate superior "D" in only three days. They need to quell the riot of their layout so they can continue receiving much-needed support and funding. They want to expand their organization internationally, where the number of incidents is growing rapidly.

IDENTIFYING SUSPECTS

Even before seeing Agent Andrew's pages, simply by noticing her high level of twitchiness, I surmised that her problems were all from IE. Her screen shots proved as much: the IE8 and IE7 shots are very close, but the site in IE6 is vastly different from them both.

Because the current browsers have dramatically improved their CSS support and rendering, pronounced layout issues are usually the product of the typical IE bugs. Sadly, these problems will exist until the use of these browsers dies out completely.

MUG SHOTS

True to form, APoSD employed an XHTML 1.1 Strict doctype:

```
<!DOCTYPE html PUBLIC "-//W3C//DTD XHTML 1.0 Strict//EN"
➥ "http://www.w3.org/TR/xhtml1/DTD/xhtml1-strict.dtd">
<html xmlns="http://www.w3.org/1999/xhtml" xml:lang="en" lang="en">
<head>
<meta http-equiv="Content-Type" content="text/html; charset=utf-8" />
<title>The Agency for the Prevention of Spontaneous Dancing (APoSD)</title>
<link rel="shortcut icon" type="image/x-icon" href="aposd.ico" />
<style type="text/css">
/* --- general styles --- */
body {
background: #b6c4e8 url(bg_blue.jpg) repeat-x;
font: .8em/1.35em Arial, Calibri, "Trebuchet MS", Trebuchet,
➥ sans-serif;
margin: 0 0 16px 0;
padding: 0 0 16px 0;
}
➥
```

```
h1, h2, h3 {
clear: both;
font-family: Georgia, "Palatino Linotype",
➥ "Times New Roman", serif;
}

h2 {
border-bottom: 1px dotted #3655a3;
color: #ad1c37;
margin: 0;
padding: 8px 0 6px 0;
text-transform: uppercase;
}

h3 {
color: #173187;
margin: 14px 0;
}

h4 {
color: #3655a3;
}

h5 {
font-size: 1em;
margin: 0;
}

ul {
list-style-type: square;
margin: 0;
padding: 0 0 0 16px;
}

ol {
margin: 0 0 0 8px;
padding: 0 0 0 16px;
}

a, a:link {
color: #293F6F;}

  a:hover {
  font-style: italic;
  text-decoration: none;
  }
```

```
  a:visited {
  color: #345193;}

a img {
border: none;}

li img {
vertical-align: middle;}

img {
border: 1px solid #D3D5D7;}

.morelink {
clear: both;
float: right;
font-size: .8em;
margin-bottom: 4px;
}

.clear {
clear: both;}

.clearoff {
clear: none;}

/* --- page layout styles --- */
#ubercontainer {
background: transparent url(bg_body.gif)
center repeat-y;
margin: 0 auto;
padding: 0;
width: 1000px;
}

#head {
background: transparent url(bg_head2.gif)
center no-repeat;
height: 324px;
margin: 0 auto;
overflow: hidden;
padding: 0;
width: 1000px;
}
```

```
h1 {
background: transparent url(bg_aposd.gif)
➥no-repeat;
float: left;
height: 58px;
margin: 0;
padding: 0;
text-indent: -10000px;
width: 214px;
overflow: hidden;
}

  h1 a {
  display: block;
  height: 100%;
  width: 100%;
  }

#searchbox {
float: right;
height: 58px;
margin: 0;
overflow: hidden;
padding: 0;
width: 214px;
}

  #searchbox p {
  margin: 0;
  padding: 0;
  }

  #searchbox input {
  float: left;
  font-size: .9em;
  margin: 16px 0 0 0;
  }

  #searchbox input.textinput {
  color: #aaa;
  margin-left: 8px;
  margin-right: 4px;
  width: 150px;
  }
```

```
#mainnav {
clear: both;
font: bold 1.3em/58px Georgia, "Palatino
➥Linotype", "Times New Roman", serif;
list-style-type: none;
height: 55px;
margin: 235px auto 0 auto;
padding: 0;
text-align: center;
text-transform: uppercase;
width: 936px;
}

  #mainnav li {
  display: inline;
  float: left;
  margin: 0;
  padding: 0;
  width: 156px;
  }

  #mainnav a {
  color: #fff;
  display: block;
  height: 100%;
  margin: 0;
  padding: 8px 0;
  text-decoration: none;
  }

  #mainnav a:hover {
  border-top: 8px solid #d9dde7;
  border-bottom: 8px solid #d9dde7;
  color: #d9dde7;
  font-style: normal;
  padding: 0;
  }

#maincontain {
margin: -15px 0 0 0;
overflow: hidden;
padding: 0 0 16px 0;
width: 1000px;
} ➞
```

```
#primaryinfo {
float: left;
margin: 0 0 0 31px;
padding: 0 16px 0 16px;
width: 584px;
}

    #about {
    background: #e5eaf7 url(bg_about.gif)
    ➥no-repeat;
    height: 237px;
    margin: 0 auto 16px auto;
    padding: 0 8px;
    width: 572px;
    }

        #about img {
        margin-top: -42px;}

    img.example {
    background-color: #fff;
    border: 1px solid #D3D5D7;
    float: right;
    margin: -10px 0 8px 10px;
    padding: 2px;
    }

    object {
    float: right;
    margin: 0 0 0 8px;
    }

    ul#circumstances {
    float: left;
    margin: -12px 0 10px 0;
    padding: 0;
    width: 390px;
    }

        #circumstances li {
        margin: 0;
        padding: 0;
        }
```

```
#circumstances li.title {
list-style-type: none;}

#circumstances li h4 {
font-family: Georgia, "Palatino
➥ Linotype", "Times New Roman", serif;
margin: 10px 0 0 0;
}

ul#illustration {
float: right;
list-style-type: none;
margin: -4px 0 0 0;
padding: 0;
text-align: center;
width: 182px;
}

    #illustration li {
    border: 1px solid #D3D5D7;
    height: 180px;
    margin: 0 0 8px 0;
    padding: 0;
    width: 182px;
    }

    #illustration li img {
    border: 1px solid #D3D5D7;
    margin: 4px auto 0 auto;
    }

    #illustration p {
    font-size: .75em;
    margin-top: 2px;
    }
#sidebar {
float: right;
margin: 0 33px 0 0;
padding: 0 16px 0 16px;
overflow: hidden;
width: 282px;
}
```

```
#mission {
background: #d8d9dc url(bg_mission.gif)
➥top left no-repeat;
height: 188px;
margin: 0 auto 16px auto;
padding: 0 8px;
width: 270px;
}

   #mission blockquote {
   font-size: 1.4em;
   margin: 32px 30px 0;
   text-align: center;
   }

   /* --- curly quote styles --- */
   .bqstart {
   color: #eee;
   float: left;
   font-family: Georgia, "Palatino
➥Linotype", "Times New Roman",
   serif;
   font-size: 500%;
   height: 45px;
   margin: -20px -5px -50px -30px;
   padding: 45px 0 0 0;
   }

   .bqend {
   color: #eee;
   float: right;
   font-family: Georgia, "Palatino
➥Linotype", "Times New Roman", serif;
   font-size: 500%;
   height: 25px;
   margin: -30px -30px 0 0;
   padding: 45px 0 0 0;
   }

.chart {
text-align: center;}
```

```
dl {
line-height: 1.2em;
overflow: hidden;
margin: 0 0 12px 0;
}

dt {
float: right;
margin: 3px 0 0 0;
}

   dt img {
   padding: 2px;}

dd {
float: left;
font-size: .9em;
margin: 0 12px 0 0;
width: 165px;
}

   dd p {
   margin: 0;}

#sociallinks {
list-style-type: none;
margin: 0;
padding: 0 0 0 16px;
}

#sociallinks li {
padding: 4px 0;}
```

```
#fatfooter {
background: transparent url(bg_footer.gif)
bottom left no-repeat;
clear: both;
margin: 0 auto;
padding: 0 0 16px 0;
width: 968px;
}
➥
```

```css
#containedfoot {
background-color: #fff;
border-top: 1px solid #E4E4E4;
font-size: .95em;
margin: 0 auto;
padding: 8px 16px 16px 16px;
width: 904px;
overflow: hidden;
}

    #containedfoot h4 {
    margin: 4px 0;}

    #contactus {
    float: left;
    width: 620px;
    margin: 0;
    padding: 0;
    }

        #containedfoot ul {
        list-style-type: none;
        padding: 0;
        }

        #contactlinks li {
        padding: 4px 0;}

    address {
    font-style: normal;}

    #linklist a {
    text-decoration: none;}

        #linklist a:hover {
        text-decoration: underline;}

</style>
</head>
<body>

<div id="ubercontainer">
    <div id="head">
        <h1><a href="#">APoSD.gov - The Agency
        ➥ for the Prevention of Spontaneous
        ➥ Dancing</a></h1>
```

```html
        <form id="searchbox" action="post">
            <p><input type="text" size="20"
            ➥ class="textinput" value="Search
            ➥ APoSD.gov" /><input type="submit"
            ➥ value="Go!" class="submit" /></p>
        </form>

        <ul id="mainnav">
            <li><a href="#">About</a></li>
            <li><a href="#">Policies</a></li>
            <li><a href="#">Programs</a></li>
            <li><a href="#">News</a></li>
            <li><a href="#">Get Involved</a></li>
            <li><a href="#">Contact</a></li>
        </ul>
</div><!-- end head -->

<div id="maincontain">
    <div id="primaryinfo">
        <div id="about">
            <h2>About Us</h2>
            <div id="whois">
                <h3>Who is <acronym
                ➥ title="The Agency for the
                ➥ Prevention of Spontaneous
                ➥ Dancing">APoSD</acronym>?
                ➥ </h3>
                <img src="pic_whois.jpg"
                ➥ class="example" alt="The
                ➥ APoSD Team" />
                <p>The Agency for the
                ➥ Prevention of Spontaneous
                ➥ Dancing (<acronym title="The
                ➥ Agency for the Prevention of
                ➥ Spontaneous Dancing">APoSD
                ➥ </acronym>) was created as a
                ➥ proactive national security
                ➥ measure in response to the
                ➥ tragic spontaneous train
                ➥ station dance in Liverpool
                ➥ in early 2009, the after-
                ➥ effects of which are still
                ➥ being felt to this day. </p>
```

```
<p>Because of the very
➥ serious threat that it
➥ poses, rather than being
➥ apposed, we are <em>opposed
➥ </em> to spontaneous dancing
➥ in any way, shape, or
➥ form.</p>
</div><!-- end whois -->
</div><!-- end about -->

<div id="policy">
<h2><acronym title="The Agency for
➥ the Prevention of Spontaneous
➥ Dancing">APoSD</acronym> Policy
➥ </h2>
<div id="rising">
<h3><acronym title="The Agency
➥ for the Prevention of
➥ Spontaneous Dancing">APoSD
➥ </acronym>: Rising from the
➥ Ashes of Tragedy</h3>
<object width="232" height=
➥ "143" type="application/
➥ x-shockwave-flash"
➥ data="http://www.youtube.com/
➥ v/mUZrrbgCdYc&amp;
➥ hl=en_US&amp;fs=1&amp;">
<object data=
➥ "pic_traindancevideo.jpg"
➥ type="image/jpeg">Your
➥ browser is not displaying
➥ the video. Sorry.</object>
<param name="movie"
value="http://www.youtube.com/
➥ v/mUZrrbgCdYc&amp;hl=en_US
➥ &amp;fs=1&amp;"/>
<param name="allowFullScreen"
➥ value="true"/>
<param
➥ name="allowscriptaccess"
➥ value="always"/>
</object>
```

```
<p>Midmorning one day in January
➥ 2009, the Liverpool train
➥ station was overrun by a group
➥ of incognito dancers, who
➥ shocked the public with a
➥ flagrant display of spirited
➥ funky dance moves to catchy
➥ popular tunes. Since this
➥ incident, spontaneous dancing
➥ has exploded worldwide, with
➥ brief surprise takeovers of
➥ stores, public squares, parks,
➥ train stations, and other
➥ public gathering places. </p>
<p>We at <acronym title="The
➥ Agency for the Prevention of
➥ Spontaneous Dancing">APoSD
➥ </acronym> believe that
➥ dancing is serious business.
➥ Shaking your groove thing is
➥ fine every once in a while,
➥ but it must be done when
➥ everyone knows it is going to
➥ happen at pre-determined
➥ times. There is true danger in
➥ unexpectedly having a
➥ ridiculous amount of fun.</p>
<p>We have gathered together a
➥ team of rigorously trained
➥ elite agents who are the
➥ product of a highly
➥ competitive selection process.
➥ We have the resources and the
➥ commitment at APoSD to keep
➥ dancing controlled and in its
➥ rightful place.</p>
</div><!-- end rising -->

<div id="mandatedlist">
<h3>List of Mandated Dancing
➥ Circumstances</h3>
<ul id="circumstances">
<li class="title"> ➥
```

```
<h4>Sanctioned</h4>
  <ul>
    <li>Performances:
    ⇒musicals, ballet,
    ⇒contemporary, jazz,
    ⇒ethnic</li>
    <li>Dance classes,
    ⇒troupes, parties,
    ⇒clubs </li>
    <li>Cheerleading squads,
    ⇒drill teams, dance
    ⇒teams, and spirit and
    ⇒glee teams</li>
    <li>Religious dancing:
    ⇒whirling dervishes,
    ⇒temple, fancy dancing
    ⇒("Getting Happy" under
    ⇒investigation)</li>
  </ul>
</li>
<li class="title"><h4>Pending
⇒Decision</h4>
  <ul>
    <li>Carnival/Carnivale/
    ⇒Mardi Gras</li>
    <li>Capoeria and any
    ⇒other martial art
    ⇒practiced to music</li>
    <li>Break and hip-hop
    ⇒dancing</li>
    <li>Sport sack-dances</li>
    <li>Quasi-choreographed
    ⇒personal greetings
    ⇒(use of "The Bump" is
    ⇒under a dedicated task
    ⇒force review)</li>
  </ul>
</li>
<li class="title"><h4>Strictly
⇒Verboten</h4>
```

```
  <ul>
    <li>Impromptu boogying,
    ⇒shimmying, or hip-
    ⇒shaking</li>
    <li>Extemporaneous
    ⇒dancing in public
    ⇒areas, especially in
    ⇒train stations, street
    ⇒intersections, parks,
    ⇒beaches, sidewalks,
    ⇒rooftops, and
    ⇒bridges</li>
    <li>Dance fights/dance-
    ⇒offs - getting
    ⇒"served" and/or being
    ⇒the server</li>
  </ul>
</li>
</ul><!-- end circumstances -->

<ul id="illustration">
  <li>
  <img src="illust_fancydancing
  ⇒.jpg" alt="Fancy Dancer" />
  <p>OK: Fancy Dancing</p>
  </li>
  <li>
  <img src="illust_breakdancing
  ⇒.jpg" alt="Breakdancers" />
  <p>Pending: Breakdancing</p>
  </li>
  <li>
  <img src="illust_parkdance.jpg"
  alt="Dancing in the park" />
  <p>Right out: Park dancing</p>
  </li>
</ul>
```

```
<p>All groups and venues must be
registered with <acronym title=
"The Agency for the Prevention
of Spontaneous Dancing">APoSD
</acronym>. Circumstances
listed apply to those both
professional and amateur
unless otherwise noted.</p>
<p>We are always accepting new
categories of dancing for
review. Read the full set of
<a href="#">criteria for
acceptable forms of dance</a>.
</p>
</div><!-- end mandatedlist -->
</div><!-- end policy -->

<div id="origins">
<h2>Origins</h2>
<div id="roots">
<h3>Historical Roots of
Spontaneous Dancing</h3>
<img src="pic_ringrosy.jpg"
class="example"
alt="Children playing ring
around the rosey" />
<p>Scholars suggest that
spontaneous dancing (<acronym
title="spontaneous dancing">
SD</acronym>) has its roots
in children's games, notably
those such as "Ring Around
the Rosey" and "Simon Says."
But from innocent beginnings
can come unpredictable
outcomes. We all know what
happens after a pocket full
of posey: it's ashes and we
all fall down.</p>
```

```
<p>While they may seem harmless,
games such as these lay a
foundation for future
tendencies toward spontaneous
dancing. Just as your parents
always warned you: it's all
fun and games until someone
pokes an eye out.</p>
</div><!-- end roots -->

<div id="dangers">
<h3>The Dangers of <acronym
title="spontaneous dancing">SD
</acronym></h3>
<img src="pic_asianladies.jpg"
class="example" alt="Ladies
dancing" />
<p>Spontaneous dancing looks
benign, nay, even delightful
at first glance. However,
all of the surface fun and
ebullience that it imparts
actually masks the
underlying dubious tenets of
spontaneity, love of fun,
and the sheer joy of being
alive. Spontaneous dancing
often causes huge smiles,
laughter, and enjoyment, all
of which is highly
contagious. </p>
<p>Freely expressing and
epitomizing joyous thoughts
and feelings -- even if only
for a few minutes -- is
extremely risky behavior. It
is for this reason that we
take our role so seriously:
to protect the public from
SD and its far-reaching
effects.</p>
```

```
<p>It is our goal to keep
➥outbreaks of <acronym
➥title="spontaneous
➥dancing">SD</acronym> to a
➥minimum at present, and for
➥as long as we are able.</p>
</div><!-- end dangers -->

<p><span class="morelink">
➥<a href="#">Read more about the
➥problem of <acronym title=
➥"spontaneous dancing">SD
➥</acronym> &raquo;</a></span></p>
</div><!-- end origins -->

<div id="news">
    <h2>APoSD NEWS</h2>
    <div class="lateststory">
        <h3> Top Story</h3>
        <img src="pic_response.jpg"
        ➥class="example" alt=
        ➥"Spontaneous dance pizza
        ➥party" />
        <h4><a href="#">Recent YouTube
        ➥Uploads from Train Station
        Dance Trigger <acronym
        ➥title="post-traumatic stress
        ➥disorder">PTSD</acronym>-like
        ➥Symptoms</a></h4>

        <p>Approximately one year since
        ➥tragedy struck, just as the
        ➥public was finally starting to
        ➥forget the lingering traumatic
        ➥memories of the joyous train
        ➥station dance, the latest
        ➥crop of spectator-uploaded
        ➥YouTube videos illicits a
        ➥unexpectedly strong emotional
        ➥response...<br />
```

```
        <span class="morelink clearoff">
        ➥<a href="#">read more&gt;</a>
        ➥</span></p>
</div><!-- end lateststory -->

<h3 class="clearoff">Other Stories
➥</h3>
<ul id="storylist">
    <li><a href="http://www.youtube
    ➥.com/watch?v=OLj5zphusLw">
    ➥100 Single Lady <acronym
    ➥title="spontaneous dance">SD</
    ➥acronym>-ers Sashay Through
    ➥Picadilly Square Without
    ➥Recourse</a></li>
    <li><a href="#">Security
    ➥Measures at Trains Stations
    ➥Increased Worldwide, All Boom
    ➥Boxes Confiscated</a></li>
    <li><a href="http://www.youtube
    ➥.com/watch?v=NZW92lEzBAs">Stop
    ➥Hammertime: LA Clothing Store
    ➥Overrun by Crowd in Gold
    ➥"Hammer" Pants</a></li>
    <li><a href="http://www.youtube
    ➥.com/watch?v=7EYAUazLI9k">How
    ➥Do You Solve a Problem Like a
    ➥Train Station in Antwerp?
    ➥Belgium Latest Victim to
    ➥<acronym title="spontaneous
    ➥dancing">SD</acronym></a></li>
    <li><a href="#">German Telecom
    ➥Company Entering Trial for
    ➥Sponsoring and Promoting
    ➥<acronym title="spontaneous
    ➥dancing">SD</acronym> for
    ➥Commercial Gain</a></li>
```

```
      <li><a href="http://www.youtube
   .com/watch?v=I_DBKZQsldU">
   Worldwide Thriller SD Gives
   Credence and Raison D'Etre to
   New Agency</a></li>
      <li><a href="#">Hundreds of New
   Bystander-Victims Surface in
   Liverpool</a></li>
   </ul>

   <p><span class="morelink"><a href="#">
   See all news &raquo;</a></span>
   </p>
   </div><!-- end news -->

</div><!-- end primaryinfo -->

<div id="sidebar">
   <div id="mission">
      <h2>Mission</h2>
      <blockquote>
         <p><span class="bqstart">
   &ldquo;</span>To fearlessly
   provide the public the best
   prevention of spontaneous
   dancing that is humanly
   possible.<span class="bqend">
   &rdquo;</span></p>
      </blockquote>
   </div><!-- end mission -->

   <div id="getfacts">
      <h2>Get the Facts</h2>
      <div id="progress">
         <h3><acronym title="The Agency
   for the Prevention of
   Spontaneous Dancing">APoSD
   </acronym> vs. <acronym
   title="spontaneous dancing">SD
   </acronym>s</h3>
```

```
      <p>Since our inception, we have
   prevented more than ten
   serious outbursts of
   spontaneous dancing, and we
   project that our prevention
   rates will only grow in years
   to come.</p>
      <p class="chart"><img src=
   "chart_aposd.gif" alt="dance
   prevention figures" /></p>
      <p><span class="morelink">
   <a href="#">Read more &raquo;
   </a></span></p>
</div><!-- end progress -->

<div id="risks">
   <h3>Know the Risks</h3>
   <p>The general public simply
   does not have the means to
   handle massive groups of
   people dancing out of nowhere.
   It is far too interesting and
   thrilling for most people and
   can cause an aftermath that
   needs to be dealt with.</p>
   <p>Know ahead what effects being
   caught in an SD situation
   might have on you by <a href="#">
   taking our brief personality
   type quiz</a>.</p>

   <p><span class="morelink">
   <a href="#">Read more &raquo;
   </a></span></p>
</div><!-- end risks -->

<div id="quickref">
   <h3><acronym title="spontaneous
   dancing">SD</acronym>
   Prevention Quick Reference
   Guide</h3>
```

```
<p>In our eyes, an ounce of
➥prevention is worth a true ton
➥of cure. We have assembled a
➥quick reference guide to help
➥you learn the following:</p>
<ul id="reflist">
   <li><a href="#">What to look
   ➥for</a> - recognizing the
   ➥signs of impending <acronym
   ➥title="spontaneous
   ➥dancing">SD</acronym></li>
   <li><a href="#">What to do</a>
   ➥- if you suspect an <acronym
   ➥title="spontaneous
   ➥dance">SD</acronym> taking
   ➥place</li>
   <li><a href="#">Preventative
   ➥measures</a> - steps to
   ➥take</li>
   <li><a href="#">How to report
   ➥suspicious activity</a> -
   ➥contacting us and what
   ➥information to supply</li>
   </ul>

   <p><span class="morelink">
   ➥<a href="#">Read more &raquo;
   ➥</a></span></p>
   </div><!-- end quickref -->
</div><!-- end getfacts -->

<div id="getinvolved">
   <h2>Get Involved</h2>
   <p>We have agents working around
   ➥the world, but <acronym title=
   ➥"spontaneous dancing">SD
   ➥</acronym> can happen anywhere
   ➥and at any time. Here's how you
   ➥can get involved:</p>
   <div id="ways">
```

```
   <h3>Do Your Part</h3>
   <ol id="name">
      <li><a href="#">Report problems
      ➥</a> before they happen</li>
      <li>Join a <a href="#">
      ➥citizen's coalition</a>,
      ➥like CAPoSD (Citizens
      ➥Against PDSD's [public
      ➥displays of spontaneous
      ➥dancing])</li>
      <li><a href="#">Organize your
      ➥own group</a> or meetup
      ➥(dancing allowed only if it
      ➥is planned in advance)</li>
      <li><a href="#">Join our team
      ➥</a> - become an APoSD
      ➥agent</li>
   </ol>

   <p><span class="morelink">
   ➥<a href="#">Read more &raquo;
   ➥</a></span></p>
</div><!-- end ways -->

<div id="offenders">
   <h3>Report a Repeat Offender</h3>
   <p>Have you seen any of these
   ➥people? If sighted, please
   ➥report their whereabouts to
   ➥<acronym title="The Agency for
   ➥the Prevention of Spontaneous
   ➥Dancing">APoSD</acronym> as
   ➥soon as possible.</p>
   <dl class="wanted">
      <dt><img src="pic_wanted_
      ➥pinqie.jpg" alt="Maaike
      ➥Speijers" /></dt>
      <dd><h5>Maaike "Pinqie"
      ➥Speijers</h5>
```

```
<p>Last seen practicing
⇒<acronym title="spontaneous
⇒dancing">SD</acronym> in
⇒malls in Northern Europe.
⇒May be the mastermind behind
⇒several Michael Jackson
"Beat It" tribute <acronym
⇒title="spontaneous dance">
⇒SD</acronym>s in Sweden.</p>
<p class="readmore"><a href="#">
⇒read more &gt;</a></p>
</dd>
</dl>

<dl class="wanted">
<dt><img src="pic_wanted_
⇒bhuller.jpg" alt="Bhuller
⇒Darshan" /></dt>
<dd><h5>"Bhuller" Darshan</h5>
<p>Former <acronym title="The
⇒Agency for the Prevention of
⇒Spontaneous Dancing">APoSD
⇒</acronym> certified
⇒choreograper and agent gone
⇒renegade. He now encourages
⇒kung fu practioners to break
⇒into dance as part of their
⇒"practice".</p>
<p class="readmore"><a href="#">
⇒read more &gt;</a></p>
</dd>
</dl>

<dl class="wanted">
<dt><img src="pic_wanted_
⇒thelud.jpg" alt="The Lud" />
⇒</dt>
<dd><h5>The Artist Formerly
⇒Known as "The Lud"</h5>
```

```
<p>True name and whereabouts
⇒unknown. Is often spotted
⇒at senior athletic
⇒tournaments inciting
⇒those disinclined to
⇒dance to impetuously "cut
⇒a rug". Leader of
⇒<acronym title="Moms
⇒Opposed to The Agency for
⇒the Prevention of
⇒Spontaneous Dancing">MOtA
⇒</acronym> (Moms Opposed
⇒to APoSD). Frequently
⇒disguises herself with
⇒hats.</p>
<p class="readmore">
⇒<a href="#">read more &gt;
⇒</a></p>
</dd>
</dl>

<p><span class="morelink">
⇒<a href="#">See more offenders
⇒&raquo;</a></span></p>
</div><!-- end offenders -->
</div><!-- end getinvolved -->

<div id="getsocial">
<h2>Get Social</h2>
<h3>Stay Connected</h3>
<p>There are many ways to keep up
⇒with what we are doing. Check us
⇒out on:</p>
<ul id="sociallinks">
<li><a href="#"><img src=
⇒"twitter_16.png" alt="twitter
icon" /></a> <a href="#">
⇒twitter</a></li>
<li><a href="#"><img src=
⇒"facebook_16.png"
⇒alt="facebook icon" /></a>
⇒<a href="#">facebook</a></li>
```

```
      <li><a href="#"><img src=
      ➥ "dopplr_16.png" alt="dopplr
      icon" /></a> <a href="#">
      ➥ dopplr</a></li>
      <li><a href="#"><img src=
      ➥ "youtube_16.png" alt="youtube
      ➥ icon" /></a> <a href="#">
      ➥ youtube</a></li>
    </ul>
  </div><!-- end getsocial -->
 </div><!-- end sidebar -->

</div><!-- end maincontain -->

<div id="fatfooter">
  <div id="containedfoot">

    <div id="contactus">
      <h4>Contact Us</h4>
      <address>
        <acronym title="The Agency for
        ➥ the Prevention of Spontaneous
        ➥ Dancing">APoSD</acronym> - The
        ➥ Agency for the Prevention of
        ➥ Spontaneous Dancing<br />
        1123 A Street, suite #2010<br />
        Washington, DC 20032<br />
      </address>
      <p><a href="#">Map</a> to our
      ➥ office | <a href="#">Get
      ➥ directions</a> to our office</p>
```

```
      <ul id="contactlinks">
        <li><img src="icon_phone_16.gif"
        ➥ alt="phone icon" />
        ➥ Phone: 202.010.0101 |
        ➥ Fax: 202.010.0110</li>
        <li><img src="email_16.png" alt=
        ➥ "email icon" /> Send email to:
        ➥ <a href="#">director@aposd.gov
        ➥ </a></li>
      </ul>
    </div><!-- end contactus -->

    <div id="relatedlinks">
      <h4>Related Sites</h4>
      <ul id="linklist" >
        <li><a href="#">Bureau of
        ➥ International Joy Management
        ➥ and Mitigation</a></li>
        <li><a href="#">Workplace
        ➥ Dancing Task Force</a></li>
        <li><a href="#">Citizens Against
        ➥ PDSD's (CAPoSD.org)</a></li>
        <li><a href="#">Flashmobbers
        ➥ Anonymous</a></li>
      </ul>
    </div><!-- end relatedlinks -->

  </div><!-- end containedfoot -->

 </div><!-- end fatfooter -->
</div><!-- end ubercontainer -->

</body>
</html>
```

The Evidence Never Lies

Agent Andrew verified that she'd validated the page and that the code had passed with flying colors. So now we have to get clever about the source of the problems.

CONFIRMING SUSPICIONS AND NAMING THE CULPRIT

One nice thing you can say about IE6 bugs is that a lot of them are not subtle. Many of the common ones will jump right out of the page at you. Let's be systematic and start with one of the issues common to both IE6 and IE7: the gap at the top of the page (**Figure 9.5**).

The code looks fine at first glance, validates, and shows up well in most of the modern browsers (Firefox, IE8, Safari and Google Chrome) so we will definitely have to widen our sights to find the problem.

Figure 9.5 *Where is that gap at the top coming from?*

Any ideas yet? It would be nice if it were as simple as a margin or padding error. But if that were the case, the problem would show up in all of the browsers, right?

Following my own advice, I say we go right to the CSS of the element in question: #head. Both the top margin and padding are set to zero, and the height is the same as the image, so what gives? Now I see it: there's only one value established to tell the browser the position (center) of the image. Ha!

```
#head {
background: transparent url(bg_head.gif) center no-repeat;
height: 324px;
margin: 0 auto;
overflow: hidden;
padding: 0;
width: 1000px;
}
```

If you don't supply two coordinate values to determine where to place items on the screen, then the browser may default to a value that you didn't intend. In this case, because one coordinate is specified but the second coordinate is omitted, the browser has defaulted to a value of center center (or 50% 50%) so the background image will be both horizontally *and* vertically centered. So let's add an additional value, which was implied, but not explicitly stated:

```
#head {
background: transparent url(bg_head.gif) top center no-repeat;
height: 324px;
margin: 0 auto;
overflow: hidden;
padding: 0;
width: 1000px;
}
```

Eureka! The background image for the #head is now in its proper place, and the gap at the top of the screen is gone (**Figure 9.6**).

Figure 9.6 *Now the gap is gone.*

Next order of business: what's up with the navigation bar? It looks like it's trying to hide itself behind the main body section in IE6 and IE7 (**Figure 9.7**).

Figure 9.7 *The hover indicator is all we can see of the navigation bar.*

Whereas, in Opera, it is completely out of a place, right out in the open
(**Figure 9.8**).

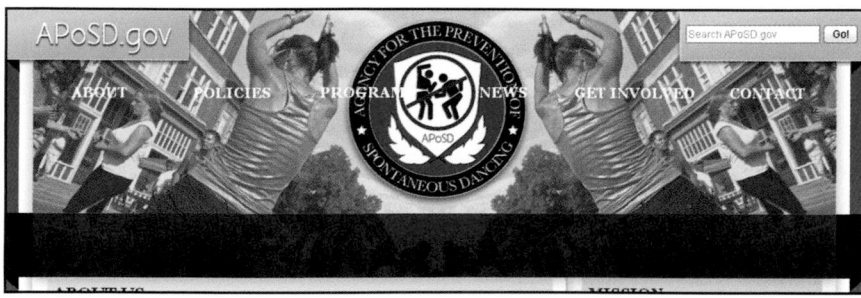

Figure 9.8 *The navigation in Opera is doing its own thing*

I'm sure that these two extremes of "going into hiding" and flying free are
forced rather than freely chosen. Let's take a closer look at what's going on:

```
#mainnav {
clear: both;
font: bold 1.3em/4.5em Georgia, "Palatino Linotype",
➥ "Times New Roman", serif;
list-style-type: none;
height: 73px;
margin: 235px auto 0 auto;
padding: 0;
width: 936px;
text-align: center;
text-transform: uppercase;
}
```

Doesn't that look fine to you? There is a `clear: both;` to accommodate the element being in the container with the two floated elements prior to it. The value for the top margin is exactly the number of pixels from the top of the browser window to the navigation area of the background image. What could the problem be?

Let's do this: let's clear the slate for the margins and see if that will reveal what is eluding us.

Changing the margin values to this: `margin: 0 auto;` gives us this onscreen (**Figure 9.9**).

Figure 9.9 *Now we can see the lay of the land.*

I don't know about you, but I believe I see the source of the problem. Did you notice just how far down the navigation element was pushed in the earlier screen shot (**Figure 9.7**)? Doesn't it look as if it has the same height as that of the two top floated elements? I've got it: the earlier versions of IE are interpreting the margin source-point location differently than the more current browsers! Those older browsers are pushing the element down 235px from the bottom of the two floats, rather than from the top of the browser window.

So, let's even the playing field, shall we? We have two options to push the element down to the correct position: we can either position #mainnav relatively, or we can give #searchbox a bottom margin of 177px.

To relatively position #mainnav, these changes will do the trick:

```
#mainnav {
clear: both;
font: bold 1.3em/58px Georgia, "Palatino Linotype",
➥"Times New Roman", serif;
list-style-type: none;
height: 55px;
margin: 0 auto;
padding: 0;
```

```
text-align: center;
text-transform: uppercase;
width: 936px;
position: relative;
top: 177px;
}
```

By adding position: relative to the element, we are telling all of the browsers that the starting point is the location where #mainnav would be if it stayed in its place in the flow after clearing the prior floats.

Similarly, we could also make an adjustment to the bottom margin of #searchbox, which is the element immediately before #mainnav in the source code. Changing the bottom margin value will push #mainnav down the desired amount, with the added advantage of keeping #mainnav in the flow of the page:

```
#searchbox {
float: right;
height: 58px;
margin: 0 0 177px 0;
overflow: hidden;
padding: 0;
width: 214px;
}

...

#mainnav {
clear: both;
font: bold 1.3em/58px Georgia, "Palatino Linotype",
➥ "Times New Roman", serif;
list-style-type: none;
height: 55px;
margin: 0 auto;
padding: 0;
text-align: center;
text-transform: uppercase;
width: 936px;
}
```

Success! With either of these solutions, all of the browsers will now start from the same coordinates, push the element down 177px from this point, and align the element in the correct location on the page (**Figure 9.10**).

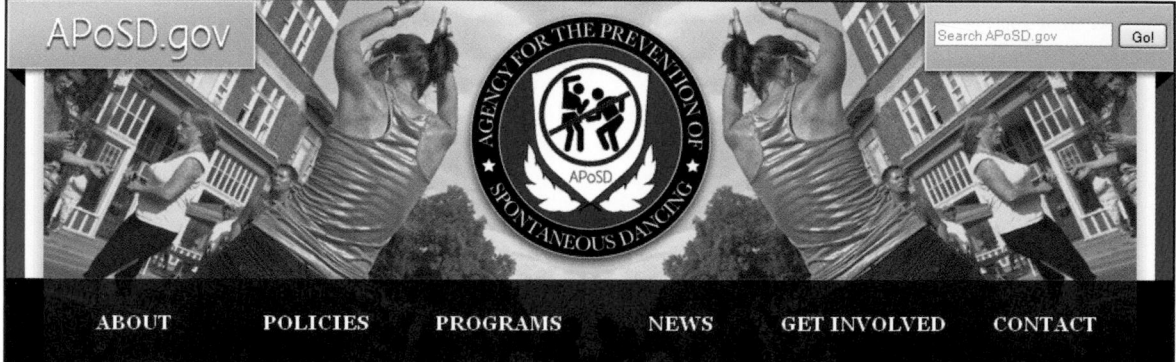

Figure 9.10 *The head of the document: everything fixed*

With Opera completely fixed and IE7 mostly taken care of, let's turn our sights solely to the IE6 issues.

If the serious case of float drop is the first thing that jumps out at you, then we're on the same page. Here's my educated guess: the double margin float bug (again!)—but this time on *both* the left and the right (**Figure 9.11**).

The two elements in question are #primaryinformation and #sidebar. The double margin float bug returns to make a cameo appearance. Since we just dealt with this issue extensively in Chapter 8, let's put these floats back in place with display: inline;.

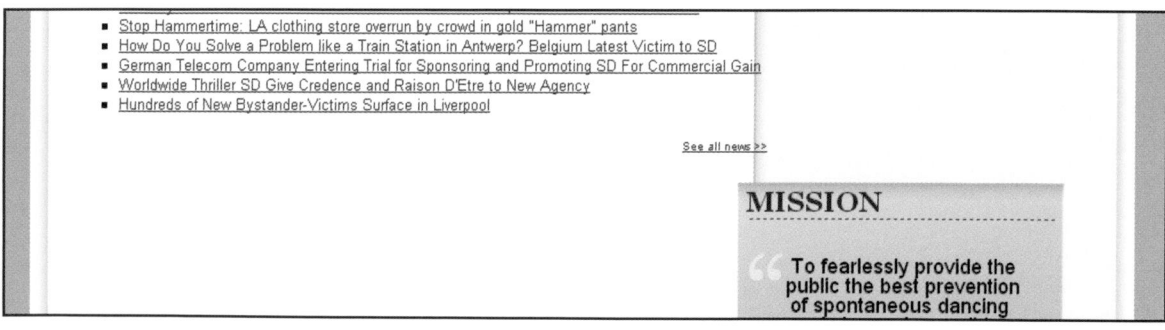

Figure 9.11 *The double-oh-margin float problem*

```
#primaryinfo {
display: inline;
float: left;
margin: 0 0 0 31px;
padding: 0 16px 0 16px;
width: 584px;
}

...

#sidebar {
display: inline;
float: right;
margin: 0 33px 0 0;
padding: 0 16px 0 16px;
width: 282px;
overflow: hidden;
}
```

This does the trick perfectly. Now, we have a couple more items to address.

In the right column, the mugshots of the recent offenders and their descriptions are controlled by definition lists. Although the `<dl>` tag has the margin defined with the declaration `margin: 0 0 12px 0`, which is respected by other browsers, IE6 completely ignores the value and collapses this bottom margin. The floated list items don't clear those before them and we get this (**Figure 9.12** on the next page).

The solution? Be explicit and make sure the floats all clear in every browser, by adding `clear: both;` to the `dl` style declaration:

Figure 9.12 *The bottom margin is ignored and is collapsed*

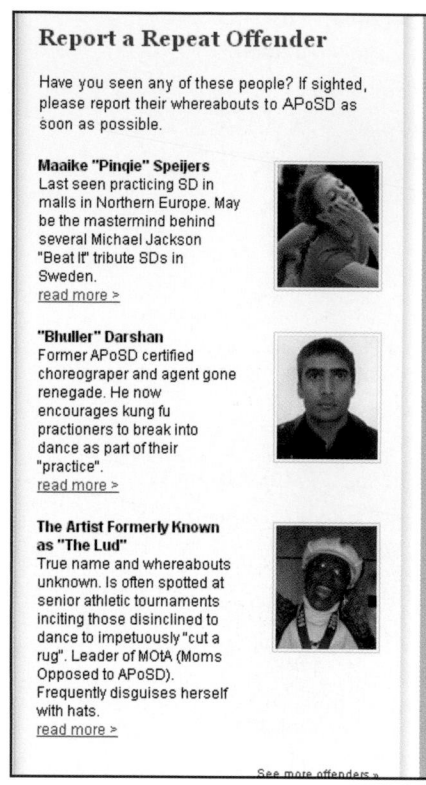

Figure 9.13 *Now the space is respected*

```
dl {
clear: both;
overflow: hidden;
margin: 0 0 12px 0;
line-height: 1.2em;
}
```

Now the lineup of repeat offenders, uh, lines up across all the browsers (**Figure 9.13**, above right).

For the page overall, there is the issue of how the size of the text renders on the page. There is enough of a difference cross-browser that it detracts from the user experience (**Figures 9.14** and **9.15**).

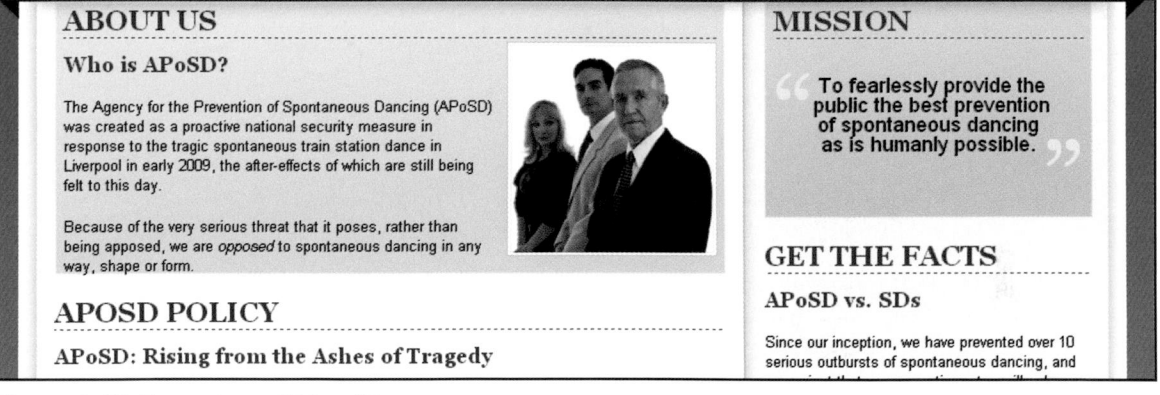

Figure 9.14 *Text sizing in modern browsers*

Figure 9.15 *Text sizing in IE 6 and 7*

I propose a change that is not so much a bug fix, but rather a technique for ensuring—as in the earlier example with the margin of the navigation bar— that we establish the same sizing starting point for all of the browsers.

In order to get the consistency we want and still have relative sizes, let's make these few small adjustments:

```
body {
background: #b6c4e8 url(bg_blue.jpg) repeat-x;
font: 12px/18px Arial, Calibri, "Trebuchet MS", Trebuchet, sans-serif;
margin: 0 0 16px 0;
padding: 0 0 16px 0;
}

...
```

```
h2 {
border-bottom: 1px dotted #3655a3;
color: #ad1c37;
font-size: 1.6em;
margin: 0;
padding: 8px 0 6px 0;
text-transform: uppercase;
}

h3 {
color: #173187;
font-size: 1.4em;
margin: 14px 0;}

h4 {
color: #3655a3;
font-size: 1.2em;
}
```

Once we do this, we have fixed all of the problems, and the pages show up essentially the same in Firefox and in IE 6, 7, and 8.

The footer of the page looks fine, except—wait, what just happened?! Did you *see* that? Where is the bottom of the page (**Figure 9.16**)?

My goodness, it's no small wonder that Agent Andrew is so tense—this kind of unplanned interactivity would not shine a favorable light upon their organization, in the footer of the page or otherwise. My friend, we are looking at none other but the infamous guillotine bug.

If you remember from Chapter 4, the elements that need to be in place for the guillotine bug to appear are as follows: a parent container element, a floated element inside of that container that is not cleared, links inside the parent container in non-floated content after the float, and finally, style rules for those links that change certain link properties on hover. What happens is that hovering over the links causes part of the floated element inside of the parent container to get cut off and become inaccessible.

This particular IE6 bug stumped front-end developers for years. However, this bug has now met its match: from years of trial and error, we have several solid code solutions to thwart it.

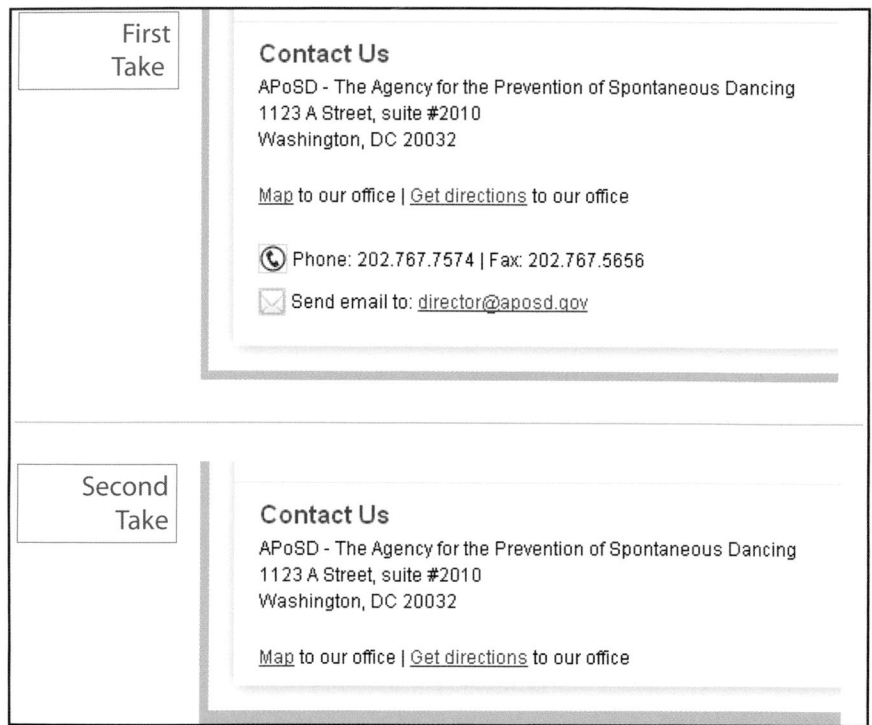

Figure 9.16 *The guillotine bug cut the footer short*

Thankfully, this version of the guillotine bug was particularly obedient to the IE6–specific Star HTML hack delivering a height of 1% to all of the divs on the page, including the ones containing the bug: `* html div {height: 1%;}`.

Once this code is added as the second declaration in the CSS, the footer of the page is neutralized and stays agreeably still.

However, just as APoSD is dedicated to prevention, I feel it is my patriotic duty to show how this particular bug could have been avoided entirely. Let's take a look at the basic markup first:

```
<div id="fatfooter">
  <div id="containedfoot">
    <div id="contactus">
      ...
    </div><!-- end contactus -->
```

```
        <div id="relatedlinks">
          ...
        </div><!-- end relatedlinks -->
      </div><!-- end containedfoot -->
    </div><!-- end fatfooter -->
```

And now let's look at the pertinent area of the CSS:

```
#contactus {
float: left;
width: 620px;
margin: 0;
padding: 0;
}
```

Hmm. It seems to me that whoever did the coding pushed the #relatedlinks div over to the desired position by making #contactus really wide. While that works, there are other ways of achieving the same visual outcome that are a bit more elegant.

I suggest making the width of #contactus a more reasonable width, and then floating #relatedlinks to the right:

```
#contactus {
border: 1px dotted red;
display: inline;
float: left;
width: 350px;
margin: 0;
padding: 0;
}

...

#relatedlinks {
display: inline;
float: right;
width: 280px;
}
```

This also solves the guillotine bug, and is more in line with current coding practices.

We can breathe a sigh of relief. We have the satisfaction of knowing that we prevented yet another coding situation that had the potential to threaten national security and maybe even shift the axis of global political power. However, for the rest of the world, it is just another ordinary day.

Case Closed!

From years of training, Agent Single-Oh-Ten (Andrew) managed to maintain a calm exterior during the whole debugging process, but the faintest hint of moisture on her brow belied her true anxieties over the way IE was rendering her organization's site. Once all of the fixes were in the document, however, her tension dissipated and she was truly satisfied with the outcome.

Staying on the trail of bugs and divining the cause of their errant behavior requires fortitude. However, getting around all of the intrigue and subterfuge that IE 6 and 7 provide is what keeps this job interesting. Well, that plus all the travel to foreign lands and getting entangled with a vast array of characters. CSS detectives and special government agents have much more in common than one would initially think.

As in the previous cases, our process starts with validating to see if we have missed some small yet necessary detail. Once that knowledge is established, we start looking for the problems in the area of the pages located. This time, because the browser differences were dramatic, we could use this fact to help us further zero in on the source—browser-specific bugs—thereby ruling out other possibilities and limiting the number of solutions.

This case also underlines the necessity of taking cross-browser testing seriously. We focused on certain major browsers based on the primary audience of the site. Having an idea of your target users—specifically, which browsers they are using and to what degree they are using them—provides the parameters for your coding, debugging, and QA processes.

Luckily for us, we were already aware of the bugs that presented themselves, but that won't always be the case. Whenever the page behaves strangely, see yourself as duty-bound to research and find the true source of the problem and then dispatch it with laser-like precision rather than flail around haphazardly trying random fixes.

Taking all of these steps into consideration and putting them into action should give you some major bug-fixing confidence. Instead of getting wrapped up in any given browser's sly buggy-ness, use your keen eye to see right through the façade and pinpoint the problems quickly. You will have all the browsers you are coding for dancing to the same tune, so to speak.

Your training is almost complete. You'll put your skills to the final test in Chapter 10, The Case of the LOL Layout.

10

The Case of the LOL Layout

IN THIS CASE, WE'LL SEE HOW YOU CAN USE hasLayout when you need it and effectively prevent your pages from lapsing into IE bug silliness, as well as provide solutions for all browsers that will make everyone smile.

The Crime Scene

Despite a successful career as VP for a small innovative industrial design company, Andrea Christine has decided to combine two of her passions into a single website. While looking for a covered litter box for her cats that was stylish enough to have out in the open in her apartment, she became frustrated by the dearth of classy, well-designed cat accessories available. She realized that not only did few options exist, but no sites congregated them all for other consumers. Additionally, while she loved the content on the popular LOLcats sites, she cringed a little at their cartoonish look and feel.

She feels that the time is right for Oh-Hai.com, a site that combines more intelligent LOLcats with reviews of well-designed cat products for owners hungry for chic quality décor.

Getting the business off the ground is going well. However, while embarking on the development of the site, she finds that the problems she is experiencing with getting her site to look the same in all browsers, and with certain IE hasLayout bugs, are no laughing matter.

INITIAL SNAPSHOTS

Andrea was shooting for classy, but with fun elements sprinkled in for the design. The close rendering of her prototyped design in Firefox, Safari, Google Chrome made her smile (**Figure 10.1**).

It's true that IE8 was missing the cool text effects, rounded corners, and drop shadows, but it still maintained the correct layout, so Andrea gathered up her courage to look at IE7 and IE6.

As to be expected, the site in IE6 (**Figure 10.2**) and IE7 (**Figure 10.3**, on the next page) failed to crack even the smallest grin.

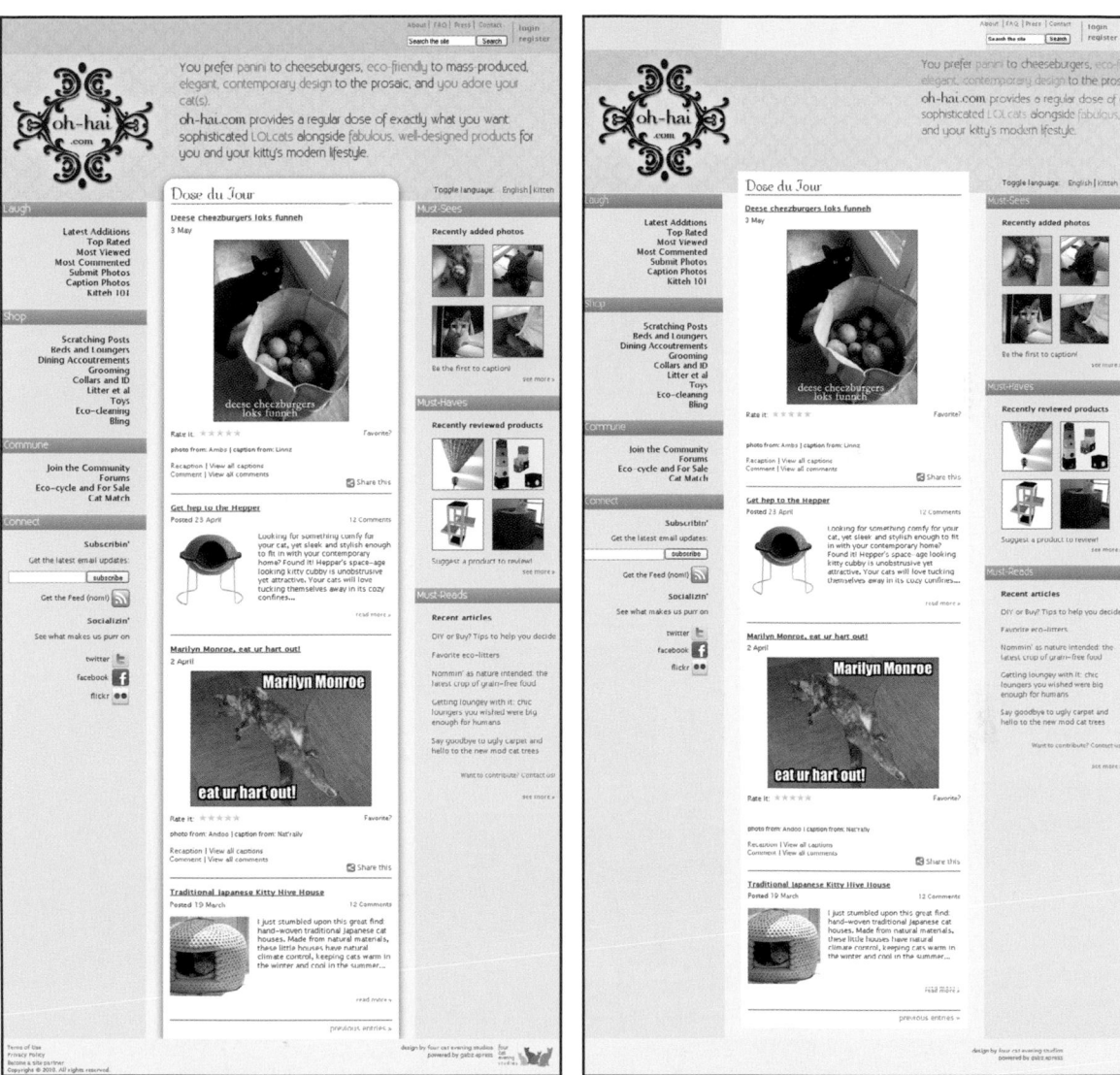

Figure 10.1 *The Oh-Hai.com original design*   **Figure 10.2** *Oh-Hai.com in IE6*

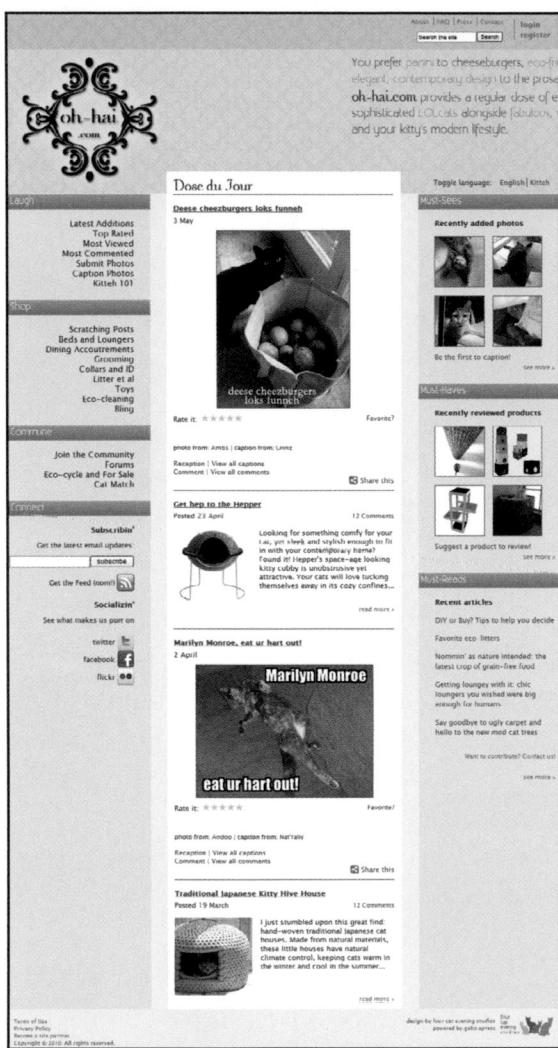

Figure 10.3 *Even in IE7, there wasn't much to laugh about.*

In both browsers, the intro text was out of place, and Andrea was getting strange results in the footer, where the links caused the background to change considerably (**Figure 10.4**).

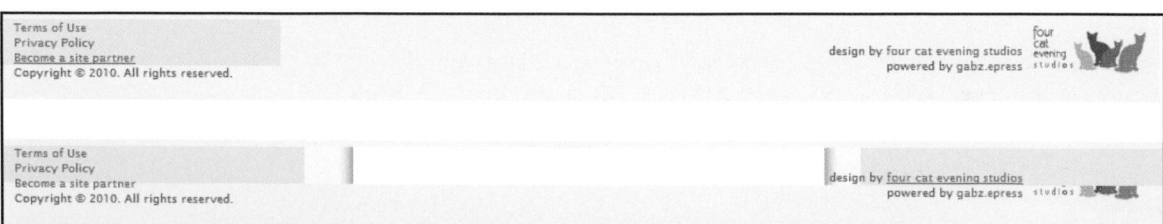

Figure 10.4 *Unstable footer links*

Follow the Evidence

Andrea is building this website as a labor of love. While she has worked for years in the design industry professionally, she is relatively new to web development. She is aware of some of the more common and easily avoided bugs in the older IEs, such as the double margin float bug, so she was surprised that her page would have so much difference in rendering, especially given that she made an effort to code proactively against potential problems.

She also is up to date on the "newer" properties of CSS3 and made an effort to not only incorporate some jazzy display properties, but build in progressive enhancement. Andrea understands that many of these properties are not fully supported by all the modern browsers, knows that the page will not render the same across all browsers, and realizes that she will have to get clever to serve up the same look-and-feel for all of them. She doesn't know exactly where to start with that process, but is eager to learn.

IDENTIFYING SUSPECTS

We'll start with her rendering problems. Because they are almost solely in IE6 and 7 and are involved with some of the larger elements on the screen, I have a hunch that hasLayout may be the source of her chagrin. The disappearing and reappearing of the footer link text are a dead giveaway, as are some of the spacing problems.

As for the getting the same look-and-feel cross-browser, we'll tackle that once we have some of the other fixes in place.

MUG SHOTS

Despite the light-hearted nature of the site, Andrea has employed a XHTML 1.0 strict doctype. Here is her code:

```
<!DOCTYPE html PUBLIC "-//W3C//DTD XHTML 1.0 Strict//EN"
➥ "http://www.w3.org/TR/xhtml1/DTD/xhtml1-strict.dtd">

<html xmlns="http://www.w3.org/1999/xhtml" xml:lang="en" lang="en">
<head>
<meta http-equiv="Content-Type" content="text/html; charset=utf-8" />
<title>Oh-Hai.com: Fur teh Sofiskatd Kitteh (an Hoomanz 2)</title>
<link rel="shortcut icon" type="image/x-icon" href="ohhai.ico" />
<style type="text/css"> ➥
```

```
/* --- font face fonts -- */
@font-face {
font-family: "Existence Light";
src: url(Existence-Light.eot);
src: url(Existence-Light.otf)
format("truetype");
}

@font-face {
font-family: "COM4t Nuvu Regular";
src: url(COM4NRG_.eot);
src: url(COM4NRG_.TTF) format("truetype");
}

/* --- minor css reset --- */
html, body, div, p, h1, h2, h3, h4, h5, h6,
a, img, ul, li, form {
margin: 0;
padding: 0;
border: 0;
font-size: 100%;
}

body {
font: 13px/18px "Lucida Sans Unicode",
"Lucida Grande", Arial,
➥sans-serif;
}

ul {
list-style: none outside;}

/* --- font sizes for elements --- */
.login, .navlinks {font-size: 115%;}
h3 {font-size: 99%;}
.postinfo, .useraction , input {font-size:
95%;}
.commentstars, .bottom {font-size: 90%;}
#mininav, .readmore, .credits {font-size:
85%;}
#footer {font-size: 80%;}
```

```
/* --- general styles --- */
body {
background-color: #eff4fb;
color: #3B3F33;
width: 100%;
}

div, h1, h2, img, a {
behavior: url(iepngfix.htc);}

h2 {
color: #fcfdf6;}

a {
color: #275B9F;
text-decoration: none;}

    .readmore a, .preventries a {
    color: #69824d;}

a:hover {
text-decoration: underline;}

.photonav img, .centeredimg img {
border: 1px solid #575d57;}

.readmore {
clear: both;
text-align: right;
margin-bottom: 20px;
}

    #mostcontent .readmore {
    margin-right: 10px;
    }

.rightalign {
text-align: right;}

.last {
border: 0;}
```

```css
/* --- main section styles ---- */
#mainwrap {
background: url(bg_faux_column_left.gif)
repeat-y 26% 0;
margin: 0 auto;
width: 100%;
overflow: hidden;
}

#secondwrap {
background: url(bg_faux_column_right.gif)
repeat-y 74% 0;
width: 100%;
}

#head {
background: url(bg_ohhai_top.gif) 0 0
repeat-x;
overflow: hidden;
}

  #mininav {
  color: #69824d;
  float: right;
  margin-top: 5px;
  width: 280px;
  }

    .login {
    border-left: 1px solid #69824d;
    float: right;
    font-weight: bold;
    line-height: 1.5em;
    list-style-type: none;
    margin-top: 5px;
    padding-left: 5px;
    width: 80px;
    }

    #mininav ul.login li {
    border: 0;
    display: block;
    }
```

```css
#mininav a {
color: #69824d;}

#mininav ul.infonav {
width: 190px;}

#mininav li, #footer li {
border-right: 1px solid #69824d;
padding: 0 5px;
display: inline;
}

#mininav li.last, #footer li.last {
border: 0;}

#search {
width: 190px;
margin-top: 10px;
}
#siteintro {
margin: 64px auto 1px;
height: 263px;
width: 994px;
overflow: hidden;
}

  h1 {
  float: left;
  margin: 0 0 0 -5px;
  width: 312px;
  }

  h1 a {
  background-image: url(logo_ohhai_glow.png);
  display: block;
  text-indent: -9999px;
  height: 263px;
  }

    h1 a:hover {
    background-image: url
    ➥(logo_ohhai_ceilingcat.png);} ➡
```

```
/* -- english/kitteh toggle styles -- */
#ekwelcome {
position: relative;
top: 235px;
left: 46%;
width: 682px;
}

   #ekwelcome a {
   text-decoration: none;}

.languages {
display: inline;
padding-left: 5px;}

li.first{
border-right: 1px solid #3B3F33;}

.introenglish, .introkitteh {
color: #3B3F33;
font: 1.58em/1.45em "Existence Light",
➡"Century Gothic", sans-serif;
text-shadow: .01em .01em 1px #666;
float: left;
height: 200px;
margin-top: 10px;
width: 97%;
position: absolute;
top: -233px;
left: -143px;
text-decoration: none;
cursor: default;
}

.accent {
color: #5B8F00;}

.nobreak {
white-space: nowrap;}

.ohhai {
font: 1.6em "COM4t Nuvu Regular", serif;
}
```

```
.introkitteh {
font: 1.5em/1.45em "Existence Light",
➡"Century Gothic", sans-serif;
visibility: hidden;
}

a.english:hover .introenglish {
visibility: visible;
}

a.kitteh:hover .introkitteh {
background: url(bg_head.gif) 11% 9%
➡repeat-x;
visibility: visible;
}

#maincontent {}

#maincontent h2 {
background-color: #fcfdf6;
clear: both;
font: 1.35em/1.6em "Existence Light",
➡"Century Gothic", sans-serif;
height: 30px;
text-indent: 5px;
text-shadow: .01em .01em 1px #fff;
}

#primarynav {
display: inline;
float: left;
overflow: hidden;
width: 26%;
}

   #primarynav h2 {
   margin: 0 -1px 15px 0;
   height: 30px;
   }
      .navheaderleft {
      background: url(bg_headers.png)
      ➡100% 0 no-repeat;}
```

```
.navheaderright {
background: url(bg_headers.png) 0
➥100% no-repeat;}

#primarynav ul {
float: right;
text-align: right;
margin: 0 30px 20px 0;
width: 221px;
}

#primarynav a {
color: #27323F;}

    #primarynav a:hover {
    font-weight: bold;
    text-decoration: none;
    }

.navlinks {
display: inline;}
➥/* avoids double margin float bug */

#connect {
margin-right: 30px;}

    #subscribe {
    margin: 10px 0;}

    #connect h3 {
    margin: 15px 0 10px 0;}

    ul#connectlinks {
    margin: 15px 0 0 0;}

    #connectlinks li {
    line-height: 2.4em;}

    #connectlinks a img, #feed a img,
    ➥.rightalign img {
    vertical-align: middle;}

#contentcolumn {
background-color: #fff;
```

```
display: inline;
➥/* avoids double margin float bug */
float: left;
margin: -40px 3% 0 3%;
overflow: hidden;
width: 42%;
-moz-border-radius: 20px 20px 0 0;
-webkit-border-top-left-radius: 20px;
-webkit-border-top-right-radius: 20px;
-moz-box-shadow: 0 5px 20px rgba(0,0,0,0.6);
-webkit-box-shadow: 0 5px 20px
➥rgba(0,0,0,0.6);
box-shadow: 0 5px 20px rgba(0,0,0,0.6);
}

    #content {
    background-color: #fff;
    margin: 1px auto;
    width: 94%;
    }

        #contentcolumn h3 {
        font: 2.5em "COM4t Nuvu Regular",
        ➥serif;
        padding-top: 10px;
        }

        #content h4 {
        margin: 15px 0 5px 0;}

        #content h4 a {
        color: #3B4F18;
        text-decoration: underline;
        }

        #content p {
        line-height: 1.2em;}

        .lolcatentry, .productentry,
        ➥.preventries {
        border-top: 1px solid #3b5b13;
        padding-bottom: 10px;
        overflow: hidden;
        } ➥
```

```css
.postinfo {
margin-bottom: 15px;
line-height: 1em;
overflow: hidden;
}

.postdate {
float: left;}

.commentstars {
float: right;}

.credits {
clear: both;
margin-bottom: 15px;
padding-top: 15px;}

.centeredimg, #search p {
text-align: center;}

.centeredimg {
clear: both;
text-align: center;
margin: 10px 0;
}

.productentry img {
float: left;
margin-right: 15px;
}

.useraction {
line-height: .7em;}

p.preventries   {
padding-top: 5px;
text-align: right;}

/* --- star rating code --- */
.star ul {
float: left;
height: 14px;
width: 75px;
}

.star li {
display: block;
float: left;
height: 14px;
margin-right: -25px;
width: 75px;
}

.star li.curr {
background-image: url('ystar.gif');}

#mostcontent {
background-color: #e1e9e5;
display: inline;
float: right;
overflow: hidden;
width: 26%;
}

#mostcontent h2 {
clear: both;
margin-left: -1px;
}

#mostcontent h3 {
margin: 15px 0 0 30px;}

#mostcontent p {
margin-left: 30px;
clear: both;}

#mostcontent ul {
margin: 0 auto 10px 30px;
float: left;
width: 222px;
}

ul.photonav li {
display: inline;
float: left;
margin: 15px 15px 0 0;
}

ul.photonav li img {
display: block;}
```

```
          ul.articles li {
          margin: 15px 0;}

#footer {
background: #ecf1ee url(logo_fourcatevening_
➥rect.gif) 99% 5px no-repeat;
clear: both;
color: #616F6A;
line-height: 1.3em;
margin-top: -55px;
padding: 8px 120px 5px 0;
position: relative;
text-align: right;
}

   #footer a {
   color: #69824d;}

   #footer ul {
   margin-top: -5px;}

.importantlinks {
float: left;
width: 26%;
text-align: left;
padding-left: 10px;
}

.clearer {
clear: both;
}
</style>
</head>

<body>
<div id="mainwrap">
<div id="secondwrap">
   <div id="head">
      <div id="mininav">
        <ul class="login">
          <li><a href="#">login</a></li>
          <li><a href="#">register</a></li>
        </ul>
```

```
      <ul class="infonav">
        <li><a href="#">About</a></li>
        <li><a href="#">FAQ</a></li>
        <li><a href="#">Press</a></li>
        <li class="last"><a href="#">
        ➥Contact</a></li>
      </ul>
      <form id="search" action="post">
        <p><input type="text" size="20"
        ➥value="Search the site"
        ➥class="textinput" /><input
        ➥type="submit" value="Search"
        ➥class="submit"/></p>
      </form>

</div><!-- end mininav -->

<div id="siteintro">
   <h1><a href="#">Oh-Hai.com</a></h1>

   <div id="ekwelcome">
   <div class="languages">Toggle
   ➥language:
      <ul class="languages">
        <li class="languages first">
          <a href="#" class="english ">
          ➥English
          <span class="introenglish">
          You prefer <span class=
          ➥"accent">panini</span>
          ➥to cheeseburgers, <span
          ➥class="accent">eco-friendly
          ➥</span> to mass-produced,
          ➥<span class="accent">
          ➥elegant, contemporary
          ➥design</span> to the
          ➥prosaic, and <span class=
          ➥"accent">you adore your
          ➥<span class="nobreak">
          ➥cat(s)</span></span>.<br />
                                     ➥
```

```
<span class="ohhai">oh-hai.com
➥</span> provides a regular
➥dose of exactly what you
➥want: sophisticated <span
➥class="accent">LOLcats
➥</span> alongside <span
➥class="accent">fabulous,
➥well-designed products
➥</span> for you and your
➥kitty's modern lifestyle.
</span>
</a>
</li>
<li class="languages">
  <a href="#" class="kitteh">
  ➥Kitteh
  <span class="introkitteh">
  U liek nommin on <span class=
  ➥"accent">fancee sammiches
  ➥</span> nstead of cheezburgers
  ➥(kitteh dont undrstnd dat,
  ➥srsly), u also liek <span
  ➥class="accent">thanz frum
  ➥natur</span> not maed in
  ➥factries (kitteh agree),
  ➥<span class="accent">purty
  ➥thanz in teh hauze</span>
  ➥(all teh same 2 kitteh), an
  ➥<span class="accent">u luv
  ➥kittehz</span> (of
  cuors)!<br />
  wif <span class="ohhai">
  ➥oh-hai.com</span> site
  ➥hoomanz can haz funnys an
  ➥purties evrydy: <span
  ➥class="accent">sofiskatd
  ➥LOLcats</span> (wahtz dat?)
  ➥an <span class="accent">niec
  ➥made thanz</span> fur
  ➥stylesh kittehz an hoomanz
  ➥2. kthxbai!
```

```
          </span>
        </a>
      </li>
    </ul>
  </div>
</div><!-- end ekwelcome -->
</div><!-- end siteintro -->

</div><!-- end head -->

<div id="maincontent">
  <div id="primarynav">
    <h2 class="navheaderleft">Laugh</h2>
    <ul class="navlinks">
      <li><a href="#">Latest Additions
      ➥</a></li>
      <li><a href="#">Top Rated</a></li>
      <li><a href="#">Most Viewed</a>
      ➥</li>
      <li><a href="#">Most Commented</a>
      ➥</li>
      <li><a href="#">Submit Photos</a>
      ➥</li>
      <li><a href="#">Caption Photos</a>
      ➥</li>
      <li><a href="#">Kitteh 101</a>
      ➥</li>
    </ul>
    <!-- end laugh section -->

    <h2 class="navheaderleft">Shop</h2>
    <ul class="navlinks">
      <li><a href="#">Scratching Posts
      ➥</a></li>
      <li><a href="#">Beds and Loungers
      ➥</a></li>
      <li><a href="#">Dining
      ➥Accoutrements</a></li>
      <li><a href="#">Grooming</a></li>
      <li><a href="#">Collars and ID
      ➥</a></li>
```

```
<li><a href="#">Litter et al</a>
➥</li>
<li><a href="#">Toys</a></li>
<li><a href="#">Eco-cleaning</a>
➥</li>
<li><a href="#">Bling</a></li>
</ul>
<!-- end shop section -->

<h2 class="navheaderleft">Commune
➥</h2>
<ul class="navlinks">
    <li><a href="#">Join the Community
    ➥</a></li>
    <li><a href="#">Forums</a></li>
    <li><a href="#">Eco-cycle and For
    ➥Sale</a></li>
    <li><a href="#">Cat Match</a></li>
</ul>
<!-- end commune section -->

<h2 class="navheaderleft">Connect
➥</h2>
    <div id="connect" class="rightalign">
        <h3>Subscribin'</h3>
        <p>Get the latest email updates:
        ➥</p>
        <form id="subscribe" action=
        ➥"post">
          <p><input type="text" size="23"
          ➥class="textinput" />
          ➥<input type="submit"
          ➥value="subscribe"
          ➥class="subscribe"/></p>
        </form>

        <p id="feed"><a href="#">Get
        ➥the Feed (nom!) <img src="rss_
        ➥green.png" alt="RSS" /></a></p>
```

```
        <h3>Socializin'</h3>
        <p>See what makes us purr on</p>
        <ul id="connectlinks">
            <li><a href="#">twitter
            ➥<img src="twitter_32.png"
            ➥alt="" /></a></li>
            <li><a href="#">facebook
            ➥<img src="facebook_32.png"
            ➥alt="" /></a></li>
            <li><a href="#">flickr
            ➥<img src="flickr_32.png"
            ➥alt="" /></a></li>
        </ul>
    </div><!-- end connect section -->

</div><!-- end primarynav -->

<div id="contentcolumn">
    <div id="content">
    <h3>Dose du Jour</h3>

    <div class="lolcatentry">
        <h4><a href="#">Deese cheezburgers
        ➥loks funneh</a></h4>
        <p>3 May</p>

        <p class="centeredimg"><img src=
        ➥"lol_mangocheezburgers.jpg"
        ➥alt="Deese cheezburgers loks
        ➥funneh" /></p>

        <div>
            <ul class="star" title="Rate
            ➥this photo!">
                <li>Rate it:</li>
                <li id="starcur"
                ➥class="curr"></li>
            </ul>
            <p class="commentstars">
            ➥<a href="#">Favorite?</a></p>
        </div> ➡
```

```
<p class="credits">photo from:
<a href="#">Ambs</a> | caption
from: <a href="#">Linnz</a></p>
<div class="useraction">
    <p><a href="#">Recaption</a> |
    <a href="#">View all captions
    </a></p>
    <p><a href="#">Comment</a> |
    <a href="#">View all comments
    </a></p>
</div>

<p class="rightalign">
<a href="#"><img src="sharethis.png"
alt="" /> Share this</a>
</p>
</div>

<div class="productentry">
    <h4><a href="#">Get hep to the
    Hepper</a></h4>
    <p class="postinfo"><span class=
    "postdate">Posted <a href="#">
    23 April</a></span><span class=
    "commentstars"><a href="#">
    12 Comments</a></span></p>
    <p class="clearer"><a href="#">
    <img src="prod_hepper.jpg"
    alt="Hepper cat house" /></a>
    Looking for something comfy for
    your cat, yet sleek and stylish
    enough to fit in with your
    contemporary home? Found it!
    Hepper's space-age looking kitty
    cubby is unobstrusive yet
    attractive. Your cats will love
    tucking themselves away in its
    cozy confines...</p>
    <p class="readmore"><a href="#">
    read more &raquo;</a></p>
</div>
```

```
<div class="lolcatentry">
    <h4><a href="#">Marilyn Monroe,
    eat ur hart out!</a></h4>
    <p>2 April</p>

    <p class="centeredimg"><img src=
    "lol_marilyn.jpg" alt="Marilyn
    Monroe, eat ur hart out!" /></p>

    <div>
        <ul class="star" title="Rate
        this photo!">
            <li>Rate it:</li>
            <li id="starCur" class=
            "curr"></li>
        </ul>
        <p class="commentstars"><a
        href="#">Favorite?</a></p>
    </div>

    <p class="credits">photo from:
    <a href="#">Andoo</a> | caption
    from: <a href="#">Nat'rally</a>
    </p>
    <div class="useraction">
        <p><a href="#">Recaption</a> |
        <a href="#">View all captions
        </a></p>
        <p><a href="#">Comment</a> |
        <a href="#">View all comments
        </a></p>
    </div>

    <p class="rightalign">
    <a href="#"><img src="sharethis.png"
    alt="" /> Share this</a>
    </p>

</div>

<div class="productentry">
    <h4><a href="#">Traditional
    Japanese Kitty Hive House</a></h4>
```

```
        <p class="postinfo"><span class=
    ➥"postdate">Posted <a href="#">
    ➥19 March</a></span><span class=
    ➥"commentstars"><a href="#">
    ➥12 Comments</a></span></p>
        <p class="clearer"><a href="#">
    ➥<img src="prod_japanese.jpg"
    ➥alt="Traditional Japanese Kitty
    ➥Hive House" /></a> I just
    ➥stumbled upon this great find:
    ➥hand-woven traditional Japanese
    ➥cat houses. Made from natural
    ➥materials, these little houses
    ➥have natural climate control,
    ➥keeping cats warm in the winter
    ➥and cool in the summer...</p>
        <p class="readmore"><a href="#">
    ➥read more &raquo;</a></p>
    </div>

    <p class="preventries"><a href="#">
    ➥previous entries &raquo;</a></p>
    </div><!-- end content -->
</div><!-- end contentcolumn -->

<div id="mostcontent">
    <h2 class="navheaderright">Must-Sees
    ➥</h2>
    <h3>Recently added photos</h3>
    <ul class="photonav">
        <li><a href="#"><img src=
        ➥"th_whee.jpg" alt="sleeping
        ➥kitty-Aashika" /></a></li>
        <li><a href="#"><img src=
        ➥"th_gheri.jpg" alt="lounging
        ➥kitty-Gheri" /></a></li>
        <li><a href="#"><img src=
        ➥"th_daisy.jpg" alt="alert kitty-
        ➥Day-Z" /></a></li>
        <li><a href="#"><img src=
        ➥"th_sheets.jpg" alt="hiding
        ➥kitty-Zealand" /></a></li>
    </ul>
    <p><a href="#">Be the first to
    ➥caption!</a></p>
    <p class="readmore"><a href="#">
    ➥see more &raquo;</a></p>
    <!-- end mustsee section -->

    <h2 class="navheaderright">Must-
    ➥Haves</h2>
    <h3>Recently reviewed products</h3>
    <ul class="photonav">
        <li><a href="#"><img src=
        ➥"th_tree.jpg" alt="eco cat
        ➥climbing tree" /></a></li>
        <li><a href="#"><img src=
        ➥"th_cubes.jpg" alt="stylish
        ➥cat cubes" /></a></li>
        <li><a href="#"><img src=
        ➥"th_climber.jpg" alt="bamboo
        ➥cat climber" /></a></li>
        <li><a href="#"><img src=
        ➥"th_modkat.jpg" alt="modkat
        ➥litter box" /></a></li>
    </ul>
    <p><a href="#">Suggest a product to
    ➥review!</a></p>
    <p class="readmore"><a href="#">
    ➥see more &raquo;</a></p>
    <!-- end musthave section -->

    <h2 class="navheaderright">Must-
    ➥Reads</h2>
    <h3>Recent articles</h3>
    <ul class="articles">
        <li><a href="#">DIY or Buy? Tips
        ➥to help you decide</a></li>
        <li><a href="#">Favorite
        ➥eco-litters</a></li>
        <li><a href="#">Nommin' as nature
        ➥intended: the latest crop of
        ➥grain-free food</a></li> ➥
```

```
            <li><a href="#">Getting loungey with it: chic loungers you
            ➡wished were big enough for humans</a></li>
            <li><a href="#">Say goodbye to ugly carpet and hello to
            ➡the new mod cat trees</a></li>
        </ul>
        <p class="readmore"><a href="#">Want to contribute? Contact us!
        ➡</a></p>
        <p class="readmore"><a href="#">see more &raquo;</a></p>
        <!-- end musthave section -->

    </div><!-- end mostcontent -->
  </div><!-- end maincontent -->

  <div id="footer">
    <p class="importantlinks">
    <a href="#">Terms of Use</a><br />
    <a href="#">Privacy Policy</a><br />
    <a href="#">Become a site partner</a><br />
    Copyright &copy; 2010. All rights reserved.<br />
    </p>

    <p>design by <a href="#">four cat evening studios</a><br />
    powered by <a href="#">gabz.epress</a></p>
    <div class="clearer"></div> <!--deleting this is is part of
    ➡the fix too -->
  </div><!-- end footer -->
</div><!-- end secondwrap -->
</div><!-- end mainwrap -->
</body>
</html>
```

The Evidence Never Lies

We'll start by making certain there are no problems in the markup and CSS code. Validation of the HTML yields no errors. However, the CSS validator produces several errors (**Figure 10.5**).

```
Sorry! We found the following errors (7)
URI : TextArea
45    div, h1, h2, img, a  Property behavior doesn't exist :
      ➥url(iepngfix.htc)
291   #contentcolumn  Property -moz-border-radius doesn't exist :
      ➥20px 20px 0 0
292   #contentcolumn  Property -webkit-border-top-left-radius doesn't
      ➥exist : 20px
293   #contentcolumn  Property -webkit-border-top-right-radius doesn't
      ➥exist : 20px
294   #contentcolumn  Property -moz-box-shadow doesn't exist :
      ➥0 5px 20px rgba(0,0,0,0.6)
295   #contentcolumn  Property -webkit-box-shadow doesn't exist : 0
      5px 20px rgba(0,0,0,0.6)
296   #contentcolumn  0 is not a box-shadow value : 0 5px 20px
      rgba(0,0,0,0.6)
```

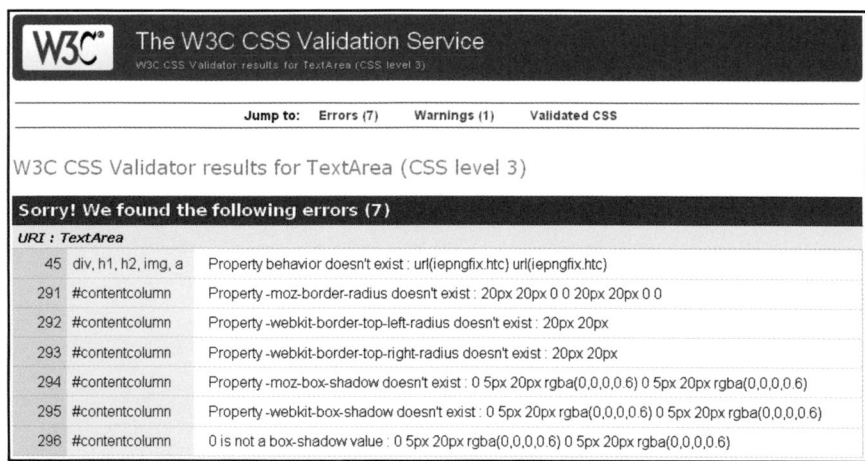

Figure 10.5 *CSS3 validation: the newer properties don't validate (yet)*

This is one situation where having code that doesn't validate is entirely legitimate. Parts of Andrea's design relies upon transparent .png image files (PNG-24), which aren't supported by IE6 without the help of workaround scripts or proprietary filters. Andrea used a popular script that helps the images render correctly but the script requires the use of IE proprietary properties which are not part of the CSS specs and therefore are not valid in any browser but IE.

Additionally, to be able to employ the cool CSS3 effects that she wanted, she had to use Mozilla- and Webkit- (Safari and Google Chrome) specific properties, as well as a property that is still in draft form, but is slated to be approved in the not-so-distant future. To future-proof the styles, she included the anticipated CSS3 specification syntax.

These validation errors, therefore, are to be expected and can be ignored.

CONFIRMING SUSPICIONS AND NAMING THE CULPRIT

Now that I have had a look at the code, I am eager to see the hasLayout status of the page elements that are out of place. hasLayout may have a funny name, but instead of bringing amusement, the problems that stem from an element either having or not having layout can bring a front-end developer close to tears. If you remember, hasLayout is a quality in both IE6 and IE7 that elements have either intrinsically based on what element they are, or when certain properties are applied to them. Layout can be removed by later properties once it is applied if necessary, but if it is intrinsic to the element it can't ever be removed.

While the problems in IE6 are not as important because of its low usage by the demographic of her audience, IE7 is still widely used, and therefore Andrea is taking the issues in that browser particularly seriously.

Let's see what is going on with Andrea's misplaced and strangely behaving page sections, shall we?

At the very top of the page in IE6, there is a mysterious gap (**Figure 10.6**).

Figure 10.6 *In IE6, ceiling gap says "Oh, hi—I'm at the top of your page, messing up your layout."*

Now, while IE6 is not of major importance to Andrea, this is a big enough issue to warrant fixing. The CSS for the head of the page is this:

```
#head {
background: url(bg_ohhai_top.gif) top left repeat-x;
overflow: hidden;
}
```

Do you notice anything about this code? Since there are only two lines, I think the telling thing about this code is what is missing, and that is this: a property that will give the #head element layout.

I think the most effective way to activate hasLayout would be to make the height explicit. If you'll harken back to your earlier training, height is on the list of properties that give layout. So let's add this:

```
#head {
background: url(bg_ohhai_top.gif) top left repeat-x;
height: 328px;
overflow: hidden;
}
```

To Andrea's delight, the explicit height works as hoped, and keeps the top navigation from pushing the #head div down (**Figure 10.7**).

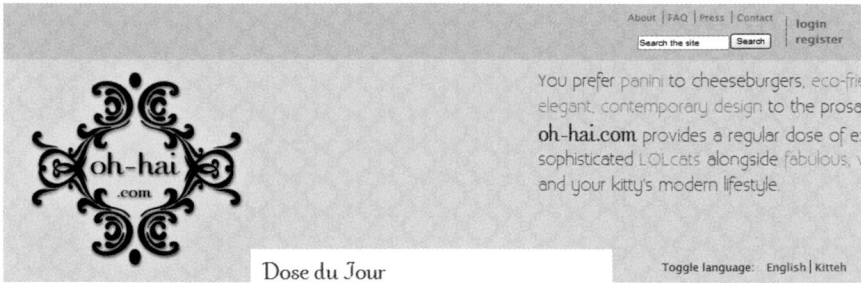

Figure 10.7 *Ceiling gap has left the building, but the intro text is pushed right off the page—in both English and Kitteh*

Now, on to the rest of the page.

The most troubling problem for both the early IEs is the misplaced introductory text. What seems to be happening is that the text in the other browsers is acting like it has a property of float: left, but the IEs are not on board with that. Any time an element acts out of character compared to other browsers in IE7 and IE6, you can pretty much bet your kitty toys that it is due to hasLayout. Indeed, I recall (from the very detailed treatise on hasLayout at http://www.satzansatz.de/cssd/onhavinglayout.html) that if an element with layout is next to a floated element, then essentially the element is displaced, as if the element with layout were a float itself. Well, that sounds like a viable explanation, especially when I test the theory by adding float: left; to the code on the next page, which moves the element in all of the other browsers to the same place it is in the IEs:

```
#ekwelcome {
float: left;
position: relative;
top: 235px;
left: 46%;
width: 682px;
}
```

This helps me formulate a plan: instead of getting IE to conform, I decide to make the other browsers play along instead. I add this extra bit of code to change the value from -143px to -450px here:

```
.introenglish, .introkitteh {
color: #3B3F33;
font: 1.58em/1.45em "Existence Light","Century Gothic", sans-serif;
text-shadow: .01em .01em 1px #666;
float: left;
height: 200px;
margin: 10px 0 0 0;
width: 97%;
position: absolute;
top: -233px;
left: -450px;
text-decoration: none;
cursor: default;
}
```

And voila! Now all of the browsers have the introductory text in the correct place (**Figure 10.8**)!

Figure 10.8 *Now the welcome message is fully accessible*

Andrea shows me another puzzler: when changing the width of the page in the IEs, the right column flickers from float drop and then mysteriously goes back into place. Weird!

As you know, float drop is usually caused by a float being too wide to fit into the given space on the page, and therefore the float drops below the adjacent element to the next available space. The double margin float bug is usually the culprit behind float drop, and is easily fixed by adding display: inline to the declaration. However, display: inline is already there! I imagine that you, like myself, were expecting that to be the answer, but it isn't.

Furthermore, there are two properties that give the element layout: float and width. I have to conclude that the issues with this element may actually be due to having layout rather than lacking it, but we do need both the float and width properties and values, so getting rid of them is not the solution.

I suggest to Andrea that we slightly alter the size of the middle column for the IEs, and deliver this new value through conditional statements. The other browsers will ignore the conditional statements and render the CSS that they can see.

We try a small adjustment, nothing major, and change the width of the center column from 42% to 41.9%:

```
#contentcolumn {
width: 41.9%;}
```

With this change, the columns seem much better behaved, and no longer drop at the slightest provocation.

Finally, we get to the footer of the page, where all sorts of interesting things are happening (**Figure 10.9**).

Can you guess what is causing the mysterious comings and goings of the elements in the footer? That's right, it is none other than the infamous peekaboo bug in all of its splendor and glory. Unlike the famed LOL ceiling cat peeking down at you, there is little cute about this bug.

The peekaboo bug is caused by an element not having layout, so the fix is straightforward. I suggest giving the footer a height, which it lacked:

```
#footer {
background: #ecf1ee url(logo_fourcatevening_rect.gif) 99% 5px no-repeat;
clear: both;
color: #616F6A;
height: 55px;
line-height: 1.3em;
padding: 8px 120px 5px 0;
position: relative;
text-align: right;
}
```

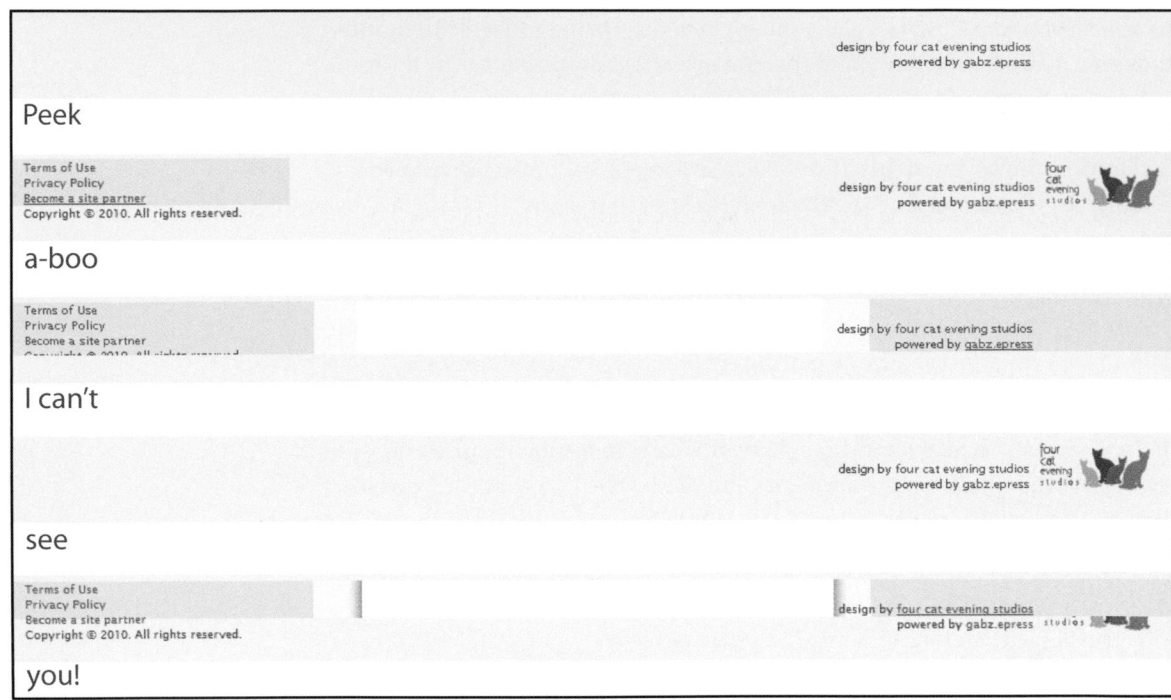

Figure 10.9 *Variations on a buggy theme*

With the addition that small line of code, the footer is stable and the page looks as it should in both IEs (**Figure 10.10**).

Figure 10.10 *Bugless in the footer*

With everything fixed and showing up correctly in all browsers, it seemed like an opportune moment to let Andrea know that she could have avoided this bug completely by coding this section of the page differently.

Here is her original code:

```
<div id="footer">
    <p class="importantlinks">
    <a href="#">Terms of Use</a><br />
    <a href="#">Privacy Policy</a><br />
    <a href="#">Become a site partner</a><br />
    Copyright &copy; 2010. All rights reserved.<br />
    </p>
```

```
<p>design by <a href="#">four cat evening studios</a><br />
powered by <a href="#">gabz.epress</a></p>

<div class="clearer"></div>
</div><!-- end footer -->
```

In terms of good page semantics, she could do a bit better by making the
.importantlinks paragraph an unordered list:

```
<div id="footer">
<ul class="importantlinks">
  <li><a href="#">Terms of Use</a></li>
  <li><a href="#">Privacy Policy</a></li>
  <li><a href="#">Become a site partner</a></li>
</ul>
<p>Copyright &copy; 2010. All rights reserved.</p>

<p>design by <a href="#">four cat evening studios</a><br />
  powered by <a href="#">gabz.epress</a></p>
<!-- delete <div class="clearer"></div> -->
</div><!-- end footer -->
```

This code makes a lot more sense from a page semantics standpoint, and she
still would be able to control the placement on the page and styling easily. Also,
ironically, having the links as list items in a <ul>, prevents the peekaboo bug entirely.

Andrea thanked me for my suggestion and assured me that she would think
about making that change before launching the site.

We're making great progress, and Andrea is truly pleased that we have
squashed all of the major bugs. Now we have to make sure the rounded
corners and drop-shadow of the center column looks the same in as many
browsers as possible.

Currently, Firefox, Safari, and Google Chrome render the CSS3 text drop
shadows, rounded corners and drop-shadow on the center column, and
@font-face correctly. Opera renders the text effects just fine, but falls short
on the center column rounded corners and drop shadows. Andrea doesn't
expect that much of her audience will use Opera, so is fine with letting that
one go for now.

However, IE7 and IE8 are a different story. She feels it is important that these
users see the site the way she intended it. Since we are serving the IEs some
specific code already, we decide to make separate CSS files for them and use
conditional comments to give each version their own tailor-made CSS.

We create two background images for the center column in order to employ
a technique that uses one image for the left, and a repeating image for the
right. Once we get those two in place, we need to make some small adjustments to the margins and widths of the center column and some of its children to make it show up correctly:

```
#contentcolumn {
background: url(bg_content_left.png) top left no-repeat;
display: inline;
margin: -40px 3% 0 3%;
padding: 0;
width: 41.9%;
}

#content {
background: url(bg_content_right.png) top right no-repeat;
margin: 1px auto 0 26px;
padding: 0 0 50px 0;
}

.lolcatentry, .productentry, .preventries {
width: 94%;}
```

As for IE6, while we know the browser is gasping its final breaths, some of
Andrea's audience could still be using it. Chic cat decor is not just for the tech-
nologically savvy. While the scripts that handle PNG-24 support for IE can be
a great workaround for single images, they are not infallible, and there is still
a problem with rendering PNGs as repeating background images. Therefore,
instead of using the same PNG background images with a drop shadow that
we were able to use in IE7 and IE8, we will simply use plain old .gifs without
a drop shadow, which won't have a problem with repeating.

Here is the code we will serve to IE6:

```
div, h1, h2, img, a {
behavior: url(iepngfix.htc);}

#contentcolumn {
background-image: url(bg_content_left_nds.gif);
margin: -40px 3% 0 3%;
width: 41.9%;}
```

```
#content [
background: transparent url(bg_content_right_nds.gif) top right no-
repeat;
margin: 0 -5px 0 17px;
padding: 0 0 0 8px;
}
```

The last requirement is to add the conditional comments in the regular page. I advise her to put the code after the page CSS, so that it won't be overridden by the styles meant for modern browsers:

```
<!--[if lte IE6]>
<link rel="stylesheet" type="text/css" href="ohhai_ie6.css" />
<![endif]-->
<!--[if gte IE6]>
<link rel="stylesheet" type="text/css" href="ohhai_ie78.css" />
<![endif]-->
```

With these final changes in place and the site looking really good in all of the browsers, Andrea finally lets out a huge smile and laugh, and even shows me the mini Easter egg she put in the site just for kicks (**Figure 10.11**).

Figure 10.11 *A little surprise in the logo*

Case Closed!

With the final changes completed, Andrea is thrilled. Now she has the beginnings of a web presence and the site may give her the opportunity to implement, produce and market some of her own well-designed product ideas.

We saw how hasLayout issues can cause pretty dramatic problems with the rendering of elements on the page, but also how some of the fixes are as simple as making height explicit. There are several in-depth articles about hasLayout on the web, so it is a good idea to familiarize yourself with its ins and outs. Although IE6 is on its way out, it's not quite dead yet, and is still being used enough to warrant being cordial to it. But even when IE6 is completely defunct, its more refined sibling IE7 still harbors vestigial bugs that will render parts of a page incorrectly.

It is seductive to think that you can code proactively against IE bugs—but you may end up getting them anyway. Just as Andrea consciously coded against the double margin float bug and employed properties that gave layout in most of the major section containers on the page, she was not immune to other bugs that she did not foresee.

If you want to start incorporating the increasingly popular CSS3 properties, know in advance that getting your pages to render similarly cross-browser may be a challenge. While it is admirable to want your pages to look exactly the same in all, that aspiration needs to be balanced with a willingness to be flexible and potentially have alternatives for less-compliant browsers. Also, by knowing the limitations beforehand, you may be able to proactively design for such possibilities.

Finally, it is important to note that some issues will require unconventional solutions or those in which you may have to rework the structure of your markup to be able to achieve your page layout. Employing good, semantic markup will sometimes be the key to never coming up against old browser bugs! By coding proactively against IE6 and IE7 bugs and by keeping web standards in mind, you will most likely avoid many IE bug headaches.

Fantastic work! And congratulations are in order. You have faithfully stuck to your training and have assisted me in solving several cases with tough CSS mysteries. I am proud to say that you have passed your trial with flying colors, and thus fully earned your new title of CSS Detective! Now you can fearlessly go forth and more easily find the culprits behind your own CSS conundrums, and maybe even those of other people.

Good luck to you, and remember—let's be careful out there.

Appendix

Resources

See? I've kept my word to you. Here is a compilation of resources—more in-depth information than could be covered in the main part of this book—that will provide food for thought and advanced techniques. Enjoy!

CHAPTER 1: INVESTIGATING THE SCENE OF THE CRIME

Having a shallow foundation in web design and development is acceptable, but possessing a deeper knowledge of the languages, properties, and browser support thereof can really help you understand the source of problems down the line, and may even help to prevent them.

Differences between HTML & XHTML

If you want to delve further into the differences between HTML and XHTML, these pages will lend great history, comparisons, and opinions on which one to use.

HTML & XHTML frequently answered questions

http://www.w3.org/MarkUp/2004/xhtml-faq

Nice overview of the differences between HTML and XHTML from the W3C itself. If you can't trust this source, I'm not sure who you can trust.

Frequently asked questions about XHTML vs. HTML

http://www.sitepoint.com/forums/showthread.php?t=393445

Another great resource comparing the markup languages that also gives a bit of clarification about which is better.

HTML

http://en.wikipedia.org/wiki/HTML

A great overview on Wikipedia, with important history behind the versions of HTML and XHTML, plus a nice breakdown of the differences between transitional and strict doctypes.

XHTML

http://en.wikipedia.org/wiki/XHTML

Good explanation on Wikipedia of why XHTML was developed, as well as some criticisms about it.

Properties inherited by default

Simply knowing that some style properties are automatically inherited isn't enough; you should also know *which* ones are inherited so you won't create unnecessary declarations.

Cascading order & inheritance in CSS

http://monc.se/kitchen/38/cascading-order-and-inheritance-in-css

Nice article explaining order and inheritance, plus a comprehensive list of all of the CSS properties inherited by default.

CSS cheat sheet: inheritance, cascade, specificity

http://www.communitymx.com/content/article.cfm?cid=2795D

Another article that lists the properties. Not as thorough as the article above, but still provides valuable content on the cascade and specificity.

CSS selector browser support

Browser-support charts are critical to have at your fingertips when creating your code, especially when trying to achieve cross-browser compatibility or targeting specific browsers.

CSS browser support

http://www.evotech.net/blog/2009/02/css-browser-support

A concise, up-to-date chart that gives you the information you need about which selectors are supported by the popular browsers.

CSS selectors: basic browser support

http://dev.l-c-n.com/CSS3-selectors/browser-support.php

Similar to the chart on Evotech.net, but also adds the CSS version number of the selector and lists CSS3 selectors.

CSS contents & browser compatibility

http://www.quirksmode.org/css/contents.html

Provides some additional information such as support of multiple selectors.

Web browser CSS support

http://www.webdevout.net/browser-support-css

Another good chart on the browser support for CSS properties and selectors.

Comparison of layout engines (Cascading Style Sheets)

http://en.wikipedia.org/wiki/Comparison_of_layout_engines_(CSS)

Great Wikipedia article for geeking out on information about CSS support for the engines driving the browsers rather than the browsers themselves. Gives a better idea of which browsers are related to each other based on their code engine.

CSS differences in Internet Explorer 6, 7, & 8

http://www.smashingmagazine.com/2009/10/14/css-differences-in-internet-
➥explorer-6-7-and-8/

Good summary of the differences in CSS support between the major versions of Microsoft Internet Explorer.

CHAPTER 2: TOOLS OF THE TRADE

How can you get better at figuring out CSS problems or stopping them before they start? You should know what the default styles are for the browsers, and you need a good reference that lists all of the CSS properties and values for common elements, as well as the whys and wherefores of CSS resets.

User agents' style sheets

The user agents' default style sheets are a key aspect in the CSS cascade. Being aware of the differences between them is not only illuminating, but also provides a good foundation for troubleshooting. These articles show the importance of making some values explicit in your styles as well as the argument for a CSS reset.

CSS2.1 User-agent style sheet defaults

http://css-class.com/test/css/defaults/UA-style-sheet-defaults.htm

A superb resource for familiarizing yourself with the default style values for the various browsers. A compelling and informative read as well.

User-agent style sheets: basics & samples

http://meiert.com/en/blog/20070922/user-agent-style-sheets/

A fantastic compiled list of links to the actual CSS files of the popular browsers.

CSS properties & values charts

You don't need to memorize all of the CSS properties, but you do need a reliable source to check if you are unsure of a property's structure or values.

Full property table (CSS2)

http://www.w3.org/TR/CSS21/propidx.html

The full list of CSS2 properties from the W3C.

CSS reference

http://www.w3schools.com/css/css_reference.asp

A site where you can look up a CSS property and get the information you need about its terms of use, values, and examples.

CSS properties index

http://meiert.com/en/indices/css-properties/

Another great listing of CSS properties, boasting CSS3 properties as well as the default value for all properties listed.

90 CSS properties, values, & browser support

http://www.evotech.net/blog/2009/05/css-properties-values-and-
➥ browser-support/

Another useful chart from Evotech.com; lists the CSS properties and their browser support.

Introduction to CSS3

http://www.w3.org/TR/2001/WD-css3-roadmap-20010523/

An introduction to the new properties coming in CSS3.

CSS reset

Whether or not to use a CSS reset is purely a matter of choice, and there are pros and cons to all approaches. Here are some great resources for the most popular CSS resets.

A killer collection of global CSS reset styles

http://perishablepress.com/press/2007/10/23/a-killer-collection-of-global-
➥ css-reset-styles/

Fantastic compilation of just about every CSS reset available, with reviews of the pros and cons of each. Includes Eric Meyer's very popular CSS reset.

CSS frameworks & CSS reset: design from scratch

http://www.smashingmagazine.com/2007/09/21/css-frameworks-css-reset-
➡ design-from-scratch/

Many of the CSS resets listed in the PerishablePress.com article (above) are in this listing from Smashingmagazine.com. The information on CSS frameworks is useful for familiarizing yourself with the concepts.

Yahoo's YUI

http://developer.yahoo.com/yui/

Along with Eric Meyer's reset, YUI is one of the most popular CSS resets out there. There is YUI 2 and YUI 3—you can get to either from this index page.

Creating your own CSS reset

I have always had a strong leaning toward DIY. If you choose to use a CSS reset, it may be worth it to make one that perfectly fits your needs rather than tweaking a premade one.

To CSS reset or not to CSS reset

http://www.peachpit.com/blogs/blog.aspx?uk=To-CSS-Reset-or-Not-to-
➡ CSS-Reset

Gives the pros and cons of CSS resets, the thinking you need to create one of your own, and further explanations of the popular resets.

Weekend quick tip: create your own simple Reset.css file

http://net.tutsplus.com/tutorials/html-css-techniques/weekend-quick-tip-
➡ create-your-own-resetcss-file/

This is another great tutorial on creating a CSS reset that fits your needs and coding style.

Is your CSS reset doing more harm than good?

http://www.fivefingercoding.com/xhtml-and-css/create-custom-css-reset

Nice overview of how to create your own unique CSS reset customized for the needs of each project.

CHAPTER 3: GIVING THE THIRD DEGREE

Part of giving the third degree is knowing what makes your subjects tick. Knowing what to do when a browser switches into a different mode will help you do just that.

Doctypes & browser modes

Doctype switching is important to consider when troubleshooting. These articles outline which browser mode each doctype triggers. They also provide background about how doctype switching came about.

Activating browser modes with doctype

http://hsivonen.iki.fi/doctype/

Outlines the modes, what triggers them, and their effects. An up-to-date chart with the doctypes and browser engines is presented at the end of the article.

Quirks mode & strict mode

http://www.quirksmode.org/css/quirksmode.html

Very good overview of the background behind browser modes, and a chart of the differences in properties between the various modes.

Mozilla's doctype sniffing

https://developer.mozilla.org/en/Mozilla%27s_DOCTYPE_sniffing

Doctype modes in Mozilla.

CSS enhancements in Internet Explorer 6

http://msdn.microsoft.com/en-us/library/bb250395%28VS.85%29.aspx# ➡ cssenhancements_topic2

Doctype modes in IE and their effects on page elements.

The Opera 9 doctype switches

http://www.opera.com/docs/specs/doctype/

Doctype modes in Opera and comparisons with other browsers.

Validators

If you have a hunch about your code, you must get validation. Here are the industry-standard validators.

Markup validation service

http://validator.w3.org/

The markup validator, provided by the W3C.

CSS validation service

http://jigsaw.w3.org/css-validator/

The CSS validator, provided by the W3C.

HTML & CSS validator Firefox extensions

https://addons.mozilla.org/en-US/firefox/

Do a search on the Mozilla Firefox extension site to install the validators of your choice right into Firefox. It'll save you the trouble of going to the W3C site.

Accessibility checkers

While accessibility isn't covered as a topic in the book, keeping it in mind is extremely important and will help you design and develop more effective websites.

WAVE: Web accessibility evaluation tool

http://wave.webaim.org/

The WAVE provides visual feedback by showing the semantics of the page and the content of the link and image files (alt text, and so on). This will help you remember to put meaningful information in your tags for all users.

Color blindness simulator

http://www.vischeck.com/vischeck/vischeckURL.php

I love tools that simulate color blindness, because it keeps designers on their toes when creating color schemes for sites. Contrast and readability are key for usability and accessibility, so checking with this simulator can be extremely useful.

CHAPTER 4: THE USUAL SUSPECTS

Conditional comments and the `display` property are two methods you can use to deal with the cast of buggy characters.

CSS conditional comments

Conditional comments and their syntax, values, hacks, and the style sheets you should serve with them—it's all here.

About conditional comments

http://msdn.microsoft.com/en-us/library/ms537512%28VS.85%29.aspx

Microsoft Developer Network's full explanation of conditional comments, their syntax and values, and how to construct them.

How to create an IE-only style sheet

http://css-tricks.com/how-to-create-an-ie-only-stylesheet/

Ready-made conditional comments (and CSS hacks) for all versions of IE.

Hack-free CSS for IE

http://virtuelvis.com/archives/2004/02/css-ie-only

Similar to the article above, but with additional information about source order for serving multiple IE-specific style sheets.

Supporting IE with conditional comments

http://dev.opera.com/articles/view/supporting-ie-with-conditional-comments/

Opera is kind enough to outline CSS IE hacks, conditional comments, and how to construct an IE-specific style sheet that targets the main browser bugs and issues.

The display property

The `display` property can be a powerful tool in many situations. The articles below provide deeper information on what it does and how it works.

Visual formatting model

http://www.w3.org/TR/CSS2/visuren.html

A thorough list of all of the values of the `display` property from the W3C.

The display declaration

http://www.quirksmode.org/css/display.html

A useful chart of the support for the `display` property by the popular browsers as well as good visual examples of how each value works.

CHAPTER 9: THE CASE OF THE BROWSER WHO HATED ME

No matter what your feelings are about IE6 (and to some degree, IE7), it is here to stay for a little while longer. Best to bone up on all the information out there, so you'll know what to expect from the little dear and how to deal with it.

IE bugs

It would be so nice if IE bugs didn't exist, but they are what keep us on our toes and push our brains to innovate solutions. Know your bugs so you can code proactively or develop a new solution that no one else has thought of yet.

Explorer Exposed!

http://www.positioniseverything.net/explorer.html

Position Is Everything is one of the most well-respected sources on browser bugs on the web. This website examines major IE bugs in depth and provides solid fixes for all of them.

Internet Explorer Bugs

http://css-class.com/test/bugs/ie/ie-bugs.htm

Another good repository of IE bugs, bug examples, and fixes.

Internet Explorer & CSS issues

http://www.webcredible.co.uk/user-friendly-resources/css/internet-explorer.shtml

Light, easy-to-read overview of some of the more popular bugs in IE. Good to read before digging into more in-depth, technical articles.

CSS & Developing for IE6/7

It's best to have tricks up your sleeve for developing for IE6 and IE7 before you even have to do any troubleshooting and adjusting.

Developing CSS for IE6 & IE7

http://www.edgeofmyseat.com/blog/developing-css-for-ie6-and-7

Great overview of the steps necessary for building a page and then fixing all the IE problems that come up.

Universal Internet Explorer 6 CSS

http://forabeautifulweb.com/blog/about/universal_internet_explorer_6_css/

Relevant points about how to answer "the IE question" and a solution in the form of a style sheet that addresses the known issues.

Cross-browser testing resources

If you don't look at your pages in other browsers, then how will you know if your code is solid? Cross-browser testing isn't an option, it is an absolute necessity. All you need are some reliable ways to accomplish it.

Multiple IE installer

http://tredosoft.com/Multiple_IE

I thanked the heavens when Estelle Weyl of Evotech.com turned me on to this. Awesome to have all versions of IE on one machine. A little bugginess with IE7, but functional.

IETester

http://www.my-debugbar.com/wiki/IETester/HomePage

An application that simulates multiple versions of IE in one place.

Seven fresh and simple ways to test cross-browser compatibility

http://freelancefolder.com/7-fresh-and-simple-ways-to-test-cross-browser-
↦ compatibility/

Reviews of multiple apps and sites that do cross-browser testing or provide it as a service.

CHAPTER 10: THE CASE OF THE LOL LAYOUT

An issue like hasLayout, PNG support by IE6, or cross-browser rendering is no laughing matter. However, these resources will help you feel more confident when tackling such problems, and at least one may even make you smile.

hasLayout

Oh, how I love the excitement that hasLayout brings to working with IE6! Below are some must-reads to really understand the ins and outs of giving layout or taking it away as the situation warrants.

HasLayout overview

http://msdn.microsoft.com/en-us/library/bb250481%28VS.85%29.aspx

Microsoft's explanation of the hasLayout quality and its implications.

On having layout

http://www.satzansatz.de/cssd/onhavinglayout.html

This article seems to be the premier source on hasLayout, its effects, and ways to deal with it. A very detailed and long read, but invaluable in terms of content.

Welcome to hasLayout.net

http://haslayout.net/

Despite the name, haslayout.net not only covers hasLayout issues, but also provides examples and fixes for many other CSS bugs.

The Internet Explorer hasLayout property

http://reference.sitepoint.com/css/haslayout

This article is a condensed version of the information in the "On Having Layout" article (above), and thus a good starter article to familiarize yourself with the issues around hasLayout.

PNG-24 support for IE

PNG is really a wonderful image format, and it's a wonder that it has only fairly recently become widely adopted. One of the main culprits is the lack of support by IE6, but the following scripts provide viable workarounds.

PNG transparency for Internet Explorer (IE6 & beyond)

http://christopherschmitt.com/2007/10/30/png-transparency-for-internet-
➥ explorer-ie6-and-beyond/

Good article on the background of PNGs, how they work, and how to put PNG support into your pages for IE6.

IE PNG Fix 2.0 Alpha 4

http://www.twinhelix.com/css/iepngfix/

One of several great and easy solutions for getting PNGs to show up correctly in IE6.

Transparent PNGs in Internet Explorer 6

http://24ways.org/2007/supersleight-transparent-png-in-ie6

Another script to enable PNGs to show up in IE6.

Unit PNG fix

http://labs.unitinteractive.com/unitpngfix.php

And yet another script to enable PNGs to show up in IE6. It is good to have multiple options, try them all, and see what works best for you.

Websites looking the same cross-browser

As designers and developers, we may be inclined to think that having your pages show up 100 percent identical across browsers is the ultimate goal, but that aspiration may be unrealistic. Here are some tips on how to get as close as possible, but also some ideas on when to stop.

Tutorial: ten tips for building cross-browser websites

http://www.elated.com/articles/cross-browser-website-tips/

Good, generalized tips for getting your website to be as close as possible cross-browser.

The cross-browser conundrum

http://www.worthwhile.com/blog/the-cross-browser-conundrum/

Some thoughts on cross-browser closeness in design, and thoughts for dealing with others' expectations of how the sites will look in different browsers.

Do websites need to look exactly the same in every browser?

http://dowebsitesneedtolookexactlythesameineverybrowser.com/

I believe you will appreciate the answer that this website provides.

Page semantics & lists

There may be a situation where you opted for paragraph text but a list would be better. These articles will help you determine where to implement lists and their proper structure.

Using HTML lists properly

http://green-beast.com/blog/?p=185

Good explanation of lists, their construction, and the situations that each type of list is used for.

HTML lists

http://dev.opera.com/articles/view/16-html-lists/

Especially relevant is the section "The difference between HTML lists and text."

Image Credits/Attributions

CHAPTER 4: THE USUAL SUSPECTS

Graphics:

- 3D version of box model from HicksDesign.co.uk: http://www.hicksdesign.co.uk/ ➥boxmodel/, CC BY 2.0

- Fingerprints of Anna Timiriova: http://commons.wikimedia.org/wiki/File: Fingerprints_of_Anna_Timiriova_3.jpg, part of the public domain.

CHAPTER 5: THE CASE OF THE DEVILISH DETAILS

Graphics:

- Logos designed by the author.

CHAPTER 6: THE CASE OF THE SINGLE WHITE SPACE

Site design inspiration from Etsy.com.

Photos:

- Photo of Stefani Whylie taken by the author. Used with permission.

- Photo of Angelia Betancourt taken by the author. Used with permission.

- Video still of Stephanie Troeth, from http://hippiesque.com. Used with permission.

- All jewelry photos came from Flickr.com users, and are all Creative Commons licensed, CC BY 2.0.

- Blue and brown necklace: http://www.flickr.com/photos/madzik/36801146/

- Teal and green glass earrings: http://www.flickr.com/photos/juniperberry/2106502090/, and http://www.flickr.com/photos/juniperberry/2108578751/

- Amethyst and rhodolite garnet earrings: http://www.flickr.com/photos/ ➥mmadden/

- Turquoise necklace: http://www.flickr.com/photos/expressyourself-7/ ➥3847134534/

CHAPTER 7: THE CASE OF THE MISTAKEN IDENTITY

Photos:

- Main photo of author, courtesy of Bill Wisser Photos, http://billwisserphoto.com. Used with permission.

- Community pictures are the avatars of friends of the author on Twitter.

- All food and restaurant photos taken by the author.

Other:

- Design element for logo from istockphoto.com

CHAPTER 8: THE CASE OF THE FLOAT WITH A MIND OF ITS OWN

This site is dedicated to the memory of my father, Dennis Raymond Jacobs.

Photos:

- Walking Away: http://www.flickr.com/photos/saneboy/3811734996/, CC BY 2.0

- Twin Maples: http://www.flickr.com/photos/laserstars/623654566/, CC BY 2.0

- All other photos are stock photography from istockphoto.com.

CHAPTER 9: THE CASE OF THE BROWSER WHO HATED ME

Site concept inspiration from T-mobile "Life is for Sharing" video: http://www.youtube.com/watch?v=mUZrrbgCdYc

Photos:

- All dance photos came from Flickr.com users, and are all Creative Commons licensed, CC BY 2.0

- Dancing at the Bedouin Lounge: http://www.flickr.com/photos/
  ➥ itzafineday/3812947642/

- Dance! http://www.flickr.com/photos/ kkendall/3613416741/

- Spontaneous Dance party: http://www.flickr.com/photos/jordanfischer/
  ➥ 3583935971/

- Fancy/Fringe Dancer: http://www.flickr.com/photos/78428166@N00/
  ➥ 873166776/

- 6–10 year old Breakdancers: http://www.flickr.com/photos/m500/
  ➥ 3541920725/

- Parkdancing (The Dirty Urchins): http://www.flickr.com/photos/yourdon/
  ➥ 3903019257/

- Holland Dance Festival Preview: http://www.flickr.com/photos/
  ➥ haagsuitburo/4046910999/

- Photo of Darshan Bhuller used with permission.

- Photo of Deloria Jacobs (mother of the author) used with permission.

- All other photos are stock photography from istockphoto.com.

Other:

- Design elements for logo from istockphoto.com

CHAPTER 10: THE CASE OF THE LOL LAYOUT

Site concept inspiration from: icanhazcheeseburger.com, lolcat.com, lolcats.com,
and moderncat.net.

Photos:

- Product photos from sites listed on moderncat.net.

- All cat photos are those of the author. No cats were harmed in the making
  of this website, and no kitty labor laws were broken.

Other:

- Design elements for logo from istockphoto.com

Index